STUDY GUIDE FOR

PSYCHOLOGY

THE SCIENCE OF BEHAVIOR

THIRD EDITION

MARY CARLSON

NEIL R. CARLSON

University of Massachusetts

ALLYN AND BACON

Boston • London • Sydney • Toronto

ISBN 0-205-12172-1

Printed in the United States of America

10 9 8 7 6 5 4 3   94 93 92 91

Table of Contents

To the Student

Introductions are rarely read, so consider yourself one of the exceptional few. So as not to abuse your patience, we will keep this one short. Some of you have just started your college career and have had little or no experience with college courses. Others have had much more experience and have settled on a routine of studying that seems to work well. But before you start work on your psychology course this semester, we would like to make a few suggestions — to both groups. Studying is a behavior that most of us just "happen" into. We begin sometime in elementary school. Year by year, more and more is expected of us, and we learn to work harder and harder. Along the way we pick up a set of study habits, but few of us ever stop to reflect about what we do. And almost none of us will try experiments, studying one way for one test and another way for another and seeing which produces the best results. So although you may be firmly committed to your approach to studying, at least consider the possibility that there may be some ways to improve it.

Your instructor will, of course, give you the assignments. He or she will ask you to read chapters from the book and will probably give lectures, which may or may not follow the outline of the book. The quizzes and exams will probably be based partly on the lectures and partly on the readings; of course, you will want to learn the relative weights given to these two sources of information as soon as you can.

We would like to offer the following advice about taking lecture notes. *Don't simply be a stenographer.*

That is, try to understand what the instructor says and think about what you are writing. A serious mistake is to realize that you don't understand what he or she is saying and to tell yourself that you will write it all down and then figure it out later. Too often, "later" comes the night before an exam, and you find, to your chagrin, that you cannot understand your notes. If you do not understand what your instructor says, ask for clarification, either during or after the lecture (depending on the size of the class and your instructor's preferences). If you are able to ask questions in class, do not be afraid of looking stupid. Unless you really *are* the densest student in the class (and the fact that you are reading this proves that you are not), you will have company in your puzzlement. Your more timid fellow-students will be relieved that you asked the question, and your instructor will know that a topic is causing difficulty and needs further explanation.

We have a second suggestion, which really works. As soon as you can (preferably, immediately after class, if you have the time), go over your notes. Read them again while your instructor's words are fresh in your mind, and elaborate on them. If you wrote down a few cryptic phrases, flesh them out with complete sentences. If your instructor gave examples of some concepts, add some more of your own. The advantages of taking the time to go over your notes this way are enormous. Now, you will have a really good set of notes, which you can review when you study for an exam. In addition, just going over them and elaborating on them will put much of that information into your long-term memory. When you study your notes for the exam you will find that you already know most of what you have written in your notebook, and you will find the task much less of a chore.

Now, what about the textbook? This study guide has several functions. For one thing, it guides you through the text and makes sure that you don't miss anything important. Even better, it makes you put things in your own words, which is extremely important for long-term retention. Just as you should not simply be a stenographer, passing the instructor's words from your ears to your pen, without anything happening along the way, you should not simply read a question, find the answer in the book, and then copy it. The point in answering a question is putting the information in your own words.

Here is what we think is the best approach. Our advice is based on a combination of the results of psychological research and our own experience. *Read the chapter* as if you were reading an interesting story. (Actually, we hope that you will find it to be just that.) Don't worry about all the details now. Then, *work with the study guide*, preferably, a day or two later. In Chapter 1, you will see that the first thing you find, after the title of the chapter, is a heading, "Lesson I." Each chapter is divided into two lesons, and we recommend that you take a break between them to reward your own efforts. Talk to a friend, have a snack (if that won't violate your diet), or do something else that you enjoy. You might even want to work on the two lessons on different days. The second thing you will see is the following statement: "Read the interim summary on pages 7-8 to reacquaint yourself with the material in this section." Each chapter of the text has several interim summaries that do just what their name implies — sum up what has been said in the section. Having read the chapter a day or two earlier, you will find the interim summary helpful in reminding you about what that section discusses. So, *read the interim summary*.

Each lesson is divided into learning objectives, which are written in italics and highlighted with a pair of horizontal lines. After each learning objective is presented, you will be asked to read a few pages from the book and then answer the questions. *Read these pages*, and then *start answering the questions*. As much as you can, answer them from memory. If you find that you don't remember enough details to answer a question, read the book, then prepare your answer and write it. Do not simply copy an answer from the text into your study guide. Put the answer in your own words. *If you have to copy the information, you do not know it yet.* If you cannot remember the information long enough to look away from the book, phrase it in your own words, and then write it down, you will certainly not remember the information long enough to do well on an exam. Often, students think of a study guide as a good place to put useful items of information that they can study later on the eve of an examination. That is true, of couse. But a much more impor-

tant use of the study guide is *having to put the information into your own words*; once you do so, it is yours forever. (Well, some of it, anyway.)

At the end of each lesson you will find a self test, which presents ten multiple-choice questions, the answers of which are found at the end of the chapter. So obviously, the next step is to *take the self test*. These questions will help you see how well you are doing, and will give you a bit of practice for the exams — if they contain multiple-choice questions, that is. If they contain essay questions, the answers you have given to the questions in the study guide will have given you plenty of practice. If you get some questions on the self test wrong, go back and find out why. The number of the relevant learning objective is indicated along with the answer, and this information will make it easy for you to find the information in the study guide or in the text.

We wish you the best of luck this semester. We think that you will find that psychology is an interesting topic. There is a lot to learn, and what you do learn will serve you well — in other courses, and in the world outside of the classroom. Some of you are taking this course to see whether you would like to pursue a career in psychology, and we hope that the course will help you make an informed decision. If you have any comments or suggestions, please write, addressing your letters to Neil R. Carlson, Department of Psychology, Tobin Hall, University of Massachusetts, Amherst, Massachusetts 01003.

Chapter 1
The Science of Psychology

Lesson I

Read the interim summary on pages 7-8 of your text to reacquaint yourself with the material in this section.

1-1 *Describe the goal of psychological research and outline the philosophical roots of psychology.*

Read pages 4-7 and then answer the following questions:

1. a. State the general goal of psychological research.

   b. Explain what *causal events* are and why they are important to the study of behavior.

   c. Describe the three major types of causal events that psychologists study.

2. What types of causal events (physiological, environmental, mental) are depicted in the following examples?

   a. _____Professor Lukins administered a test of anxiety to a group of subjects and compared the behavior of those who received high and low scores in a mock interview situation.

   b. _____Professor Chen explained that differences in child rearing practices accounted for the 10-point difference in the average IQ scores of infants raised in the two orphanages.

   c. _____Marcia, a graduate student, found that they could predict how much food the rat would eat by analyzing certain nutrients in the animal's blood just before it started its meal.

3. a. Explain why *animism* made intuitive sense to our ancestors.

   b. Try to think of an animistic explanation for the fact that flowers wilt after they are picked.

   c. Although animism has been replaced by other explanations of behavior, what lesson can be learned from this type of explanation?

4. The _____ _____ is the best means to insure objectivity in trying to understand natural phenomena.

5. a. Briefly summarize Descartes's approach to understanding the world, and explain how it challenged traditional religious doctrine.

   b. How, according to Descartes, were humans and animals similar and different?

   c. How did Descartes explain automatic responses, which he named *reflexes?* (Study Figure 1.1 in your text.)

   d. Explain the concept of *dualism,* distinguishing between "extended things" and "thinking things."

   e. Descartes's form of dualism proposed an _____ between _____ and
   _____ __.

   f. What early experience guided Descartes as he thought about the human body?

   g. When Descartes thought about the body in terms of a relatively simple mechanical system, he was using
   a _____ .

6. Explain the concepts of *rationalism* and *empiricism,* paying special attention to how they differ.

7. a. According to Locke, what was the source of knowledge?

   b. Briefly summarize the model Locke used to explain the workings of the human mind.

8. a. Explain the concept of *materialism* proposed by James Mill.

   b. How did Mill reconcile differing explanations for the behavior of humans and animals?

   c. In what ways did he agree and disagree with Descartes?

9. Identify the philosophy represented by the following explanation of behavior.

   _____ He picked up the stick because his mind tilted the pineal body and forced fluid into
   the muscles in his shoulder and arm.

   _____ The woman was acting crazy because the storm spirit had entered her body.

_____ The man saw that the woman was approaching him because the image of her on the back of his eyes was getting bigger.

_____ An explanation of the man's behavior can be found through reflection and reason.

Read the interim summary on page 11 of your text to reacquaint yourself with the material in this section.

1-2   *Describe the biological roots of psychology.*

Read pages 8-11 and then answer the following questions:

1. Müller advocated what method in studying physiology?

2. a. One of Müller's most important contribution to science was the doctrine of _____
   _____ _____.

   b. By what means does the brain distinguish between sources of information from the environment?

   c. What is the implication of this fact for specialization of brain function?

3. Explain how Pierre Flourens tested the implications of Müller's doctrine of specific nerve energies:

   a. Why did Flourens remove specific parts of an animal's nervous system?

   b. Following removal, what general results did he observe?

   c. What did he conclude from his observations?

   d. Name this experimental method.

4. Describe the observations and conclusions of Paul Broca, who applied Flourens's method to the study of humans with brain damage.

5. Describe the procedure of electrical brain stimulation used by Fritsch and Hitzig. (See Figure 1.2 in your text.)

6. Summarize the contributions of Hermann von Helmholtz to experimental physiology.

7. Helmholtz abandoned his attempt to measure the speed of a person's reaction to a physical stimulus, but his attempt set the stage for the development of psychophysics. Who began this field, and what was his general approach?

8. Review the historical progress of the study of the human mind presented in the interim summary by completing this chart. Identify Comte's three stages and indicate the dominant explanations of the human mind during each stage.

Comte's Stages	*Explanations of the Human Mind*
1.	1.
2.	2.
3.	3.

Lesson I Self Test

1. In general, psychologists try to explain behavior by studying its

   a. causes.
   b. consequences.
   c. implications.
   d. meaning.

2. The best means we have for ensuring scientific objectivity is

   a. the mathematical model.
   b. the scientific method.
   c. historical precedent.
   d. logic.

3. Descartes reasoned that

   a. all reality could be divided into good and evil.
   b. the body's master gland was the pituitary.
   c. the mind and body interacted.
   d. to understand the mind one had to understand God's will.

4. Empiricism says that knowledge comes through

   a. the study of consciousness.
   b. introspection and self-report.
   c. contemplation.
   d. observation and experience.

5. Johannes Müller is most closely associated with

   a. the doctrine of specific nerve energies.
   b. experimental ablation.
   c. interactionism.
   d. materialism.

6. Pierre Flourens developed the method of experimental ablation

   a. to stimulate the cerebral cortex.

b. to test the doctrine of specific nerve energies.
c. and began the field of psychophysics.
d. to study the functions of different parts of the brain.

7. Paul Broca used the logic of experimental ablation to

a. measure the speed of nerve conduction.
b. demonstrate the scientific value of autopsy.
c. discover a brain region specialized for speech.
d. electrically stimulate parts of the brain.

8. Fritsch and Hitzig discovered that the body appeared to be "mapped" on the surface of the brain. They used

a. the psychophysical method.
b. the doctrine of specific nerve energies.
c. the method of electrical brain stimulation.
d. the method of experimental ablation.

9. Helmholtz abandoned his attempt to measure the speed of a person's reaction to physical stimuli because

a. there was too much individual variability.
b. ethical considerations were posed by the testing procedure.
c. the Church objected to the study of the human mind.
d. self-reports proved more reliable.

10. Weber's psychophysical studies

a. showed that perceptions can break down due to sensory fatigue.
b. indicate that perceptual phenomena can be studied scientifically.
c. are largely of historical interest with the development of more sophisticated testing methods.
d. were used to calculate that the speed of the nerve impulse is about 90 feet per second.

Lesson II

Read the interim summary on pages 18-19 of your text to reacquaint yourself with the material in this section.

1-3 *Discuss the major trends in the early development of psychology: structuralism, the work of Ebbinghaus, functionalism, and the influence of Freud.*

Read pages 11-15 and then answer the following questions:

1. Psychology began in _____ (country) in the late _____ century, with the work of _____ _____, who was the first to call himself a psychologist. His book _____ of _____ _____ was the first psychology text.

2. List three reasons that encouraged intellectual development in Germany paying special attention to the influence of the scientific method.

1.   2.

3.

3. a. Wundt called his approach to the study of psychology _____.

   b. Briefly explain this approach. Be sure to use the term *introspection* in your answer.

   c. List two reasons why structuralism was replaced.

   1.

   2.

   d. Although structuralism was abandoned, Wundt made other important contributions to psychology. List two.

   1.

   2.

4. a. What earlier scientist influenced the work of Ebbinghaus?

   b. What research problem did Ebbinghaus investigate?

   c. Describe the difficulty he soon encountered.

   d. Describe his solution. Be sure to use the term *nonsense syllables* in your answer.

   e. Use one word to describe Ebbinghaus' approach to the study of memory.

   f. Identify and explain the research principle he introduced.

5. a. Functionalism developed in the United States largely as a protest against what method?

   b. Briefly explain *functionalism,* paying special attention to

   1. the influence of Darwin and the principle of *natural selection* and the evolution of behaviors.

   2. the role of observable behaviors and mental events.

6. a. Name the psychologist who was the most important advocate of functionalism.

   b. What were his major contributions to psychology?

   c. Summarize the three basic principles of functionalism.

   1.   2.

   3.

7. Describe the similarities and differences in the approaches of Freud and Wundt.

1-4 *Describe the development of behaviorism and the cognitive revolution.*

Read pages 15-18 and then answer the following questions:

1. Briefly explain *behaviorism*, paying special attention to the importance of observable behaviors and mental events.

2. a. Describe Thorndike's experiments with the cats.

   b. Name the principle he discovered and define it.

   c. What modern names are applied to the two phenomena that the principle describes?

   d. Explain how Thorndike's principle is similar to the process of natural selection.

3. Describe the discovery that Ivan Pavlov made while he was working with hungry dogs.

4. Explain the significance of the work of Thorndike and Pavlov to psychology.

   a. Thorndike

   b. Pavlov

5. Summarize John B. Watson's view of psychology, paying special attention to the role of

   a. observable behavior.

   b. mental events.

6. Name the influential modern advocate of behaviorism who followed Watson.

7. List three practical applications based on the behaviorist approach.

   1.

2.

3.

8. What enduring contribution did Watson make? Be sure to use the term *methodological behaviorism* in your answer.

9. a. Why did some psychologists react against the behaviorism of Watson?

   b. Describe how cognitive psychologists study mental events. Be sure to use the term *information processing* in your answer.

10. Study Figure 1.3 in your text and then describe research by Kosslyn.

   a. procedure

   b. results

   c. interpretation

1-5   *Describe the different types of psychologists and the problems they study.*

Read pages 19-20 and then answer the following questions:

1. Briefly describe the work of the following types of psychologists, paying special attention to the typical subjects and research questions each group studies.

   a. Physiological psychologists

   b. Psychophysiologists

   c. Comparative psychologists

   d. Experimental psychologists

   e. Cognitive psychologists

   f. Experimental neuropsychologists

   g. Developmental psychologists

h. Social psychologists

i. Personality psychologists

j. Psychometricians

k. Clinical psychologists

2. Most clinical psychologists provide a service. Describe what they do.

3. Briefly describe the other areas of applied psychology.

a.

b.

c.

d.

e.

4. Complete each sentence to describe a group of professional psychologists.

_____ study behavioral phenomena in nonhuman subjects.

_____ usually study childhood development but sometimes study adolescents and adults.

_____ develop psychological tests.

_____ attempt to apply principles established in other fields of psychology to education.

_____ observe and measure the abilities of people with brain damage in order to determine the functions of the intact brain.

_____ look at a person's heredity, environment, and past behavior in order to explain personality differences.

Lesson II Self Test

1. Germany was the birthplace of psychology in part because

   a. German tradition emphasized the sciences over the humanities.
   b. German scientists believed the mind could be studied scientifically.
   c. national rivalry encouraged them to compete with scientists in other countries.
   d. German scientists were exceptionally well trained in philosophical approaches to the study of the mind.

2. Although advocated by influential scientists like Wundt, structuralism eventually died out because

   a. data gathered through introspection could not be verified.
   b. psychology continued to be closely associated with philosophy.
   c. of difficulties encountered in analyzing the data of sensation.
   d. of the cognitive revolution.

3. Ebbinghaus developed a system of nonsense syllables because

   a. he realized he could not compare the learning and forgetting of two prose passages.
   b. the structuralist approach avoided verbal material.
   c. he wanted to conduct cross-cultural studies and avoid language difficulties.
   d. he wanted to avoid experimenter bias in the selection of passages.

4. Functionalism

   a. rejected Darwin's theory of evolution.
   b. emphasized the importance of introspection.
   c. was supplanted by behaviorism.
   d. stressed the distinction between mind and body.

5. William James

   a. was a brilliant research scientist.
   b. formulated an influential and enduring theory of emotion.
   c. pioneered the field of behaviorism.
   d. based his theories on observations of patients.

6. Behaviorists differed from functionalists in their belief that

   a. all mental events are available through introspection.
   b. behavior can be shaped more successfully through punishment than through reinforcement.
   c. evolution affected only the body, not behaviors.
   d. mental events were beyond the scope of psychology.

7. Thorndike is most closely associated with the

   a. concept of variable errors.
   b. first journal of psychology.
   c. law of effect.
   d. concept of multiple experiments.

8. Pavlov's research on digestion demonstrated

   a. the utility of electric shock as a stimulus.
   b. that animals can learn to respond to a previously neutral stimulus.
   c. that hunger is a more powerful drive than thirst.
   d. that digestion begins in the mouth when the food is mixed with saliva.

9. One of the most influential modern behaviorists is

   a. Sigmund Freud.
   b. Jean Piaget.
   c. Carl Rogers.

d. B.F. Skinner.

10. Modern cognitive psychologists have demonstrated that

a. behaviors that are based upon mental images can be objectively measured.
b. the experience of imagery can be shared.
c. the ability to recognize images cannot be studied objectively.
d. dualism is the most useful approach to the mind-body problem.

Answers for Self Tests

Lesson I			Lesson II		
1.	a	Obj. 1-1	1.	b	Obj. 1-3
2.	b	Obj. 1-1	2.	a	Obj. 1-3
3.	c	Obj. 1-1	3.	a	Obj. 1-3
4.	d	Obj. 1-1	4.	c	Obj. 1-3
5.	a	Obj. 1-2	5.	b	Obj. 1-3
6.	d	Obj. 1-2	6.	d	Obj. 1-4
7.	c	Obj. 1-2	7.	c	Obj. 1-4
8.	c	Obj. 1-2	8.	b	Obj. 1-4
9.	a	Obj. 1-2	9.	d	Obj. 1-4
10.	b	Obj. 1-2	10.	a	Obj. 1-4

1.1 animism	1.10 dualism
1.2 behaviorism	1.11 educational psychologist
1.3 causal event	1.12 empiricism
1.4 clinical psychologist	1.13 engineering psychologist
1.5 cognitive psychologist	1.14 experimental ablation
1.6 comparative psychologist	1.15 experimental neuropsychologist
1.7 counseling	1.16 experimental psychologist
1.8 developmental psychologist	1.17 functionalism
1.9 doctrine of specific nerve energies	1.18 industrial psychologist

1.10

The belief that all reality can be divided into either mind or matter and that humans have a physical body and a nonmaterial thinking mind.

1.11

A psychologist who usually applies well-established psychological principles to education.

1.12

The belief that all knowledge can be obtained through observation and experience.

1.13

A psychologist who assists in the design of products so that they can be used more quickly and accurately.

1.14

An experimental technique developed by Flourens; a portion of the brain is removed; missing behavioral functions were controlled by the missing parts of the brain.

1.15

A psychologist who studies human brain functions through observation of people with brain damage.

1.16

A psychologist who studies the general principles of learning, perception, motivation, and memory in both humans and other animals.

1.17

An approach to understanding a species' structural or behavioral features by attempting to discover their biological significance (function).

1.18

A psychologist who works in industry advising management about the application of psychological principles to running a business.

1.1

A primitive belief that all animals and moving objects possessed spirits providing their motivating force.

1.2

A movement in psychology that asserts that the only proper subject matter for the scientific study of psychology is observable behavior.

1.3

An event that causes another event to occur.

1.4

A psychologist who investigates and treats abnormal behavior and mental disorders.

1.5

A psychologist who studies such processes as perception, memory, attention, and concept formation; whose subjects are almost always humans; the largest subcategory of experimental psychologists.

1.6

A psychologist who studies many of the same kinds of behavior of animals as physiological psychologists, but who explains behavior in terms of evolutionary adaptation to the environment.

1.7

A form of help given to people with minor problems of daily life including academic and vocational guidance.

1.8

A psychologist who studies the changes in behavioral, perceptual, and cognitive capacities primarily of children, but sometimes of other age groups.

1.9

Müller's observation that different nerves convey specific information between particular parts of the brain and particular parts of the body and that the message in all cases is an electrical impulse.

1.19	1.28
information processing	psychophysiologist
1.20	1.29
introspection	reflex
1.21	1.30
law of effect	school psychologist
1.22	1.31
materialism	social psychologist
1.23	1.32
model	structuralism
1.24	1.33
personality psychologist	variable error
1.25	
physiological psychologist	
1.26	
psychometrician	
1.27	
psychophysics	

1.28	1.19
A psychologist who studies the physiological reactions of people (blood pressure, heart rate, muscular tension) to stress and other emotional situations.	An approach to the study of behavior based on the model of a digital computer.
1.29	1.20
An automatic response to a stimulus such as an eye blink or rapid pulling back from a hot object.	Wundt's method of gathering information about the structure of the mind; observers were taught to "look within" and observe the kinds of changes various stimuli produced in their own experiences.
1.30	1.21
A psychologist who works as a counselor in elementary or secondary schools.	Thorndike's observation that a response will increase when followed by pleasant stimuli and will decrease when followed by unpleasant stimuli.
1.31	1.22
A psychologist who studies the effects that people have on other people.	The belief that the world (including the human mind) is composed entirely of matter and energy.
1.32	1.23
Wundt's approach to the study of psychology that emphasized studying the structures of the mind through introspection.	In science, a physical or mathematical analogy for a complex system based on a familiar system that shares some of the properties of the more complex system.
1.33	1.24
Observational error in gathering data caused by random factors such as alertness or uncontrollable changes in the environment.	A psychologist who studies individual differences in disposition and patterns of behavior by looking into a person's genetic and environmental history.
	1.25
	A psychologist who studies the physiological basis of behaviors such as memory, sensory processes, motivation, and sleep.
	1.26
	A psychologist who develops ways to measure human personality and ability.
	1.27
	The scientific study of the relation between the physical characteristics of a stimulus and the perceptions they produce.

Chapter 2
The Ways and Means of Psychology

Lesson I

Read the interim summary on pages 33-34 of your text to reacquaint yourself with the material in this section.

2-1   *Identify the four principal steps of the scientific method.*

Read pages 29-31 and then answer the following questions:

1. a. What category of natural phenomena do psychologists study?

    b. Why is the scientific method used in research?

2. List the four major steps of the scientific method.

    1.

    2.

    3.

    4.

3. a. What is a *hypothesis?*

    b. Where do hypotheses come from?

4. a. What is a *theory?*

    b. Compare theories and hypotheses.

    c. List two ways theories are useful to scientists.

    1.

    2.

5. a. What is a *variable?*

   b. Explain the difference between an *independent variable* and a *dependent variable*. (See Figure 2.1 in your text.)

   c. Why are variables stated in general terms rather than specific ones?

   d. Using the terms *independent variable* and *dependent variable,* give a more complete explanation of a hypothesis.

6. a. What is the *nominal fallacy*, and why is it an error?

   b. Give your own example of a nominal fallacy.

2-2   *Discuss the importance of operational definitions and explain the meaning of reliability and validity.*

Read pages 31-33 and then answer the following questions:

1. a. What is an *operational definition*?

   b. Why is it important to operationally define dependent and independent variables?

   c. Your town has decided to support a project to encourage voluntary recycling of newspaper and will evaluate the success of the project in six months. Write an operational definition of "success."

   d. Is your operational definition of success the only one that could have been devised? What does this answer say about the importance of making such a definition explicit and communicating it to others?

2. a. Explain the concept of *validity* and say why it is important to research.

   b. Describe two ways a researcher can attempt to assess the validity of an operational definition.

      1.

      2.

3. a. Explain the concept of reliability and say why it is important to research.

   b. If an operational definition is reliable, can we then assume it is also valid? Explain.

4. a. Why is it more difficult to make reliable measurements of children's friendly behavior than their reading speed?

b. Describe the procedure you would use to make reliable measurements of friendly interactions among children.

Read the interim summary on pages 43-44 of your text to reacquaint yourself with the material in this section.

2-3   *Discuss the manipulation and control of independent variables.*

Read pages 34-36 and then answer the following questions:

1. a. State the general purpose of an experiment, using the terms dependent and independent variable.

   b. You have already described some difficulties in formulating hypotheses and operational definitions. Explain another potential problem: *confounding of variables.*

2. If the independent variables of an experiment are confounded, what will the effects be on the interpretation of the results?

3. Briefly describe the experimental procedure used by the Zoology Department's guest speaker.

   a. In what order did the speaker show the cardboard models to the restrained birds? (See Figure 2.2 in your text.)

   b. What were the results?

   c. What potential problem did the speaker fail to anticipate and why did this flaw make the study useless?

   d. Study Figure 2.3 in your text and explain what he should have done differently and why.

   e. What is the name of the procedure he should have followed?

4. a. Explain the meaning and purpose of a *control group.*

   b. Study Figure 2.4 in your text, which outlines an experimental procedure to assess the effects on children's behavior of watching violent television shows. What kinds of variables might be confounded? Explain why the addition of a control group will help the experimenter interpret the results.

2-4   *Discuss the confounding of subject variables and the problem of subject expectations.*

Read pages 36-39 and then answer the following questions:

1. Describe a method for random selection of subjects for the various groups participating in an experiment and explain why it is important to do so.

2. a. Study Figure 2.5 in your text and briefly describe or diagram the two experimental conditions in the study on humiliation.

   1.

   2.

   b. Now study Figure 2.6 in your text and explain what the effect on the experimental design will be if some subjects become angry and leave.

3. Some experimental subjects respond differently because they know they are participating in an experiment. Describe three ways this knowledge could influence their behavior.

   1.

   2.

   3.

4. In the hypothetical experiment testing the effects of a stimulant drug on fine manual dexterity, one group of subjects is given amphetamine and a second group of subjects is given nothing, and then all subjects are tested for dexterity.

   a. What is the problem with this experimental procedure?

   b. How can the procedure be improved to overcome this problem? Be sure to use the term *placebo* in your answer.

   c. What is the name of this procedure?

5. a. Contrast *subjective* and *objective* measurements.

   b. Indicate whether the following statements refer to subjective or objective judgments.

      _____ The coach thinks his team is twice as good as the others.

      _____ Howard is funnier than Larry.

      _____ Julie weighs more than Helen.

      _____ The temperature is 30°.

      _____ It feels stuffy in here.

   c. In the hypothetical experiment studying the effects of a drug on the communicative behavior of patients with mental disorders, how might the ratings of researchers be affected by their knowing which patients received the drug?

   d. How can the procedure be improved to overcome this problem?

e. What is the name of this procedure?

2-5   *Describe observational studies, case studies, and problems encountered in generalizing their findings.*

Read pages 39-43 and then answer the following questions:

1. a. Under what conditions is an observational study the most appropriate approach?

    b. In your own words, state the basic principle underlying observational studies.

    c. If we observe a correlation between two variables that we are studying, can we conclude that a cause-and-effect relationship exists between them? Use the example in Figure 2.7 in your text in your answer.

2. a. Under what circumstances would a researcher use the *matching* procedure in an observational study?

    b. Explain the rationale behind the use of matching.

    c. List several weakness of the matching procedure even when it is carefully followed.

3. Explain what it means to *generalize* experimental results and why it is important to be able to do so. Be sure to use the term *sample* in your answer.

4. a. Define *case study* in your own words.

    b. Consider the case studies regarding food additives and the woman who could no longer read, and explain the difference in the way the independent variable was "manipulated" in each study.

    c. Case studies that attempt to correlate events that occurred in the client's past with the client's present behavior are called _____ studies.

    d. Why should the conclusions of such studies be regarded cautiously?

5. Match the following situations with the name of the appropriate concept.

    _____ "Attractive people are more likely to have their requests fulfilled."

    _____ "Attractiveness is defined by ratings of photographs made by a group of college students."

    _____ number of people who agree to give the person money for the parking meter

    _____ The researcher thought that having college students rate people's attractiveness was a reasonable procedure.

_____ Unfortunately, all of the attractive people in the experiment were under the age of twenty, and all of the unattractive people were over the age of forty-five.

_____ the mean rating received by a person's photograph

_____ Based on the results obtained from the study, the researcher concluded that an attractive person would have a better chance of getting other people to comply with a request.

a. dependent variable
b. hypothesis
c. generalization
d. face validity

e. independent variable
f. operational definition
g. confounding of variables

Lesson I Self Test

1. The independent variable is

   a. manipulated by the experimenter.
   b. measured by the experimenter.
   c. manipulated by the subject.
   d. found only in observational studies.

2. "Marlene told everyone what to bring to the party because she is bossy." This statement is an example of

   a. a generalization.
   b. a hypothesis.
   c. the nominal fallacy.
   d. manipulation.

3. An operational definition

   a. applies only to the independent variable.
   b. may be modified during the experiment.
   c. emerges from the results of the experiment.
   d. has face validity if it seems reasonable.

4. The use of two or more people to rate behavior is most appropriate when

   a. there are large groups of subjects.
   b. the subjects are either very young or very old.
   c. the variables are difficult to specify objectively.
   d. multiple variables are being studied.

5. The guest speaker to the Zoology department should have counterbalanced his experiment. That is, he should have presented the models of predators

   a. at the same speed to all birds.
   b. in different orders to different birds.
   c. in the same order to all birds.
   d. only once to each bird.

6. The addition of a control group

a. increases the validity of the operational definition.
b. permits a contrast between manipulating the independent variable and no treatment.
c. works best with human subjects.
d. assures a random sample of subjects.

7. If a researcher selects subjects randomly from a pool of student volunteers

a. retrospective studies will be impossible.
b. confounding of subject variables is less likely.
c. confounding of independent variables is less likely.
d. a control group will be unnecessary.

8. A single-blind study insures that

a. subject expectations will not affect the results.
b. researcher expectations will not affect the results.
c. only one independent variable will be manipulated.
d. drugs will be used.

9. Researchers turn to observational studies when

a. large groups of subjects are involved.
b. they are certain that subjects can remember accurately what happened to them earlier.
c. communication may be a problem.
d. variables of interest cannot be altered by the researchers.

10. Researchers are most comfortable about generalizing experimental results to a larger population when

a. the subjects' behavior was directly observed.
b. the study is an observational one.
c. the observed relationship between the independent and dependent variables is strong.
d. the subjects were unique.

Lesson II

Read the interim summary on page 52 of your text to reacquaint yourself with the material in this section.

2-6   *Describe measures of central tendency, measures of variability, and measures of relations.*

Read pages 44-48 and then answer the following questions:

1. a. Define *descriptive statistics* in your own words.

   b. Cite two ways in which they are used in scientific experiments.

2. a. Define *measure of central tendency* in your own words.

   b. The most common measure of central tendency is the _____.

c. According to Suzanne's attendance record, she was absent 3 days in September, 1 day in October, 4 days in November and 2 days in December. Calculate the mean number of absences for that semester.

3. a. Explain how the *median* is calculated.

   b. Follow the calculations in Table 2.1 in your text to explain why the median is a more representative measure of central tendency than the mean.

   c. Give three reasons why the mean is still used.

4. a. When researchers analyze experimental data, they frequently compare the scores of two groups of subjects. Name them.

   b. Why do the researchers compare these scores?

5. a. Study Table 2.3 in your text and explain how to calculate the *range*.

   b. Briefly explain what the range indicates.

6. a. What does the *standard deviation* measure?

   b. Why is it used instead of the average deviation?

7. Study the data presented in Table 2.4 and Figures 2.8, 2.9, and 2.10 in your text.

   a. The test scores and average grades of students can be graphed to make a _____ _____ to determine whether they are related.

   b. What is the range of possible values of the correlation coefficient?

   c. What does a correlation coefficient of +.5 mean?

   d. What does a negative correlation indicate about the relationship of two measures?

2-7 *Describe how to determine whether the results obtained in an experiment are statistically significant.*

Read pages 49-52 and then answer the following questions:

1. a. Explain why researchers hope that the results of their experiments will be statistically significant.

   b. If the size of the difference between the performance of two groups of subjects is large, relative to the variability, the results of the experiment are probably _____ _____, but if the difference is small the results are probably due to _____.

2. Study the data presented in Tables 2.5, 2.6, and 2.7 and Figure 2.11 in your text and describe the in-class experiment.

   a. Why was the mean height calculated so many times?

   b. Explain what a frequency distribution is and why it is useful for organizing data.

   c. Explain how the distribution of mean differences in heights from 1000 random divisions supported the original hypothesis that the last letter of the first name is related to height.

3. a. Researchers do not usually determine statistical significance this way. Explain why the special mathematical properties of the standard deviation are useful assessing the significance of results.

   b. What does a researcher mean when he or she reports that experimental results were statistically significance at the 1 percent level?

   c. Explain why statistically significant results need not be important.

Lesson II Self Test

1. The median is calculated by

   a. adding the individual values of the sample and dividing by the number of observations.
   b. arranging all scores in numerical order and finding the midpoint.
   c. subtracting the lowest score from the highest score.
   d. adding the differences between each score and the measures of central tendency and then dividing by the number of scores.

2. The mean

   a. is the most common measure of central tendency, but the median is more representative.
   b. and the median of two sets of numbers are always different.
   c. is easier to calculate than the median, but the median is more useful because it has special mathematical properties.
   d. and the median are most accurate when the sample is small.

3. The standard deviation is used instead of the average deviation because the standard deviation

   a. is easier to calculate.
   b. has been the traditional measure.
   c. and the average deviation are close to the same value.
   d. has special mathematical properties.

4. A scatter plot

   a. with points distributed along a line running from the lower left to the upper right represents a negative correlation.
   b. with points distributed along a horizontal line represents a correlation of +1.0.
   c. indicates the relation between two variables.
   d. indicates the statistical significance of differences between means.

5. What score indicates the strongest relationship between variables?

   a. +.6
   b. -.9
   c. 0
   d. +.1

6. The correlation coefficient is more convenient

   a. than the range because standard tables to determine its value have already been developed.
   b. than showing scatter plots of the scores.
   c. than calculating the average deviations of scores from both the median and the mean.
   d. than the range because it makes calculating the standard deviation unnecessary.

7. If the results of an experiment are statistically significant, we may conclude that the

   a. operational definitions were reliable.
   b. experiment was important.
   c. dependent variable had an effect on the independent variable.
   d. results were not due to chance.

8. The best way to determine whether results are statistically significant is to

   a. repeat the experiment.
   b. construct a scatter-plot.
   c. examine the performance of the control group.
   d. calculate whether the difference in mean scores was greater than chance.

9. The frequency distribution of heights of 1000 randomly chosen divisions of a set of data showed

   a. the range of the heights of students.
   b. the range of the correlation coefficient.
   c. the number of times various ranges of mean differences in height occurred.
   d. the height of each student in the sample.

10. A small difference in the performance of a control group and an experimental group can be statistically significant if

   a. the number of subjects is very large.

b. the variability within the groups is very large.
c. a single-blind experimental design is used.
d. the correlation is positive.

Answers for Self Tests

Lesson I

1. a Obj. 2-1
2. c Obj. 2-1
3. d Obj. 2-2
4. c Obj. 2-2
5. b Obj. 2-3
6. b Obj. 2-3
7. b Obj. 2-4
8. a Obj. 2-4
9. d Obj. 2-5
10. c Obj. 2-5

Lesson II

1. b Obj. 2-6
2. a Obj. 2-6
3. d Obj. 2-6
4. c Obj. 2-6
5. b Obj. 2-6
6. b Obj. 2-6
7. d Obj. 2-7
8. d Obj. 2-7
9. c Obj. 2-7
10. a Obj. 2-7

2.1 case study	2.10 face validity
2.2 confounding of variables	2.11 generalization
2.3 construct validity	2.12 hypothesis
2.4 control group	2.13 independent variable
2.5 correlation coefficient	2.14 interrater reliability
2.6 counterbalancing	2.15 manipulation
2.7 dependent variable	2.16 matching
2.8 descriptive statistics	2.17 mean
2.9 double-blind method	2.18 measure of central tendency

2.10 The assumption that the operational definitions of an experiment are accurate because they seem reasonable to the experimenter.	2.1 The observation of the behavior of a particular individual, as opposed to studies of groups; frequently used to study people with mental or neurological disorders.
2.11 The application of the results of an experiment to a population larger than the experimental subjects.	2.2 The unintentional manipulation of more than one independent variable in an experiment.
2.12 A tentative statement about a relation between two or more events.	2.3 The assumption that the correctness of an operation definition will emerge when the results of experiments using the same definition are compared.
2.13 The variable that is manipulated in an experiment. Manipulation of the independent variable may or may not affect the value of the dependent variable.	2.4 A comparison group of subjects similar to the experimental subjects who are subjected to an independent variable with a value of zero.
2.14 A technique to improve the accuracy in measuring the dependent variable by comparing independent rating of two or more people of the same behavior.	2.5 A measurement of the degree to which two variables are related; zero indicates no relation; a perfect relation is ±1.0; negative values indicates that variables are inversely related.
2.15 In research, setting the value of an independent variable for experimental purposes.	2.6 The presentation of values of the independent variable to different subjects in a way that is not correlated with other potentially important variables; avoids confounding of variables.
2.16 Selection of subjects in such as way that the composition of the groups is homogeneous with respect to important variables; in observational studies, the groups differ only with respect to the variable of interest.	2.7 The behavior of the subjects observed in an experiment; manipulation of the independent variable may or may not affect the value of the dependent variable.
2.17 The most common measure of central tendency; obtained by dividing the sum of the individual values in a sample by their number.	2.8 A set of measures that represent the characteristics of a sample of numbers.
2.18 A measure that indicates how different the scores in a sample are from each other, on the average.	2.9 An experimental procedure in which neither the subjects nor the experimenter knows the value of the independent variable for a particular subject.

2.19 median	2.28 sample
2.20 nominal fallacy	2.29 scatterplot
2.21 observational study	2.30 single-blind method
2.22 operational definition	2.31 standard deviation
2.23 placebo	2.32 statistical significance
2.24 random selection	2.33 theory
2.25 range	2.34 validity
2.26 reliability	2.35 variable
2.27 retrospective study	

2.28 A group of items selected from a larger population; can refer to subjects, stimuli, or behaviors.	2.19 A measure of central tendency; the midpoint of a group of scores arranged numerically.
2.29 A graph that demonstrates the relation between two variables; each sample is shown as a point graphed in two dimensions; one variable is plotted against the horizontal axis and the other against the vertical axis.	2.20 The false belief that one has explained the causes of a phenomenon simply by identifying and naming it.
2.30 An experimental design in which the experimenter, but not the subject, knows the value of the independent variable for that subject.	2.21 The observation of groups of subjects matched on all important variables but the one in question; often used to study effects of variables that cannot be manipulated; cannot prove the existence of causal relations.
2.31 A measure of variability; the square root of the sum of the squared deviations between each score and the mean of the sample.	2.22 A statement specifying precisely how a variable will be measured or manipulated by the experimenter.
2.32 A sufficiently low probability that an observed relation or difference between two variables was simply due to chance.	2.23 An inert substance that cannot be distinguished from a real medication by the patient or subject; may be used as the control substance in a single-blind or double-blind experiment.
2.33 An elaborate form of hypothesis that attempts to explain a set of natural phenomena or account for the results obtained in a set of related experiments.	2.24 The assignment of experimental subjects to groups by random means such as computer assignment to assure that the groups are similar in composition.
2.34 The degree to which an operational definition accurately represents a particular variable.	2.25 A measure of variability; the difference between the highest score and the lowest score in a sample.
2.35 Quantities, characteristics, or phenomena whose values are assigned by the experimenter or that are free to vary.	2.26 The repeatability of a measurement; the likelihood that if the measurement were made again it would yield the same value.
	2.27 A research technique that asks subjects to report what happened in the past.

Chapter 3
Biology of Behavior

Lesson I

Read the interim summary on pages 64-65 of your text to reacquaint yourself with the material in this section.

3-1   *Describe methods for studying the brain and for assessing brain damage and outline the basic structure of the nervous system.*

Read pages 56-64 and then answer the following questions:

1. Physiological psychologists frequently study the brain by producing brain lesions in experimental animals.

   a. What is a *brain lesion?*

   b. Explain the underlying logic of research that employs brain lesions.

2. Study Figure 3.1 in your text and explain how brain lesions are produced in the laboratory.

   a. Carefully describe a *stereotaxic apparatus* and describe the position of the animal. Be sure to explain why this equipment is used.

   b. How does the researcher actually produce the brain lesion?

3. a. Study Figure 3.2 in your text and explain how electrodes for recording or stimulation may be placed in an animal's brain.

   b. Explain the logic of electrical recording studies.

   c. Study Figure 3.3 in your text and either draw or carefully describe how an animal is prepared for recording electrical brain activity.

   d. Explain the logic of brain stimulation studies.

e. Why does electrical stimulation of the brain affect an animal's behavior?

4. Describe the use of chemicals in brain research.

5. How do researchers confirm the location of the brain lesions they have produced?

6. a. Describe how neuropsychologists study the human brain.

   b. What is the leading cause of human brain lesions?

   c. How is the location of human brain lesions confirmed?

   d. Describe the appearance of a CT scanner and explain how the patient is positioned.

   e. Now compare the CT scans in Figures 3.4 and 3.5 in your text with the photograph of a brain slice in Figure 3.4.

   f. What device is beginning to take the place of CT scanners?

   g. Describe PET and MRI scanners and the images they produce, and explain what they do. (Study Figures 3.6 and 3.7 in your text.)

7. Study Figure 3.8 in your text and list the two divisions of the nervous system and identify the major structures within each of them.

8. Study Figure 3.9 in your text, draw a profile of the human brain, and label the three major divisions.

9. Explain how the vertebrae, the meninges, and the cerebrospinal fluid protect the brain and the spinal cord from injury. (Refer back to Figure 3.8.)

10. a. The _____ _____ is believed to be the most primitive region and controls _____ _____ and _____ _____ .

b. The _____ _____ are believed to be the most recently evolved parts of the brain.

c. The _____ looks like a set of miniature _____ _____ and is involved in the control of _____ .

11. Describe the development of the central nervous system. Identify the three parts of the brain that develop around the three chambers present early in development. Note that the chamber in front divides into three ventricles and that the middle chamber becomes narrow. (Study Figures 3.10a,b, and c in your text as you go.)

12. a. Describe the appearance of the cerebral cortex.

b. What is its function?

c. Why is the human cerebral cortex full of wrinkles?

d. Study Figure 3.11 in your text and describe the gyri and fissures.

13. Describe the structure and function of the peripheral nervous system. (See Figure 3.12 in your text.)

14. What is the difference between spinal nerves and cranial nerves?

Read the interim summary on page 72 of your text to reacquaint yourself with the material in this section.

3-2   *Describe the primary sensory, primary motor, and association cortex and discuss the concept of lateralization of function.*

Read pages 65-68 and then answer the following questions:

1. Study Figure 3.14 in your text and draw a side view of the human brain, showing the location of the primary motor cortex, the primary somatosensory cortex, the primary auditory cortex, and the primary visual cortex.

2. Each cerebral hemisphere receives information from the *contralateral* side of the body. Explain what that statement means.

3. a. The portion of the cerebral cortex not occupied by the primary sensory or motor areas is known as the

_____ _____ .

 b. What does this region do?

4. a. Identify the landmark on the surface of cerebral cortex that divides the anterior and posterior regions.

 b. Identify the general activities of each of these two regions.

5. Go back to the drawing you prepared in question 1. Review Figures 3.15 and 3.16 in your text and then add the four lobes and indicate the location of the sensory and motor association cortex.

6. Describe the functions of the right and left hemisphere using these terms: *lateralization*, *analysis*, and *synthesis*.

3-3 *Describe the functions of the four lobes of the cerebral cortex.*

Read pages 68-72 and then answer the following questions:

1. a. State the principal function of the occipital lobe.

 b. Damage to _____ _____ cortex causes a "hole" in the visual field, whereas damage to _____ _____ cortex does not cause blindness, but it does cause _____ _____ .

 c. Describe visual agnosia.

2. a. State the principal function of the temporal lobe.

 b. What happens after damage to the auditory association cortex of the left temporal lobe?

 c. What happens after damage to the auditory association cortex of the right temporal lobe?

3. a. State the principal function of the parietal lobe.

 b. What happens after damage to the association cortex of the right parietal lobe?

 c. What happens after damage to the association cortex of the left parietal lobe?

 d. Study Figures 3.17 and 3.18 in your text and compare the left and right sides of the drawings of the bike with each other and with the drawing of the clock, paying special attention to the richness of detail and proportion.

 e. Use the concept of *sensory neglect* to explain the differences in detail on the two halves of each drawing.

f. Imagine how a patient with right hemisphere damage would draw a picture of a daisy. Draw one that way.

g. List some tasks that are difficult for patients who have damage to the parietal lobes:

1. left hemisphere

2. right hemisphere

4. a. State the principal function of the frontal lobe.

b. Damage to right primary motor cortex results in paralysis of which side of the body?

c. List the four categories of deficits that result from damage to motor association cortex.

1.

2.

3.

4.

Read the interim summary on pages 77-78 of your text to reacquaint yourself with the material in this section.

3-4   *Describe the control of internal functions and automatic behaviors by the brain stem, the cerebellum, the thalamus, the hypothalamus, and the limbic system.*

Read pages 72-77 and then answer the following questions:

1. Using your own words, define:

a. homeostasis.

b. species-typical behavior.

2. List the three structures of the brain stem and their principal functions. (See Figure 3.20 in your text.)

a.

b.

c.

3. State the principal functions of the cerebellum.

4. List the two kinds of information the cerebellum receives.

a.   b.

5. The white matter is a layer of _____ _____ that connect the _____ with the rest of the brain.

6. Study Figure 3.21 in your text and describe the location and appearance of the thalamus.

7. a. Describe the two basic functions of the thalamus.

   b. Which function is more primitive?

   c. What is the only kind of sensory information that does not go directly to the thalamus?

8. a. Draw a profile of the human brain and include the thalamus, hypothalamus, and pituitary gland. (Study Figure 3.22 in your text.)

   b. Describe two ways that the hypothalamus receives sensory information.

   c. Name the gland controlled by the hypothalamus.

9. Explain why the pituitary is considered the "master gland." Be sure to use the term *endocrine glands* in your answer.

10. The autonomic nervous system is also controlled by the hypothalamus. List its two branches and their functions.

    Branch   Function

    1.

    2.

11. Indicate whether each of the following responses are controlled by the sympathetic (S) or parasympathetic (PS) branch of the autonomic nervous system. (See Table 3.2 in your text.)

    _____ crying

    _____ sweaty palms

    _____ drooling

    _____ decreased heart rate

    _____ constriction of the pupil of the eye

    _____ erection

12. Explain why a person analyzing the results of a "lie detector" test must know something about the functions of the autonomic nervous system. (See Table 3.2 in your text.)

13. Study Figure 3.34 in your text and draw a profile of the human brain and include the limbic cortex, the amygdala, and the hippocampus.

14. a. These three structures together are parts of the _____ _____.

 b. List several effects of damage to these structures.

 1. amygdala

 2. hippocampus

Lesson I Self Test

1. In order to infer the function of a damaged brain region, it is most important to know

 a. the subject's age.
 b. how the damage occurred.
 c. when the damage occurred.
 d. where the damage occurred.

2. Most of the brain tissue is found in the

 a. cerebral cortex.
 b. cerebral hemispheres.
 c. ventricles.
 d. cerebellum.

3. Fissures and gyri

 a. increase the surface area of the brain.
 b. separate the brain from the skull.
 c. are pathways for cerebrospinal fluid.
 d. line the ventricles.

4. The central fissure divides the cerebral cortex into

 a. hemispheres.
 b. lobes
 c. anterior and posterior regions.
 d. primary and association cortex.

5. Lateralization of function refers to the fact that the two sides of the brain

    a. perform identical functions.
    b. do not perform identical functions.
    c. receive information from the opposite side of the body.
    d. operate independently.

6. Although he is not deaf, Mr. R. can no longer understand what people say to him. He has most likely suffered damage to the

    a. occipital lobe.
    b. temporal lobe.
    c. parietal lobe.
    d. frontal lobe.

7. The opening vignette describes how Miss S. ignores the left half of her environment and even her own body. She has most likely suffered damage to the

    a. occipital lobe.
    b. temporal lobe.
    c. parietal lobe.
    d. frontal lobe.

8. The cerebellum plays an important role in the control of

    a. movement.
    b. sleep.
    c. species-typical behavior.
    d. body temperature.

9. The pituitary gland controls the

    a. thalamus.
    b. hypothalamus.
    c. endocrine glands.
    d. limbic system.

10. The limbic system is a set of structures located in the

    a. brain stem.
    b. cerebellum.
    c. pons.
    d. cerebral hemispheres.

Lesson II

Read the interim summary on pages 87-88 of your text to reacquaint yourself with the material in this section.

3-5 *Describe the structures of neurons and the effects of synaptic transmission and explain the workings of a simple neural circuit.*

Read pages 76-83 and then answer the following questions:

1. List the four major parts of a neuron and identify their primary functions.

   1.

   2.

   3.

   4.

2. Study Figure 3.25 in your text and draw a neuron and label its parts.

3. When an _____ _____ is sent down the axon, the _____ _____ secretes a chemical called a _____ _____, which affects the activity of the cell with which it communicates.

4. a. Name the substance that almost completely surrounds axons and describe its appearance and composition. (See Figure 3.25 in your text.)

   d. What is its function?

5. Now that you are familiar with the major parts of a neuron and their functions, sketch two side-by-side neurons and join them together with several synapses. Study Figure 3.27 in your text.

6. a. Study Figure 3.28 in your text and describe a motor neuron and its relation to a muscle.

   b. What happens when the motor neuron fires?

   c. Explain the relationship between rate of firing and strength of muscular contraction.

7. Explain the following terms:

   a. excitatory synapse

   b. inhibitory synapse

   c. presynaptic neuron

   d. postsynaptic neuron

8. Study Figure 3.30 in your text and describe a simple withdrawal reflex in response to an unpleasant stimulus:

   a. Name the neurons that first detect the stimulus.

   b. What change immediately takes place in these neurons?

   c. What is the location of the terminal buttons of the axons of these neurons?

   d. What kind of transmitter substance do they release?

   e. Name the neurons they excite.

   f. Interneurons stimulate another set of neurons. Name them.

   g. What change now takes place in the muscle?

   h. What was the overall effect of this sequence of events?

9. The soup bowl was so hot that you felt it burning your fingers. Somehow you managed to put it down without dropping it. Explain how the simple withdrawal reflex that you have just described was inhibited. (Study Figure 3.31 in your text.)

3-6 *Explain the steps of synaptic transmission and the effects of drugs and neuromodulators on this process.*

Read pages 83-87 and then answer the following questions:

1. Identify

   a. the containers inside the terminal button and what they store.

   b. what happens to some of these containers when an action potential comes down the axon.

   c. the place into which the transmitter substance is released.

   d. the two kinds of effects that a transmitter substance can have on a postsynaptic neuron.

   e. the protein molecules that trigger these reactions, and their location.

2. a. Use one word to describe the duration of the synaptic effects.

   b. Describe the process that stops the effect of a transmitter substance at most synapses. (See Figure 3.34 in your text.) Be sure to describe what happens to the used transmitter substance.

   c. Explain the relationship between rate of re-uptake and duration of the effect of the transmitter substance.

3. Describe how a drug can increase the production of a transmitter substance. Give a specific example and name and describe the disease it treats.

4. a. Name a specific drug that

    1. facilitates the release of a transmitter substance.

    2. inhibits the release of a transmitter substance.

  b. Name the transmitter substance that these drugs affect, and describe the brain functions in which it is involved.

5. a. Describe two ways that drugs can effect postsynaptic receptors and give an example of a drug in each category.

    1.

    2.

  b. Name a drug used to treat schizophrenia and briefly explain why it is effective.

6. Explain how cocaine and amphetamines produce their effects.

7. a. Compare the range of action of transmitter substances and neuromodulators.

  b. Name the best known group of neuromodulators.

  c. When are these chemicals released?

  d. What is their general effect and why is it significant?

  e. Explain how opiates exert their effect on neurons.

Read the interim summary on page 93 of your text to reacquaint yourself with the material in this section.

3-7 *Describe the effects of following drugs: those that cause sedation, excitation, or alteration of perceptions, and those that alleviate the symptoms of mental disorders.*

Read pages 88-90 and then answer the following questions:

1. a. Name the principal effect of barbiturates.

  b. List the effects of barbiturate overdose.

    c. Why are barbiturates poor sleeping medications?

2. a. Name an important class of antianxiety drugs and give a specific example.

    b. How do they exert their effect on neurons in the brain?

3. a. Name the most commonly used depressant drug.

    b. The effects of a moderate dose of alcohol plus a moderate dose of barbiturates is _____ and can be _____.

    c. How does alcohol affect neurons in the brain?

4. Describe research by Suzdak and his colleagues (1986):

    a. Name the drug both rats were given by injection.

    b. Name the additional drug one of them received.

    c. Compare the appearance of the rats. (See Figure 3.38 in your text.)

    d. Compare the effects of this drug on alcohol and barbiturate intoxication and explain the difference.

    e. Explain why this drug will probably not be widely used.

5. Describe research on alcohol addiction:

    a. How have researchers succeeded in getting some rats to drink alcohol?

    b. Underline the correct response: An adopted person is more likely to become an alcoholic if his or her *biological/adoptive* parents are also alcoholics.

    c. What do these results suggest about one of the causes of alcoholism?

6. a. Briefly explain how amphetamine and cocaine mimic the effects of reinforcing stimuli.

    b. Name and describe the serious symptoms that occur after heavy, prolonged use of these drugs.

c. What are the implications of drug-induced psychosis for research on schizophrenia?

7. a. Explain why drugs that suppress serotonin-secreting neurons produce hallucinations.

 b. Compare the hallucinations produced by cocaine and LSD.

8. Psychotherapeutic drugs often affect synapses using particular types of transmitter substances.

 a. Drugs that block _____ receptors reduce or eliminate the symptoms of schizophrenia.

 b. Drugs that stimulate synapses that use _____ relieve the symptoms of depression.

 c. _____ _____ is an effective treatment for severe mood swings between depression and _____. The reason for its therapeutic effect is _____.

3-8   *Discuss the causes of opiate addiction.*

Read pages 90-93 and then answer the following questions:

1. Why do opiates affect behavior?

2. a. List the functions of three neural systems that are affected by the stimulation of opiate receptors.

  1.

  2.

  3.

 b. Of the three functions, which one is most likely responsible for opiate addiction?

3. Explain this statement: "The behavioral response to opiates shows tolerance."

4. a. Use one word to contrast the withdrawal symptoms and the primary effects of the drug.

 b. List some of the symptoms experience by heroin addicts who are trying to break their habit.

  1.

  2.

  3.

5. a. Explain the function of the brain's compensatory mechanisms.

 b. Explain why these mechanisms cause drug tolerance.

c. Explain why they cause withdrawal symptoms.

d. Explain why recovering addicts feel a strong need for drugs when they encounter people or paraphernalia that remind them of their habit. (See Figure 3.39 in your text and be sure to use the term *classical conditioning* in your answer.

6. Use the concepts of tolerance and reinforcement to explain why some addicts go "cold turkey" and why avoidance of withdrawal effects is not the primary cause of addiction.

Lesson II Self Test

1. The largest structure of the neuron is the

   a. soma.
   b. dendrites.
   c. axon.
   d. terminal buttons.

2. Neurons communicate through

   a. myelin sheaths.
   b. muscular contractions.
   c. synapses.
   d. interneurons.

3. In a simple withdrawal reflex, the noxious stimulus is detected by

   a. sensory neurons.
   b. interneurons.
   c. motor neurons.
   d. association neurons.

4. When the action potential reaches a terminal button, synaptic vesicles

   a. pull back from the presynaptic membrane.
   b. are released into the synaptic cleft.
   c. attach to the postsynaptic receptors.
   d. move, break open, and release transmitter substance.

5. The action potential is _____, but communication between neurons is _____.

   a. chemical; electrical
   b. electrical; chemical
   c. inhibitory; excitatory
   d. excitatory; inhibitory

6. L-DOPA is an effective treatment for Parkinson's disease because it

a. blocks dopamine receptors.
b. stimulates dopamine receptors.
c. blocks dopamine production by neurons.
d. stimulates dopamine production.

7. Benzodiazepines

a. have antianxiety effects.
b. are used to help people with hypersomnia stay awake.
c. are the most commonly used antidepressant drugs.
d. are lethal in moderately high doses.

8. Lithium carbonate is an effective treatment for

a. schizophrenia.
b. auditory hallucinations.
c. alternating periods of depression and mania.
d. depression.

9. A person who takes opiates regularly develops tolerance. That is,

a. increasing amounts of the drug must be taken to achieve a "high."
b. the severity of withdrawal symptoms decreases.
c. the primary effects of the drug become classically conditioned to environmental stimuli.
d. neurons involved in reinforcement become more and more activated.

10. Withdrawal symptoms

a. are generally the opposite of the effects of the drug itself.
b. account for the additive effects of drugs.
c. activate compensatory mechanisms.
d. are the primary cause of drug addiction.

Answers for Self Tests

Lesson I		Lesson II	
1. d	Obj. 3-1	1. a	Obj. 3-5
2. b	Obj. 3-1	2. c	Obj. 3-5
3. a	Obj. 3-1	3. a	Obj. 3-5
4. c	Obj. 3-2	4. d	Obj. 3-6
5. b	Obj. 3-2	5. b	Obj. 3-6
6. b	Obj. 3-3	6. d	Obj. 3-6
7. c	Obj. 3-3	7. a	Obj. 3-7
8. a	Obj. 3-4	8. c	Obj. 3-7
9. c	Obj. 3-4	9. a	Obj. 3-8
10 d	Obj. 3-4	10 a	Obj. 3-8

3.1 acetylcholine	3.10 brain stem
3.2 action potential	3.11 central nervous system
3.3 amygdala	3.12 cerebellum
3.4 antianxiety drug	3.13 cerebral cortex
3.5 autonomic nervous system	3.14 cerebrospinal fluid (CSF)
3.6 axon	3.15 contralateral
3.7 barbiturate	3.16 CT scanner
3.8 benzodiazepine	3.17 dendrite
3.9 brain lesion	3.18 dopamine

3.10

The "stem" of the brain, including the medulla, pons, and midbrain, involved in the control of functions and behaviors essential to survival of individual or species; does not include cerebral hemispheres or cerebellum.

3.1

A transmitter substance released by the terminal buttons of some neurons in the brain and peripheral nervous system; causes muscles to contract ACh neurons appear to be involved in memory.

3.11

The brain and spinal cord.

3.2

A brief electrochemical event carried by an axon from the cell body to the terminal buttons, which release a transmitter substance.

3.12

Pair of hemispheres resembling the cerebral hemispheres but smaller; receives information from the frontal cortex and assists in the control and coordination of movement, posture and balance.

3.3

A part of the limbic system of the brain located deep in the temporal lobe. Damage causes changes in emotional and aggressive behavior.

3.13

Outer layer of the cerebral hemispheres of the brain; specialized areas include the primary sensory and motor cortex, the association cortex and regions necessary for speech comprehension and production.

3.4

A "tranquilizer," which reduces anxiety. One of the most common is diazepam (Valium).

3.14

A clear liquid that fills the hollow ventricles inside the brain and the spaces between the meninges and the surface of the brain and spinal cord; serves to cushion them against injury.

3.5

Controls the internal organs, blood vessels, sweat glands, and endocrine glands; sympathetic branch is active during exercise or high arousal; parasympathetic branch is active during repose.

3.15

Located on the opposite side of the brain.

3.6

A long, thin extension of a neuron that divides into a few or many branches, ending in terminal buttons.

3.16

A diagnostic machine using computerized tomography (CT) to scan the brain by sending a narrow beam of X rays through a person's head producing a two-dimensional image.

3.7

A class of drugs that cause sedation by depressing the activity of the brain by unknown means and by stimulating benzodiazepine receptors; poor sleeping medication.

3.17

"Treelike" growths attached to the soma of a neuron; terminal buttons of other neurons form synapses there.

3.8

A class of antianxiety drugs that works by stimulating a particular type of neuromodulator receptors; sometimes prescribed to treat anxiety disorders or to promote sleep.

3.18

Transmitter substance released by the terminal buttons of some neurons in the brain; important in reinforcement and control of movement; may be involved in schizophrenia.

3.9

An injury to a particular part of the brain produced by researcher, usually by passing an electric current through a fine wire that has been inserted into the brain using a stereotaxic apparatus.

3.19 endocrine gland	3.28 meninges
3.20 frontal lobe	3.29 motor neuron
3.21 hippocampus	3.30 myelin sheath
3.22 homeostasis	3.31 neuromodulator
3.23 hypothalamus	3.32 occipital lobe
3.24 interneuron	3.33 opiod
3.25 limbic cortex	3.34 parietal lobe
3.26 limbic system	3.35 peripheral nervous system
3.27 medulla	3.36 pituitary gland

3.28

A set of three membranes that encase the central nervous system.

3.19

A gland that secretes a hormone into the blood supply; for example, the adrenal gland and the pituitary gland.

3.29

A neuron whose terminal buttons form synapses with muscle fibers. When an action potential travels down its axon, the associated muscle fibers will twitch.

3.20

Portion of the cerebral cortex lying in front of the central fissure; the anterior part is called the motor association cortex and damage impairs movement and planning; includes Broca's speech area.

3.30

An insulating substance, part protein and part fat, produced by special cells that wrap themselves around segments of an axon leaving small bare patches of axon between them.

3.21

A component structure of the limbic system of the brain, located in the temporal lobe; plays important roles in learning and expression of emotion.

3.31

Chemical released by some neurons in the brain that can travel long distances and alter the activity of other neurons.

3.22

The process by which important physiological characteristics (such a body temperature and blood pressure) are regulated so that they remain at their optimum level.

3.32

The region of cerebral cortex lying at the back of the brain behind the parietal and temporal lobes; involved in vision.

3.23

A region of the brain located below the thalamus and above the pituitary gland; controls the autonomic nervous system and behaviors related to regulation and survival.

3.33

Neuromodulator secreted by neurons in times of stress or while engaged in species-typical behaviors; decreases sensitivity to pain, heightens arousal and has reinforcing effects.

3.24

In a simple withdrawal reflex, the neuron that receives sensory information and then stimulates the motor neurons that cause the appropriate muscle to contract.

3.34

The region of the cerebral cortex behind the central fissure and in back of the frontal lobe and above the temporal lobe; contains somatosensory cortex.

3.25

The oldest part of the cerebral cortex, located around the edges; part of the limbic system.

3.35

The nerves and their associated structures; transmits information between the central nervous system and the body.

3.26

A set of interconnected structures of the brain; important in emotional and species-typical behavior and the learning; includes the limbic cortex, amygdala, and hippocampus.

3.36

An endocrine gland attached to the hypothalamus at the base of the brain; controls most of the rest of the endocrine system.

3.27

Part of the brain stem closest to the spinal cord; controls heart rate, blood pressure, rate of respiration and some organized movements such as crawling and swimming.

3.37 pons	3.46 sensory association cortex
3.38 postsynaptic neuron	3.47 sensory neglect
3.39 presynaptic neuron	3.48 sensory neuron
3.40 primary auditory cortex	3.49 serotonin
3.41 primary motor cortex	3.50 soma
3.42 primary somatosensory cortex	3.51 species-typical behavior
3.43 primary visual cortex	3.52 stereotaxic apparatus
3.44 re-uptake	3.53 synapse
3.45 receptor	3.54 synaptic vesicle

3.46

Regions of the cerebral cortex adjacent to primary sensory cortex; analyze sensory information; perception occurs here and memories related to the particular information are stored here.

3.47

A neurological disturbance in which a person fails to notice or pay attention to stimuli that he or she is physically able to perceive; usually caused by damage to the parietal lobe in the right hemisphere.

3.48

In a simple withdrawal reflex, these neurons detect the noxious stimulus and transmit this information to the spinal cord.

3.49

A transmitter substance secreted by the terminal buttons of some neurons; appears to play a role in the control of sleep and has been implicated in the occurrence of depression.

3.50

The largest part of a neuron; contains mechanisms that control the metabolism and maintenance of the cell; also called cell body.

3.51

A behavior that is seen in all or most members of a species, such as reproductive behaviors or fighting.

3.52

A device used to guide the placement of a wire or hypodermic needle into a particular part of the brain for the purpose of producing localized damage, recording electrical activity, or stimulating the brain electrically.

3.53

The junction between the terminal button of the presynaptic neuron and the membrane of the postsynaptic neuron.

3.54

A submicroscopic sac located in a terminal button that contains the transmitter substance.

3.37

One of the three structures of the brain stem anterior to the medulla; controls some of the stages of sleep.

3.38

Receives messages from another neuron through synapses with the terminal buttons of that neuron.

3.39

Sends messages to another neuron through synapses with that neuron.

3.40

The region of the cerebral cortex that receives information directly from the auditory system; located in the temporal lobes.

3.41

The region of the cerebral cortex that directly controls the movements of the body; located in the back part of the frontal lobes.

3.42

The region of the cerebral cortex that receives information directly from the somatosensory system (touch, pressure, vibration, pain, and temperature); located in the front part of the parietal lobes.

3.43

The region of the cerebral cortex that receives information directly from the visual system; located in the occipital lobes.

3.44

The process by which a terminal button retrieves the molecules of transmitter substance that it has just released; terminates the effect of the transmitter substance on the receptors of the postsynaptic neuron.

3.45

A special protein molecule in the membrane of the postsynaptic neuron; responds to molecules of a transmitter substance or neuromodulator.

3.55

temporal lobe

3.56

terminal button

3.57

tolerance

3.58

transmitter substance

3.59

ventricle

3.60

visual agnosia

3.61

white matter

3.62

withdrawal symptom

3.55

The portion of the cerebral cortex below the frontal and parietal lobes; contains the auditory cortex; damage results in deficits in audition and production and perception of speech.

3.56

Rounded swelling at the end of the axon of a neuron; releases a transmitter substance.

3.57

A behavioral response to opiates that forces a person to take increasing amounts of a drug in order to achieve the same effect.

3.58

A chemical released by the terminal buttons that causes the postsynaptic neuron to be excited or inhibited.

3.59

One of the hollow chambers in the brain that are filled with cerebrospinal fluid.

3.60

Defect in the ability to identity an object by means of vision despite normal visual acuity; caused by damage to visual association cortex.

3.61

Portions of the central nervous system abundant in axons rather than cell bodies of neurons; the color derives from the myelin sheaths surrounding the axons.

3.62

A physiological response that occurs when a person with drug tolerance stops taking the drug; generally the opposite of the primary effect of the drug.

Chapter 4
Basic Principles of Learning

Lesson I

Read the interim summary on page 106 of your text to reacquaint yourself with the material in this section.

4-1   *Define learning and describe short-term and long-term habituation.*

Read pages 99-100 and then answer the following questions:

1. a. Define learning in your own words. Your definition should state what changes and why, and the duration of the change.

    b. Why do some psychologists distinguish between learning and performance?

    c. State their preferred definition of learning.

    d. List two circumstances that influence the performance of a behavior.

2. a. Mike was reading when he heard the banging. His head immediately turned in the direction of the sound which, he realized, was simply knocking of the heating pipes. What formal name is given to Mike's response?

    b. The pipes continued to knock now and then, but Mike no longer looked toward them. What formal name is given to the change in Mike's response?

3. Compare short-term and long-term habituation.

4. Why is habituation beneficial to a species?

4-2   *Describe the discovery of classical conditioning by Pavlov and discuss its characteristics.*

Read pages 100-106 and then answer the following questions:

1. a. Study Figures 4.1 and 4.2 in your text and explain why the child in Figure 4.2 is grimacing and drawing up his shoulders even before the balloon bursts.

b. Now explain the child's behavior using these terms: defensive reaction, neutral stimulus, important stimulus, classically conditioned.

2. a. Briefly retell how Pavlov original research interests led to his classic work in conditioning. Be sure to note what event suggested that salivation was not an automatic reflexive response.

b. Study Figure 4.3 in your text and describe Pavlov's original apparatus.

c. Describe the original conditioning procedure. Be sure you mention the time interval between sounding the tuning fork and giving the dog food.

d. How did Pavlov change his testing procedure in later studies?

e. What response did he observe when food was presented

   1. a short time after the tone?

   2. a long time after the tone?

   3. before the tone sounded?

3. Psychologists have given formal names to the stimuli and the responses. Study Figure 4.4 in your text and give a more formal name for the

   a. original eliciting stimulus (taste of food):

   b. salivation caused by the taste of food:

   c. neutral stimulus (tuning fork or bell):

   d. salivation caused by the sound of the tuning fork or bell:

4. In Pavlov's studies, the dog's response was unchanging; it always salivated. Learning was demonstrated by what sort of change?

5. The following situations illustrate some of the concepts you have just reviewed. Name them.

   a. John, a house painter, is often stung by wasps. Last week, just after setting his ladder against a house, he heard a buzzing noise and ducked his head. His response is a(n) _____. The buzzing noise is a(n) _____.

   b. John does not remember the first time he was stung by a wasp. Describe what must have happened, using the correct terms for the stimuli and responses that occurred then.

6. List the two important functions of classical conditioning.

7. What specific physical change did Hebb (1949) suggest occurs during classical conditioning?

8. To study how learning occurs during classical conditioning, researchers often record the nictitating membrane response.

   a. Describe the nictitating membrane.

   b. Use these terms to describe the conditioning procedure below: US UR CS CR

   > A puff of air to the eye (the _____) always causes the nictitating membrane to close (the _____). If a bell is sounded just before the puff of air, the animal will eventually learn to close its nictitating membrane as soon as it hears the bell. The sound of the bell has become the _____ and closing the membrane has become the _____.

   c. Study Figure 4.5 in your text and then draw the hypothesized changes that may take place in the neuron following classical conditioning.

   d. Initially, what are the relative strengths of the synapses on neuron A in your drawing?

   e. What must happen for the weak synapse to become strengthened? Be specific, and include the time sequence.

   f. Carefully explain why the tone alone can now cause the nictitating membrane to close.

9. a. Name the phenomenon illustrated by Figure 4.5.

   b. Summarize research on the existence of heterosynaptic facilitation and the search for the parts of the brain involved in classical conditioning of the nictitating membrane response.

10. A conditional response will continue to occur only if the _____ _____ occurs occasionally with the _____ _____.

11. a. Define *extinction* in your own words.

    b. How did Pavlov extinguish a dog's salivary response? (See Figure 4.6 in your text)

    c. If the dog had been permitted to rest after Trial 9 and then the CS had been presented again, what would have happened?

d. Name this phenomenon.

12. a. Suppose that seeing some fossils in a museum reminds you of the times you went fossil hunting with your grandfather, and gives you a feeling of nostalgia. How would you explain this event in terms of classical conditioning?

b. Relate this phenomenon to the research of Staats and Staats (1958).

c. ... and to the research of Berkowitz (1964).

13. a. Define:

1. phobia

2. fetish

b. Briefly explain how these behaviors can develop.

c. Summarize research by Rachman and Hodgson (1968) on classical conditioning of a fetish. Be sure you identify the CS, US, CR, and UR.

Read the interim summary on pages 114-115 of your text to reacquaint yourself with the material in this section.

4-3   *Describe instrumental conditioning, the nature of reinforcement and punishment, and the phenomenon of extinction.*

Read pages 106-110 and then answer the following questions:

1. Restate Thorndike's law of effect and explain its relationship to instrumental conditioning. (You may wish to review the discussion in Chapter 1.)

2. a. Explain the relationship between an animal's behavior and the types of events that immediately follow that behavior. Be sure to use the term *contingency* in your answer.

b. Why is this particular kind of learning is called *instrumental* conditioning?

3. a. The role that appetitive and aversive stimuli play in reinforcement and punishment is important. Begin by defining

   1. appetitive stimulus.

   2. aversive stimulus.

   b. Is it the preferences of the researcher or the organism that determines whether a particular stimuli will be aversive or appetitive? Explain and give an example.

   c. The presence of an appetitive stimulus immediately after a behavior _____ the probability that the behavior will be repeated. This phenomenon is called _____. The termination of an aversive stimulus immediately after a behavior will _____ the probability that the behavior will be repeated. This phenomenon is called _____ _____. The presence of an aversive stimulus immediately after a behavior will _____ the probability that the behavior will be repeated. This phenomenon is called _____.

   d. One type of reinforcement or punishment was not covered in paragraph c. Name and define it.

4. Name the four types of reinforcement/punishment and give an example of each of them. For each, identify the response and the reinforcing or punishing stimulus.

   1.

      response:

      reinforcing/punishing stimulus:

   2.

      response:

      reinforcing/punishing stimulus:

   3.

      response:

      reinforcing/punishing stimulus:

   4.

      response:

      reinforcing/punishing stimulus:

5. Describe the study by Logan (1965) on the importance of the immediacy of reinforcement.

6. Explain the difference between forgetting and extinction.

7. Study Figure 4.8 in your text. Explain what the experimenter did and what the results were.

8. Explain the phenomenon of spontaneous recovery of an extinguished response.

4-4   *Describe conditioned reinforcement and punishment, the role of classical conditioning in instrumental conditioning, the conditioning of complex behaviors, and the procedure called shaping.*

Read pages 110-113 and then answer the following questions:

1. State the essential difference between primary reinforcers and punishers and conditioned reinforcers and punishers.

2. a. A neutral stimulus that regularly occurs just before an appetitive stimulus will become a conditioned
   _____.

   b. A neutral stimulus that regularly occurs before an aversive stimulus will become a conditioned
   _____.

   c. List two reasons why it is important that neutral stimuli can become classically conditioned reinforcers or punishers.

3. For each of these examples decide whether the stimulus is a reinforcer or a punisher, and whether it is conditioned or primary.

   a. _____   the smell of the perfume/after-shave lotion of someone very close to you

   b. _____   the warmth of a fire after having been out in the cold

   c. _____   a bite of pizza that burns the roof of your mouth

   d. _____   a speeding ticket

   e. _____   a fine for returning your library books after the due date

   f. _____   acceptance to graduate school

   g. _____   nods of agreement from classmates

4. For each of the following situations suggest what kind of stimulus might have reinforced the person's behavior.

   a. Nancy worked long hours even in the hot summer because she enjoyed her reputation as the best gardener in the neighborhood.

b. Matt's parents were amazed at how long their young son would stay outside shooting baskets.

c. Susan worked hard at her paper route and hoped to be named a "Carrier of the Month."

d. Mr. Brown always took responsibility for organizing winter camping trips for the Boy Scouts.

5. Explain the shaping procedure:

a. Describe an operant chamber. (See Figure 4.9 in your text.)

b. From what does the operant chamber get its name?

c. Restate the principle of instrumental conditioning that explains why a food pellet delivered after the first accidental lever press will not be enough to reinforce the behavior.

d. Number these eight steps so that they can be read in the proper sequence and describe the solution to this problem.

_____ wait until the rat turns even more, almost touching the lever, and then activate pellet dispenser

_____ wait until the rat touches the lever with any body part and then activate pellet dispenser

_____ find auditory stimulus to serve as conditioned reinforcer

_____ wait for rat to eat the food, then deliver a few more food pellets while rat is near food dish so the noise will become an appetitive stimulus

_____ now wait until rat leaves dish and turns in direction of lever before activating pellet dispenser

_____ turning movement is now well established

_____ activate pellet dispenser for the first time

_____ wait until rat presses lever hard enough to operate switch itself

6. Give a more formal name for the shaping procedure.

4-5   *Describe and discuss the Premack Principle.*

Read pages 113-114 and then answer the following questions:

1. Why is it important to find a stimuli that is reinforcing for a particular organism before attempting to change that organism's behavior?

2. According to Premack (1965), what procedure can help a researcher make an accurate choice?

3. a. What unexpected behavior did Premack (1965) observe when he used M&Ms to reinforce the behavior of children in one of his studies?

b. The _____ and not the _____ determines which stimuli can actually reinforce behavior.

4. State the Premack principle.

a. part I

b. part II

5. Summarize the case of the severely retarded man reported by Tyson:

a. Which behavior was higher on the man's preference hierarchy--bed making or bathing?

b. Describe the contingency Tyson used to change the man's behavior.

Lesson I Self Test

1. Jill remarked to her neighbor that her newborn son used to cry every time the phone rang but no longer does. The absence of a response is an example of

a. species-typical behavior.
b. long-term habituation.
c. extinction.
d. classical conditioning.

2. A child who has a balloon burst in his or her face quickly cringes and squints whenever he or she blows up a balloon. The first time the child saw an expanding balloon it served as a(n) and the second time it was a(n)

a. CS; US
b. UR; neutral stimulus
c. neutral stimulus; CS
d. UR; CR

3. Hebb suggested that learning may take place because

a. of changes in the strength of synaptic connections between neurons in the brain.
b. automatic protective responses are "wired into" the brain.
c. some stimuli have more reinforcing value than others.
d. organisms make value judgments about the importance of particular stimuli.

4. _____ occurs when the conditional stimulus is repeatedly presented without being followed by the unconditional stimulus.

a. Spontaneous recovery
b. Heterosynaptic facilitation
c. Extinction
d. Reinforcement

5. Whether or not a particular stimulus is reinforcing depends on the

a. preferences of the researcher.
b. the number of times it is presented.
c. the experimental task.
d. preferences of the organism.

6. The _____ of an aversive stimulus is _____ and _____ of an appetitive stimulus is _____ .

a. termination; reinforcing; termination; punishing
b. termination; punishing; termination; reinforcing
c. occurrence; reinforcing; continuation; punishing
d. occurrence; punishing; occurrence; reinforcing

7. Reinforcement

a. is a technique developed by psychologists to strengthen synaptic connections associated with learning.
b. has yet to be observed in the natural world.
c. is probably not a natural consequence of behavior.
d. is most often a direct result of organism's behavior.

8. Which one of these statements about shaping is correct?

a. Experience indicates that food is the best reinforcer to use when shaping a behavior.
b. Shaping is the reinforcement of successive approximations at regular time intervals.
c. Shaping can be used to train an animal to perform just about any response it is physically capable of.
d. The criteria for a successful response remains constant throughout the shaping procedure.

9. A preference hierarchy

a. is established by allowing an organism free access to an operant chamber.
b. is based on the notion that an organism has different preferences for performing different behaviors.
c. groups all behaviors into two classes: preferred and less preferred.
d. suggests that the target behavior is the most desirable behavior.

10. Tyson's success in getting the severely retarded man to bathe regularly is an example of the application of

a. the Premack principle.
b. negative reinforcement.
c. response cost.
d. classical conditioning.

Lesson II

Read the interim summary on pages 127-128 of your text to reacquaint yourself with the material in this section.

4-6   *Describe the phenomena of discrimination and generalization.*

Read pages 115-118 and then answer the following questions:

1. To review: Give a brief definition of these types of stimuli.

   a. unconditional stimulus

   b. conditional stimulus

   c. reinforcing stimulus

   d. punishing stimulus

   and now add

   e. discriminative stimulus

2. Review the description of teaching a dog to bark on command and name the discriminative stimulus.

3. Briefly explain why the ability to discriminate among stimuli is beneficial to an organism.

4. Describe how a rat, who had previously learned to press a lever to receive a food pellet, was then taught a discrimination task:

   a. What is the meaning of "light on" and "light off?"

   b. Early in training on the discrimination task, how will the number of responses the rat makes when the light is on compare with the number of responses the rat makes when the light is off?

   c. Later, how will these numbers compare?

5. Describe one practical application of discrimination tasks.

6. Define *generalization* in your own words.

7. a. Briefly describe the original discrimination task that Honig and his colleagues (1963) taught pigeons. (See Figure 4.11 in your text.)

b. How did they test for generalization?

c. Describe the results.

8. The procedure for teaching animals to recognize similarities among stimuli is called _____ _____.

9. To test whether pigeons could recognize the concept of a human being, Herrnstein and Loveland (1964) first trained pigeons to peck at a translucent disk (a procedure you are already familiar with).

   a. How did they then present the concept of a human to the pigeons? (See Figure 4.12 in your text.)

   b. Which trials were reinforced and which were not?

   c. What was the discriminative stimulus?

10. List some practical uses of the ability to generalize.

4-7   *Describe the nature and limitations of aversive control in instrumental conditioning.*

Read pages 118-120 and then answer the following questions:

1. To review: The occurrence of an aversive stimulus _____ behavior and the termination of an aversive stimulus _____ behavior.

2. Punishment can be explained as a form of classical conditioning. Briefly review the example of the dog and the porcupine and study Figure 4.13 in your text. Identify:

   a. US

   b. UR

   c. CS

   d. CR

   e. In this case the CS was a stimulus that elicited a CR that belongs to a particular class of behaviors. Name that class.

3. Carefully define these terms.

   a. negative reinforcement

b. escape response

c. avoidance response

4. What cue must be available to the organisms in order for it to make an avoidance response?

5. Discuss some of the limitations of using punishment to control behavior:

a. If punishment is regularly used to control the behavior of a child, what unwanted changes in the child's behavior might also occur?

b. Equally seriously, what unwanted feelings might the child begin to have about the caregiver who uses punishment?

c. Explain why aversive stimuli (like punishment) can negatively reinforce only a small range of behaviors. Be sure to refer to species-typical defense responses in your answer.

4-8   *Describe intermittent reinforcement, its relation to resistance to extinction, and the development of superstitious behavior.*

Read pages 120-122 and then answer the following questions:

1. a. Define *intermittent reinforcement* in your own words.

b. Describe the two major categories of schedules of reinforcement.

1.

2.

2. Describe the pattern of responding if a researcher uses a

a. fixed-ratio schedule of reinforcement.

b. variable-ratio schedule of reinforcement.

c. fixed-interval schedule of reinforcement.

d. variable-interval schedule of reinforcement.

3. Explain the difference between fixed and variable schedules by describing the likely work habits of a sales

person whose sales manner is evaluated

a. every six months by the department manager.

b. twice a year by a team of professional shoppers who make unannounced visits at any time to each department.

4. Two pigeons are being trained to peck at a disk in order to receive food. The responding of one is reinforced on a one-to-one ratio, while the other one receives, on the average, one reinforcer every fifty responses.

a. When we put the pigeons on an extinction schedule, which one responds more?

b. What is this phenomenon called?

c. How do most psychologists explain it?

d. What personality variable may be related to experience with different schedules of reinforcement?

5. a. What does a psychologist mean by the term *superstitious behavior?*

b. Describe the demonstration based on Skinner's research.

4-9   *Discuss flavor aversions and other phenomena related to the compatibility of responses with reinforcers or punishers.*

Read pages 122-123 and then answer the following questions:

1. a. After successfully learning to pick up and deposit a coin in a piggy bank and performing that sequence correctly for several weeks, how did the behavior of the pig begin to change? (Breland and Breland (1961)

b. How can this "misbehavior" be explained?

2. Describe the phenomenon of *conditioned flavor aversion.* Be sure to use the term aversive stimulus in your answer.

3. In the research by Garcia and Koelling (1966), how successful were the following attempts at aversive control?

   a. taste stimulus followed by illness

   b. taste stimulus followed by shock

   c. auditory stimulus was followed by illness

   d. auditory stimulus was followed by shock

4. Explain why the fact that some birds can form a conditioned aversion to the sight of foods that have made them sick does not contradict the research with rats.

5. Describe two examples of conditioned flavor aversions in humans.

   1. spearmint gum before take-off

   2. ice cream before chemotherapy

6. Explain what research on conditioned flavor aversion indicates about the evolution of neural circuits involved in learning.

7. Indicate how the role of the same stimulus--flavor of a food that causes nausea--can be correctly interpreted in two different ways:

   a. If food aversion results through instrumental conditioning, what is the role of flavor?

   b. If food aversion results from classical conditioning, then what is the role of flavor?

4-10 *Describe learning that occurs through observation, imitation and insight.*

Read pages 123-127 and then answer the following questions:

1. Describe some examples of learning through observation and imitation:

   a. pigeons learning a complex operant task

   b. birds learning a song

   c. developing a fear of dogs

2. Describe the research with retarded children by Baer et al., 1967:

   a. Describe the subjects.

   b. When the researchers clapped their hands and said "Do this," how did the children respond?

   c. Then how did the researchers try to teach the children?

   d. How did the children respond this time?

   e. In addition to learning to clap their hands, what else did the children learn?

   f. What theoretical conclusion can be drawn from the results?

3. Define *insight* in your own words.

4. Describe studies that examined learning to solve a problem through insight:

   a. Sultan succeeded in reaching some bananas. (See Figure 4.14 in your text.)

   b. Epstein's pigeons succeeded in reaching a miniature model of a banana. (See Figure 4.15 in your text.)

   c. Sultan managed to obtain a banana that had been placed just outside the reach of either of the two rods he had in his cage.

5. According to Epstein, insight occurs only after what kind of learning has taken place?

Lesson II Self Test

1. Pigeons were trained to peck at a disk when a vertical line was present. When lines with different orientations were projected onto the disks, the birds made the most responses to vertical or near vertical lines. Their behavior is an example of

   a. an orienting response.
   b. habituation.
   c. generalization.
   d. the method of successive approximations.

2. The ability of pigeons to respond only to a slide containing a human is an example of

    a. long-term habituation.
    b. concept formation.
    c. the method of successive approximations.
    d. negative reinforcement.

3. Aversive stimuli

    a. have the same effects on behavior as appetitive stimuli.
    b. elicit species-typical defensive responses.
    c. reinforce a wide-variety of responses.
    d. accelerate training procedures.

4. Ralph is afraid of elevators; he does not even like to see people getting on or off of them. He enters a side entrance of his building and takes the stairs to his office. His behavior is an example of

    a. superstitious behavior.
    b. an escape response.
    c. an avoidance response.
    d. a species-typical defensive response.

5. If an animal's behavior is reinforced on a variable-interval schedule, it will

    a. stop responding after a reinforcer and begin again a little before the next reinforcer is due.
    b. respond rapidly, pause after the reinforcer, and begin again.
    c. respond faster than it would on a variable-ratio schedule.
    d. respond at a slow, steady rate.

6. When a bird, who has previously received a food pellet each time it pecked at a disk, is put on an extinction schedule, the bird will

    a. engage in superstitious behaviors.
    b. continue to respond for a long time.
    c. soon stop responding.
    d. show spontaneous recovery.

7. The trained pig stopped picking up a coin and depositing it in a bank because

    a. it became distracted by people who stopped to watch.
    b. reinforcement schedules were disrupted when people began to feed it.
    c. species-typical behaviors intruded on the instrumentally conditioned behavior.
    d. it developed a conditioned flavor aversion to the reinforcer.

8. Rats learned to avoid a particular taste that was followed by _____.

    a. illness.
    b. shock.
    c. noise.
    d. cold.

9. Baby birds reared apart can learn the song characteristic of their species if they hear a recording of the song. Their behavior demonstrates learning through

a. reinforcement.
b. generalization.
c. trial-and-error.
d. imitation.

10. Learning through insight

a. appears to be an innate tendency.
b. requires external reinforcement.
c. is usually reinforcing by itself.
d. requires some experience with components of the new behavior.

Answers for Self Tests

Lesson I		**Lesson II**	
1. b Obj. 4-1		1. c Obj. 4-6	
2. c Obj. 4-2		2. b Obj. 4-6	
3. a Obj. 4-2		3. b Obj. 4-7	
4. c Obj. 4-2		4. c Obj. 4-7	
5. d Obj. 4-3		5. d Obj. 4-8	
6. d Obj. 4-3		6. c Obj. 4-8	
7. d Obj. 4-4		7. c Obj. 4-9	
8. c Obj. 4-4		8. a Obj. 4-9	
9. b Obj. 4-5		9. d Obj. 4-10	
10. a Obj. 4-5		10. d Obj. 4-10	

4.1 appetitive stimulus	4.10 conditioned reinforcer
4.2 aversive stimulus	4.11 contingency
4.3 avoidance response	4.12 discrimination
4.4 classical conditioning	4.13 discriminative stimulus
4.5 concept	4.14 escape response
4.6 conditional response (CR)	4.15 extinction
4.7 conditional stimulus (CS)	4.16 fetish
4.8 conditioned flavor aversion	4.17 generalization
4.9 conditioned punisher	4.18 habituation

4.10 A process by which a previously neutral stimulus followed by an appetitive stimulus itself becomes capable, through classical conditioning, of reinforcing a response.	4.1 A stimulus that an organism tends to approach; can be used to reinforce a response
4.11 A cause-and-effect relationship between two events, such as that between a particular response and a particular stimulus.	4.2 A stimulus that an organism tends to avoid; can be used either to punish or negatively reinforce a response.
4.12 The recognition of a difference between two stimuli or a change in a stimulus, indicated by the organism's response.	4.3 The performance of a response that prevents an aversive stimulus from occurring.
4.13 In instrumental conditioning, a stimulus that indicates the nature of the current contingency between a response and appetitive or aversive stimuli.	4.4 The presentation of a stimulus (US) that naturally evokes a response (UR) followed by a neutral stimulus; eventually the neutral stimulus becomes a CS that evokes a response (CR) similar to the original one.
4.14 The performance of a response that terminates an aversive stimulus.	4.5 Recognition of similarities among a class of stimuli.
4.15 The elimination of a behavior that occurs when the CS is repeatedly presented without being followed by the US (classical conditioning) or when the response is not followed by the reinforcer (instrumental conditioning).	4.6 In classical conditioning, the response that is elicited by the conditional stimulus.
4.16 Abnormal sexual attachments to objects such as clothing that results from past associations between the objects and sexually potent stimuli.	4.7 In classical conditioning, the stimulus that elicits the conditional response, which resembles the unconditional response.
4.17 The tendency to make a response in the presence of a stimulus similar to the discriminative stimulus.	4.8 A phenomenon in which an aversive stimulus (such as one that produces nausea) is able to punish a behavior (such as eating a particular food) that occurred up to a few hours before the time of the nausea.
4.18 The disappearance of an unconditional response following the repeated presentation of the unconditional stimulus; the simplest form of learning.	4.9 A process by which a previously neutral stimulus followed by an aversive stimulus itself becomes capable, through classical conditioning, of punishing a response.

4.19	4.28
heterosynaptic facilitation	preference hierarchy
4.20	4.29
instrumental conditioning	Premack principle
4.21	4.30
intermittent reinforcement	primary punisher
4.22	4.31
interval schedule of reinforcement	primary reinforcer
4.23	4.32
method of successive approximations	punishment
4.24	4.33
negative reinforcement	ratio schedule of reinforcement
4.25	4.34
operant chamber	reinforcement
4.26	4.35
orienting response	reinforcer
4.27	4.36
phobia	response cost

4.28	4.19
A list of behaviors ranked in order of the organism's preference at a particular time.	A hypothetical phenomenon in which the activity of one synapse causes other synapses on the same neuron to be strengthened or facilitated; may be the basic element of learning in the brain.
4.29	4.20
The assertion that the opportunity to engage in a more preferred behavior can be used to reinforce the performance of a less preferred behavior.	A technique to increase or decrease the frequency of a response by establishing a contingency between the response and environmental stimuli; also called operant conditioning.
4.30	4.21
A stimulus that is naturally aversive; can be used to punish a response.	A contingency in which some, but not all, responses are reinforced; these behaviors become resistant to extinction.
4.31	4.22
A stimulus that is naturally appetitive stimulus; can be used to reinforce a response.	A pattern of intermittent reinforcement in which a response will be reinforced only after a fixed or variable interval of time since the last reinforcement.
4.32	4.23
The suppressing effect on a response of an aversive stimulus that is contingent on the occurrence of the response.	A training technique to teach an organism to perform a behavior that may not occur naturally by reinforcing behaviors that resemble more and more closely the desired behavior; also called shaping.
4.33	4.24
A pattern of intermittent reinforcement in which the reinforcer occurs after a fixed or variable number of responses is made by the organism.	The reduction or removal of an aversive stimulus that is contingent on the performance of a particular behavior; reinforces the behavior; not to be confused with punishment.
4.34	4.25
The increase in the frequency of a response caused by the presentation of an appetitive stimulus or the removal of an aversive stimulus that is contingent on the occurrence of the response.	Laboratory equipment used to train animals using instrumental conditioning, contains the means for presenting the stimulus, recording a behavior, and reinforcing or punishing the behavior.
4.35	4.26
A stimulus that increases the probability of the response that precedes it.	A response in which an organism turns the appropriate sensory organs toward the source of a stimulus.
4.36	4.27
A form of punishment in which a response is followed by the removal of an appetitive stimulus.	Unreasonable fear of specific objects or situations such as snakes or crowds.

4.37

spontaneous recovery

4.38

unconditional response (UR)

4.39

unconditional stimulus (US)

4.37

After a rest period, the reoccurrence of a behavior that had previously been extinguished.

4.38

In classical conditioning, the response elicited by the unconditional stimulus.

4.39

In classical conditioning, the unconditional eliciting stimulus.

Chapter 5
Development

Lesson I

Read the interim summary on page 137 of your text to reacquaint yourself with the material in this section.

| 5-1 | *Describe the production of gametes, conception and development of a human fetus, and environmental and genetic conditions that interfere with normal development.* |

Read pages 132-137 and then answer the following questions:

1. Chromosomes consist of thousands of _____, which specify the kinds and amounts of _____ that are produced during _____ and throughout a person's lifetime. (See Figure 5.1 in your text.)

2. The most important class of proteins are _____ which act as biological _____, determining which chemical reactions take place.

3. Gametes, or female _____ and male _____, are produced in the _____ or _____ and contain only _____ the normal number of _____ that other cells contain. All of a woman's ova are present from _____, but a man produces sperm on a _____ basis.

4. a. Where does fertilization occur? (See Figure 5.2 in your text.)

   b. Explain how each parent contributes half of an individual's chromosomes. (See Figure 5.3 in your text.)

   c. Throughout development cells become specialized in a process called _____.

   d. Carefully explain how differentiation occurs.

5. a. When cells begin to differentiate, the organism first becomes an _____, and after about eight weeks it becomes a _____.

   b. Briefly describe the birth process.

6. a. Explain how drugs, toxic chemicals, or an illness such as German measles can adversely affect fetal development.

b. Describe the causes and effects of *fetal alcohol syndrome*.

7. a. Describe the cause and consequences of *Down syndrome*.

b. What factor is related to the incidence of this abnormality?

c. What do people with Down syndrome and Alzheimer's disease have in common?

8. a. Describe the cause and consequences of phenylketonuria. (Be sure to use the terms *phenylalanine* and *tyrosine* in your answer.)

b. Describe the treatment of PKU.

9. Match the descriptions on the left with the terms on the right.

_____ site of fertilization   a. gametes

_____ membrane surrounding embryo   b. differentiation

_____ supplies nourishment to embryo and   c. Down syndrome
transports waste products to mother

                                     d. umbilical cord

_____ largest cell in the human body

                                     e. placenta

_____ inability to convert phenylalanine into
tyrosine, causing mental retardation   f. ovum

_____ specialization of cells through deactivation   g. fallopian tube
of certain genes

                                     h. amniotic sac

_____ ova and sperms

                                     i. PKU

_____ connects fetus with placenta

_____ caused by extra 21st chromosome

Read the interim summary on page 143 of your text to reacquaint yourself with the material in this section.

5-2   *Describe the physical and perceptual development of the human child.*

Read pages 137-143 and then answer the following questions:

1. a. Define the term *reflex* in your own words and describe the *rooting, sucking,* and *swallowing* reflexes of a

human infant.

    b. How does the *withdrawal* reflex differ from the three you just described?

2. Describe research on the basic motor act of walking:

    a. What response is present from birth?

    b.. What evidence suggests that this response is related to walking? (See Figure 5.6 in your text.)

    c. Why does this response temporarily disappear at about three months of age?

3. Name and explain the two general trends of motor development.

4. What are the effects of depriving an infant of the opportunity to move and explore?

5. Describe simple examples that show that the sensory systems of a newborn infant are able to function.

6. a. See Figure 5.7 in your text and describe how infant pattern perception was first studied using Fantz's (1961) technique.

    b. Describe how Salapatek (1975) refined this technique.

    c. Study Figure 5.8 in your text and describe how an infant's gaze changes at about two months of age.

    d. What capability does an infant have by five months?

7. a. See Figure 5.9 in your text and describe the visual cliff.

    b. What evidence allows us to infer that babies on visual cliffs are frightened and that depth perception develops very early?

8. a. Define *stereopsis* in your own words and explain how it is related to the development of depth perception.

   b. What important discovery about the development of depth perception did Hubel and Wiesel (1970) make?

   c. Using the example of the development of normal vision (Banks et al., 1975), explain how the concept of a critical period applies to development in general.

Read the interim summary on page 151 of your text to reacquaint yourself with the material in this section.

5-3   *Describe the importance of a responsive environment and describe and discuss the four periods of cognitive development proposed by Jean Piaget.*

Read pages 143-151 and then answer the following questions:

1. Summarize research by Watson and Ramey (1972) on factors in cognitive development:

   a. Study Figure 5.10 in your text and describe the apparatus and three testing conditions.

   b. Describe the results of a later retest and their implications for infant-rearing practices.

2. Describe research by Dennis (1973) that underscores the importance of a stimulating environment.

3. a. What similarities in children's behavior suggested to Piaget that development followed a sequence?

   b. Define *cognitive structure*, *schema*, and *concept* in your own words and give an example of each.

   c. How, in general, do children learn about schemas and concepts?

   d. Describe assimilation and accommodation, the two processes that Piaget believes help children adapt to their environment.

1. assimilation

2. accommodation

4. Summarize Piaget's four periods of cognitive development.

a. _____ Period

1. duration

2. Carefully describe how a child's concept of objects and schemas for interacting with hidden objects changes throughout the six stages of this period. Be sure to use the terms *passive expectation* and *permanence* in your answer. (See Figure 5.11 in your text.)

3. Name other cognitive structures that develop toward the end of this period.

b. _____ Period

1. duration

2. What two abilities develop rapidly during this period?

3. Contrast the meaning of the terms *signifier* and *sign* and explain why Piaget believed symbolic functions began in the sensorimotor period.

4. Describe the acquisition of the ability to perceive conservation of various characteristics of objects during this stage. (See Figures 5.12 and 5.13 in your text.)

5. Describe research by Gelman (1972) that suggests that children may conserve number earlier than Piaget suggested.

6. Define *egocentrism* in your own words and give an example of egocentric behavior characteristic of this stage.

7. Cite two observations that suggest that Piaget overestimated children's egocentrism during this stage.

c. Period of _____

1. duration

2. What three abilities develop during this stage?

3. What kinds of reasoning is still difficult for children during this stage?

d. Period of _____ _____

1. duration

2. Describe reasoning skills of children who complete this stage.

3. Explain why egocentrism takes the form of *self-consciousness* during this stage.

5. Define the concept of *cognitive disequilibrium* in your own words and explain how children progress in their cognitive development.

Read the interim summary on pages 159-160 of your text to reacquaint yourself with the material in this section.

5-4   *Describe some infant behaviors that tend to strengthen the attachment between an infant and caregiver.*

Read pages 151-156 and then answer the following questions:

1. a. What are some of the benefits of nonnutritive sucking to an infant and caregiver?

b. Cite examples of this behavior in monkeys and humans.

2. a. What do the reactions of adults who have held infants who do not cuddle suggest about the importance of cuddling to attachment? (Ainsworth, 1973)

b. Outline the *cupboard theory* explanation of attachment.

c. Carefully describe how Harlow (1974) raised infant monkeys using surrogate mothers and disproved the cupboard theory. (See Figure 5.14 in your text.)

d. Why do infant monkeys and small children cling to cuddly objects?

e. Cite research that suggests what cuddly objects may represent to children and the long-term effects of this kind of attachment.

3. Describe how Tronick et al. (1978) demonstrated the importance of looking behavior:

a. Describe how mothers and their infants usually interact together. What were mothers asked to do differently during the experiment?

b. Study Figure 5.15 in your text and describe the infant's reaction to the new contingency. How did their mothers react?

c. What do the results suggest?

4. a. What behavior of blind infants suggests that smiling is an innate behavior? How can their parents reinforce their behavior?

b. What stimuli elicit smiles during the first month? at five weeks? at three months?

c. Study Figure 5.16 in your text and describe one kind of situation that makes infants smile.

d. Describe the "contingency game." How does it strengthen infant/caregiver attachment?

5. a. According to Wolff (1969), what three situations can an infant's cry signify?

b. Cite two studies that suggest that adults can easily distinguish the cry of pain from other cries.

c. Explain why promptly responding to a young infants' cries will not spoil them.

   d. Discuss the effect of responsive caregivers on an infant's efforts to communication.

Lesson I Self Test

1. A fertilized human egg contains

    a. twice the normal number of genes.
    b. half the normal number of chromosomes.
    c. twenty-three pairs of genes.
    d. twenty-three pairs of chromosomes.

2. Dividing cells begin to specialize through the process of

    a. ovulation.
    b. fertilization.
    c. differentiation.
    d. mutation.

3. The basic walking reflex

    a. is present at birth.
    b. develops during the sensorimotor period.
    c. develops after an infant crawls.
    d. disappears as cephalocaudal development predominates.

4. Research using harmless infrared light to study which parts of a human face an infant scans indicates that one-month-old infants

    a. spend most of their time looking at the eyes.
    b. shift their gaze between the eyes and mouth.
    c. scan the exterior of the face.
    d. scan the face in a circular pattern.

5. Visual cliffs are used to study an infant's

    a. visual acuity.
    b. depth perception.
    c. fear of falling.
    d. hand-eye coordination.

6. Infant subjects who watched a stationary mobile

    a. kept trying to make it move.
    b. turned their heads to avoid looking at it.
    c. did not learn to control it when given the opportunity.
    d. were more easily frustrated by difficult problems later.

7. During the preoperational period, egocentric children

a. insist on being the center of attention.
b. believe that others see the world the way they do.
c. question authority.
d. believe their culture is superior.

8. Nonnutritive sucking

a. inhibits an infant's distress.
b. contradicts the cupboard theory.
c. relieves gas pains.
d. is discouraged in Western society.

9. Harlow's research with isolated monkeys reared with surrogates suggests that

a. infant monkeys imprint on the first object they see.
b. the most important factor in attachment is the amount of time spent interacting.
c. physical contact with cuddly objects is a biological need.
d. peer relations are irreversibly harmed.

10. Infant subjects whose mothers maintained masklike expressions

a. showed distress and turned away from their mothers.
b. seemed undisturbed.
c. kept trying to elicit a response from their mothers.
d. cried when later retesting was attempted.

Lesson II

5-5   *Describe evidence that suggests there is a critical period in the formation of attachment and discuss the importance of forming such attachments with caregivers and other people.*

Read pages 156-159 and then answer the following questions:

1. a. Define the concept of *imprinting* in your own words and explain its importance for young birds.

   b. What is the critical period for imprinting and what are the effects of isolation during this time?

2. Summarize research on a critical period for attachment in humans:

   a. What evidence suggests that there is a critical period for attachment between human parents and their infants?

   b. What do studies of infants with temporary caregivers who do not form very early permanent attachments reveal about

    1. their capacity to form permanent attachments around the first birthday? after the fourth birthday?

    2. the effects of delayed attachment on the child's personality and peer relations?

3. Define the concept of *bonding* in your own words and cite evidence for its existence in some animals, but not in humans.

4. a. In unfamiliar and frightening situations, an infant needs the reassurance of the primary caregiver acting as a kind of _____ _____.

    b. How did ten-month-old infants in a large, strange room react when their mothers were present? absent? if their mothers were in an accessible adjoining room?

    c. Describe behavior observed by Harlow in infant monkeys who had formed an attachment to a cuddly surrogate.

    d. Study Figure 5.17 in your text and compare the amount of reassurance an infant receives from the mother, a blanket, and a hard toy.

5. a. Describe the *Strange Situation Test* and the following three patterns of attachment:

    1. secure attachment

    2. ambivalent attachment

    3. avoidant attachment

    b. What two factors affect the nature of an infant's attachment with the caregiver?

    c. What is the effect of neglect? abuse?

6. If the mother is the primary caregiver, what is likely to be the role of the father? Cite research to support your answer.

7. What are the conclusions of studies of infants in day-care on patterns of attachment? importance of high quality care?

8. Summarize research by Harlow and his colleagues on the importance of interactions with peers by young monkeys:

a. How are the social interactions of isolated infant monkeys affected by the absence of primary caregiver (and the substitution of a cuddly surrogate)? and the absence of peers?

b. Describe how Harlow and his colleagues introduced isolated monkeys into peer situations. (Be sure to use the term "therapist" monkey in your answer.)

c. What was the most important factor in successful socialization?

d. What does this study suggest about a critical period for social development?

e. Describe how Fuhrman et al. (1979) adapted the "therapist" technique for work with socially withdrawn children. (Study Figure 5.18 in your text.)

Read the interim summary on page 163 of your text to reacquaint yourself with the material in this section.

5-6 *Describe and discuss Piaget's and Kohlberg's theories of moral development and describe research on teaching morality to children.*

Read pages 160-163 and then answer the following questions:

1. a. Define the concept of *moral behavior* in your own words.

b. What technique did Piaget use to assess children's moral beliefs?

2. Summarize the two stages of Piaget's description of moral development:

a. Stage I, or _____ _____

1. duration

2. How does egocentrism influence a child's behavior?

3. What do young children think is the source and force of rules? How well do they follow these rules and what motivates them to do so?

   b. Stage II or _____ ____ _____

     1. How does the shift from egocentrism influence an older child's behavior?

     2. How does increasing maturity influence the child's understanding of the source and force of rules?

3. What technique did Kohlberg use to assess children's moral beliefs? (Be sure to mention the story about Heinz.)

4. List Kohlberg's three levels and six stages of moral development. Explain the guiding principle at each stage. (Be sure to refer to the story about Heinz when appropriate.)

   a. _____ level

     1. _____

     2. _____

   b. _____ level

     3. _____

     4. _____

   c. _____ level

     5. _____

     6. _____

5. State two objections to Piaget's assertion that young children consider only the magnitude and not the intent behind an event.

   1.

   2.

6. Explain these criticisms of Kohlberg's conclusions:

   a. the validity of Heinz' story as a measure of moral development

   b. the division of moral development into stages

   c. the possibility the theory is sex-biased:

      1. State Gilligan's objections.

      2. What has more recent research suggested?

7. Describe an alternative approach proposed by Eisenberg and her colleagues and compare their findings with Kohlberg's.

8. State two factors that influence the development of moral behavior and give several examples of each.

   1.

   2.

Read the interim summary on page 169-170 of your text to reacquaint yourself with the material in this section.

5-7   *Describe physical sexual development, the nature of sex roles, and the factors that influence the development of such roles.*

Read pages 163-167 and then answer the following questions:

1. Explain how the father's sᵣ ⌐ₐ determines the sex of the child. (Be sure to use the terms *X chromosome* and *Y chromosome* in your answer.)

2. Name and describe the three categories of sex organs:

   a. _____, the first sex organs to develop, produce _____ and _____ and secrete _____. All fetuses have a pair of identical gonads that begin to develop differently about the fourth week in response to the effects of the presence or absence of a single _____ on the _____ chromosome.

b. Name and describe the other two categories of sex organs.

c. What hormone causes the development of the male internal sex organs, penis and scrotum?

d. What hormone (if any) causes the development of the internal and external female sex organs?

e. Support your answer to (d) by describing *Turner's syndrome*. (See Figure 5.19 in your text.)

3. a. _____, the period of sexual maturation, begins when the gonads are stimulated by _____ _____, produced by the _____ _____ _____.

b. Define *primary sex characteristics* and *secondary sex characteristics* in your own words.

c. What is the class name for female sex hormones and which is the most important member of this class?

4. a. Compare *sex roles* and *sex stereotypes*.

b. Describe some important male and female sex stereotypes and explain how these stereotypes are perpetuated and how they limit opportunities for both men and women.

c. Summarize research on conformity to sex stereotypes:

1. Explain how identifying tossing marbles as either a boy's or girl's game affected the enjoyment and scores of players.

2. Why do young children learn about the male sex stereotype first and why do boys conform to societal expectations before girls do?

5. Summarize research on the biological and social causes of sex-role differences:

a. Can sex hormones have an effect on the human brain?

b. According to Kimura (1987), how may the evolution of the human brain account for observed sex differences in verbal and spatial abilities?

c. Describe some of the ways parents communicate to their children "sex appropriate" and "sex inappropriate" behavior.

5-8   *Describe research on the development of sexual orientation.*

Read pages 167-169 and then answer the following questions:

1. How does human homosexuality differ from homosexual behavior observed in other species?

2. Explain why the emotional difficulties that some homosexuals experience may not be caused directly by their sexual orientation. Cite research by Bell and Weinberg (1978) to support your answer.

3. Explain why it is impossible to generalize from most of the early research on the causes of homosexuality.

4. Carefully summarize the findings of Bell et al., (1981) regarding

   a. origins of homosexuality and a reliable predictor

   b. adolescent heterosexual activity of homosexuals

   c. aversion to gender conformity and homosexuality

   d. relationship with father and mother as a predictor and possible cause of homosexuality

5. Summarize research on possible biological causes of homosexuality.

   a. role of testosterone

   b. prenatal stress

Lesson II Self Test

1. The critical period of attachment for humans is

   a. the first few hours after birth.
   b. facilitated by skin-to-skin contact.
   c. much longer than for other species.
   d. a myth.

2. Ten-month-old infants explored a strange room

   a. only if their mother was present or nearby.
   b. regardless of whether their mother was present or nearby.
   c. to look for their mother if she was not present or nearby.
   d. as long as they could hear their mother's voice through a speaker.

3. Monkeys reared in isolation never learn

   a. to copulate.
   b. to rear their young.
   c. to interact with peers.
   d. to avoid the dominant male.

4. With respect to moral development, an egocentric child

   a. believes that his or her cultural norms are superior.
   b. can imagine other people's feelings.
   c. can evaluate whether punishment is appropriate for the offense.
   d. evaluates events in terms of personal consequences.

5. Gilligan asserted that Kohlberg's conclusions were sex-biased because

   a. men and women base moral judgments on different values.
   b. his female subjects were not representative of the population as a whole.
   c. justice as a basis for moral judgment is superior to caring.
   d. caring is not more closely associated with maternal behavior.

6. The X and Y chromosomes determine

   a. gender.
   b. fertility.
   c. sexual orientation.
   d. onset of puberty.

7. Most of the reliable sex differences that researchers have found are

   a. probably biologically determined.
   b. probably the result of socialization.
   c. not being confirmed by more recent research.
   d. good predictors of individual abilities.

8. If parents encourage "sex appropriate" behavior and discourage "sex inappropriate" behavior they encourage

a. sex-stereotyping.
b. egocentric tendencies.
c. emotional stability.
d. submissive behavior.

9. The most important single predictor of homosexuality is

a. absence of adolescent heterosexual activity.
b. a passive, indifferent father.
c. self-report of homosexual feelings.
d. a domineering mother.

10. One of the conclusions of research by Bell et al. (1981) is that

a. exclusive homosexuality is an exclusively human trait.
b. there is a strong relationship between gender nonconformity and homosexuality.
c. homosexuality is a disorder that leads to emotional difficulties.
d. homosexuals often report having been seduced by older adults of the same sex.

Answers for Self Tests

Lesson I

1. d Obj. 5-1
2. c Obj. 5-1
3. a Obj. 5-2
4. c Obj. 5-2
5. b Obj. 5-2
6. d Obj. 5-3
7. b Obj. 5-3
8. a Obj. 5-4
9. c Obj. 5-4
10. a Obj. 5-4

Lesson II

1. c Obj. 5-5
2. a Obj. 5-5
3. b Obj. 5-5
4. d Obj. 5-6
5. a Obj. 5-6
6. a Obj. 5-7
7. b Obj. 5-7
8. a Obj. 5-7
9. c Obj. 5-8
10. b Obj. 5-8

5.1 accommodation/assimilation	5.10 cognitive structure
5.2 ambivalent attachment	5.11 concept
5.3 amniotic sac	5.12 conservation
5.4 androgen	5.13 critical period
5.5 avoidant attachment	5.14 differentiation
5.6 bonding	5.15 Down syndrome
5.7 cephalocaudal development	5.16 egocentrism.
5.8 cognition	5.17 enzyme
5.9 cognitive disequilibrium	5.18 estrogen

5.10

According to Piaget, rules used to understand and interact with the world; two primary types are schemas and concepts.

5.11

According to Piaget, one of the two primary types of cognitive structures; rules that describe properties of environmental events and how they relate to other concepts.

5.12

According to Piaget, the tendency to perceive quantities, mass, and volume as remaining constant even if the elements are moved or the shape is changed

5.13

Important developmental concept; an organism must have certain experiences within a certain period of time if it is to develop normally.

5.14

During development, the process by which cells begin to acquire their distinctive features and become particular organs of the body.

5.15

A genetic abnormality caused by an extra twenty-first chromosome; moderate to severe mental retardation; production of an excessive amount of a protein found in the brain of Alzheimer's patients.

5.16

The tendency of young children to believe that everyone sees the world in exactly the same way they do.

5.17

A protein that facilitates particular chemical reactions without becoming a part of the final product .

5.18

The principal class of sex hormones in females; estradiol is the primary estrogen.

5.1

According to Piaget, processes that help child adapt to environment; assimilation adds new items to a concept or schema and accommodation changes schema to incorporate new information.

5.2

A pattern of attachment identified by the Strange Situation Test; infant remains close to mother before she leaves, but shows approach and avoidance behaviors when she returns.

5.3

A membrane that encases the embryo in amniotic fluid during pregnancy; it ruptures when the head presses against it during birth.

5.4

The primary class of male sex hormones essential for the development of internal and external sex male organs and later for sexual maturation; testosterone is the most important androgen.

5.5

A pattern of attachment identified by the Strange Situation Test; infants generally do not cry when they are left alone and tend not to cling and cuddle when picked up.

5.6

A form of rapid automatic attachment between mother and offspring of some species that occurs within a few hours of birth and is stimulated primarily by the odor of the infant; appears not to occur in humans.

5.7

A general trend in the development of motor control; infant learns to control the movements of the upper body first.

5.8

The process by which infants learn information about the world and themselves.

5.9

According to Piaget, a state produced by the child's realization that new information cannot be easily assimilated into existing behavioral schemas; compels the child to pass from one cognitive stage to the next.

5.19 **fetal alcohol syndrome**	5.28 **period of formal operations**
5.20 **gamete**	5.29 **permanence**
5.21 **gene**	5.30 **phenylketonuria**
5.22 **gonad**	5.31 **placenta**
5.23 **imprinting**	5.32 **preoperational period**
5.24 **moral realism**	5.33 **primary sex characteristic**
5.25 **morality of cooperation**	5.34 **proximodistal development**
5.26 **ovulation**	5.35 **puberty**
5.27 **period of concrete operations**	5.36 **rooting**

5.28

According to Piaget, ages 12 years to adult; development of adult form of logic and symbolic reasoning.

5.29

According to Piaget, during sensorimotor period child realizes a hidden object has not ceased to exist and actively searches for it.

5.30

A genetic disorder; failure to produce the enzyme that converts phenylalanine into tyrosine; unconverted phenylalanine results in mental retardation; controlled through special diet begun soon after birth.

5.31

Organ that provides a developing embryo with nourishment from the mother and passes waste products to her body to be excreted; umbilical cord attaches fetus to placenta

5.32

According to Piaget, ages 2 to 7 years; development of language ability and ability to think of things symbolically.

5.33

The sex organs: gonads, internal sex organs, and external genitalia.

5.34

A general trend in the development of motor control; infant learns to control arms before learning to control hands and fingers.

5.35

The period that marks the transition from childhood to adulthood.

5.36

Automatic reflex, present at birth; if baby's cheek is touched lightly baby will turn the head so lips can reach object.

5.19

A drug-induced abnormality in the offspring of alcoholic mothers; characteristic facial abnormalities and mental retardation.

5.20

Collective term for ova and sperm.

5.21

The functional unit of the chromosomes; contains genetic information to produce particular proteins, including enzymes; controls an organism's development.

5.22

Testes or ovaries; one of three general categories of sex organs and the first to develop.

5.23

A form of attachment in which a baby bird learns to follow the first moving object (usually the mother) it encounters during the first day or two of life; if isolated during this critical period never learns to follow mother.

5.24

According to Piaget, first stage of moral development, ages 5 to 10 years, marked by egocentrism and rigid adherence to rules which child believes come from parents or God and cannot be changed.

5.25

According to Piaget, second stage of moral development in which child becomes less egocentric and more empathetic; follow rules less rigidly; realizes they derive from social conventions and can be changed.

5.26

The discharge of a mature ovum from the ovaries.

5.27

According to Piaget, ages 7 to 12 years; beginning of ability to reason logically, using real objects but not hypothetical ones; increased ability to empathize and understand complex cause-and-effect relationships.

5.37 schema	5.46 signifier
5.38 secondary sex characteristic	5.47 stereopsis
5.39 secure attachment	5.48 Strange Situation Test
5.40 secure base	5.49 surrogate mother
5.41 sensorimotor period	5.50 symbolic function
5.42 sex chromosome	5.51 Turner's syndrome
5.43 sex role	5.52 zygote
5.44 sex stereotype	
5.45 sign	

5.46	5.37
According to Piaget, abstract symbols such as words that represent concepts.	According to Piaget, one of two primary types of cognitive structures; a set of rules that indicates to a child how to perform a particular behavior and under what circumstances.
5.47	5.38
A form of depth perception present in animals with eyes on the front of the head arising from slightly different views of the world through each eye.	Physical characteristics that distinguish a male from a female.
5.48	5.39
A test developed by Ainsworth that determines the strength of attachment between infant and caregiver; infant reaction to eight situations that might cause some distress is observed.	A pattern of attachment identified by the Strange Situation Test; infant shows a strong preference for mother over a stranger.
5.49	5.40
From research by Harlow on development of monkeys reared in isolation; mechanical forms that substitute for the mother.	Presence of caregiver that reassures infant who is just learning to explore an unfamiliar environment; reduces infant's fear.
5.50	5.41
According to Piaget, during preoperational period, child develops ability to represent things in an abstract way with gestures and words.	According to Piaget, ages birth to 2 years; cognition is closely tied to external stimulation especially as demonstrated by the various stages of object concept.
5.51	5.42
A genetic condition; presence of only one sex chromosome (X); individuals do not develop ovaries or testes, but do develop female internal and external sex organs without the presence of sex hormones.	The X and Y chromosomes, which determine gender; XX individuals are female, XY individuals are male.
5.52	5.43
A fertilized ovum, which develops into an organism.	The particular kinds of behaviors that a society agrees are acceptable behavior for males and females.
	5.44
	Particular beliefs of a society concerning the differences in the behavior, abilities, and personalities of males and females.
	5.45
	According to Piaget, motor acts such as galloping gestures that represent concepts.

Chapter 6
Sensation

Lesson I

Read the interim summary on page 180 of your text to reacquaint yourself with the material in this section.

6-1   *Describe how sensory organs detect environmental events and convert the information into sensory codes.*

Read pages 174-177 and then answer the following questions:

1. Describe the difference between sensation and perception.

2. List the five "classical" senses and the additional components of the somatosensory system.

3. a. Define *transduction* in your own words.

   b. Study Table 6.1 and list the different stimulus characteristics that are transduced by the sense organs.

4. a. List the two general type of sensory coding and give an example of each of them.

   b. Explain how the two methods code the location and intensity of a somatosensory stimulus.

6-2   *Describe the basic principles of psychophysics.*

Read pages 177-180 and then answer the following questions:

1. Define *psychophysics* in your own words.

2. a. Explain the principle of the *just-noticeable difference (jnd)* discovered by Weber.

    b. Explain *Weber fractions*.

3. Study Figures 6.1 and 6.2 in your text and summarize research by Fechner using jnds to measure the magnitude of sensations:

    a. Describe the testing apparatus. Be sure to use the terms sample stimulus and comparison stimulus.

    b. To begin, the sample stimulus is turned _____ and the comparison stimulus is gradually turned _____ until the subject says _____. The level of the comparison stimulus is one _____.

    c. Next, the sample stimulus is turned on at a level of one _____ and the intensity of the comparison stimulus is _____ until the subject can again _____ a difference. This level is equal to _____ jnds.

4. Explain the concepts of *difference threshold* and *absolute threshold.*

5. Explain the 50 percent standard, as it applies to a threshold.

6. a. In your own words, describe the premise of the *signal-detection theory.*

    b. Describe the task outlined in your text.

    c. When it is very difficult to determine whether a tone followed the flash, a decision is affected by a person's _____ _____.

d. Study Figure 6.3 in your text and list the two events that fall under each of the following categories:

1. correct responses:

2. incorrect responses:

e. Study Figure 6.4 in your text and explain how a researcher can manipulate a person's response bias.

f. Now study Figure 6.5 in your text and explain what accounts for the difference between the two ROC curves.

Read the interim summary on pages 197-198 of your text to reacquaint yourself with the material in this section.

6-3	*Describe the anatomy of the eye.*

Read pages 180-183 and then answer the following questions:

1. List the ways the eye is protected from injury.

2. a. Study Figure 6.6 in your text. Make your own drawing of a cross-section of the eye. Label these parts: cornea, sclera, iris, pupil, aqueous humor, lens, retina, optic disk, optic nerve.

b. State the function of the:

1. cornea

2. iris

3. aqueous humor

4. cornea and lens together

5. retina

6. photoreceptors

Chapter 6

3. The change in the shape of the lens to adjust for _____ is called _____.

4. a. What is the name of the specialized cells that transduce light into neural activity?

    b. Where are they located?

    c. What is the name of the location where all axons leave the eye? (See Figures 6.7 and 6.8 in your text.)

    d. Try the demonstration illustrated in Figure 6.8 and explain your reaction by referring to photoreceptors.

    e. Describe the experiment by Scheiner that showed that an image was formed on the retina.

5. a. Return to Figure 6.6 in your text and be sure you understand where the retina is located within the eye before studying Figure 6.9 in your text.

    b. Which layer of the retina detects the presence of light?

    c. By what means do photoreceptor cells pass information to bipolar cell layer?

    d. What is the name of the cells that receive information from bipolar cells and then transmit information to the brain?

6. List the two general types of photoreceptors.

7. a. Where is the fovea located? (Refer back to Figure 6.6.)

    b. What is the name of the only kind of photoreceptors found there?

    c. Explain why our most detailed vision occurs in the fovea.

    d. Explain why sensitivity to light increases, but visual acuity decreases, at points farther away from the fovea.

6-4   *Describe the transduction of light by photoreceptors, adaptation to light and dark, and the nature and function of eye movements.*

Read pages 183-187 and then answer the following questions:

1. a. Name the vitamin from which a molecule that plays a key role in visual transduction is derived.

    b. Name the two molecules that constitute a photopigment.

    c. How many kinds of photopigments are there?

d. Where are they located?

e. What is a *photon*?

2. Now you are ready to describe how photoreceptors in the photoreceptor layer of the retina transduce the energy of light. Study Figure 6.10 in your text.

   a. When a photon strikes the photopigment of a photoreceptor cell, what happens to the photopigment?

   b. What kind of changes occur in the photoreceptor cells when the photopigment splits apart?

   c. Trace the path of the message from the photoreceptor cell to the brain.

   d. What happens to the characteristic color of a photopigment when it is split apart by a photon?

   e. What is needed for the molecules to recombine and form a photopigment again?

3. Explain dark adaptation by referring to levels of photopigment and the changing number of intact photoreceptors.

4. Study the data obtained by Hecht and Schlaer (1938) that is presented in Figure 6.11 in your text.

   a. What is the name for the change that occurs at seven minutes?

   b. Explain why this break occurs.

   c. Why does the curve drop more sharply after seven minutes?

   d. How could you verify your explanation of part c?

5. a. Define *fixation point* in your own words.

   b. List the three types of eye movements that occur even when we appear to be staring at a single point.

      1.

      2.

      3.

c. Define *stabilized image* in your own words.

d. Figure 6.12 in your text diagrams how Riggs and his colleagues (1953) were able to project stabilized images onto a subject's retina. Describe the results of this research.

e. What do the results suggest may be the purpose of the small random movements the eye makes?

6. Name and give an example of the three kinds of purposive movements the eye makes.

1.

2.

3.

6-5 *Describe the physical and perceptual dimensions of color and compare color mixing and pigment mixing.*

Read pages 187-190 and then answer the following questions:

1. The speed of radiant energy is always _____; therefore, the frequency of vibration determines the _____ of radiant energy. Slower vibrations produce _____ wavelengths. (See Figure 6.13 in your text.)

2. The entire range of wavelengths is called the _____ _____ and the portion our eyes can detect is called the _____ _____ . (See Figure 6.14 in your text.)

3. What do we mean when we say: "Each of the three types of cones in our eyes contains a different type of photopigment that responds best to a particular wavelength of light"?

4. Complete the following chart.

Physical Dimensions of Light	Corresponding Perceptual Dimensions of Light
1.	1.
2.	2.
3.	3.

5. a. What will be the result of mixing white light with a light of a single wavelength?

b. True or False: Colors of the same dominant wavelength always have the same hue and saturation. (Study Figure 6.15 in your text.)

6. Explain why we see an object as having a particular color.

7. a. Study Figure 6.18 in your text.

   b. Mixing paints together results in a _____ color, whereas mixing two or more lights together always results in a _____ color.

   c. To produce white light, is it necessary to recombine all the colors of the visual spectrum?

6-6 *Describe coloring coding by cones and ganglion cells in the retina, negative afterimages, and genetic defects in color vision.*

Read pages 190-195 and then answer the following questions:

1. a. Briefly explain Young's hypothesis of color vision by referring to the number and kind of color receptors.

   b. Later research found that the human eye does contain three kinds of cones that respond to three different wavelengths of light. List the three kinds of cones by their commonly accepted names.

   c. Study Figure 6.19 in your text and compare the number of red and green cones with number of blue cones.

2. Study Figure 6.20 in your text to understand color coding in the retina.

   a. Why does the rectangle on the television screen appear to be white?

   b. How does a television display particular colors?

3. a. List the two types of color-coding retinal ganglion cells.

   b. Describe the firing rate of these cells when they are not being stimulated.

   c. Study Figure 6.21 in your text and describe how these spots of different colored light affects the firing rate of red/green ganglion cells.

      1. red light

      2. green light

      3. yellow light

4. Try the demonstration in Figure 6.22 in your text and then explain why you saw the negative afterimage.

5. a. Why are males rather than females more frequently affected by color blindness?

   b. Briefly describe three kinds of color blindness, describe their genetics, and explain their causes.

   1. protanopia

   2. deuteranopia

   3. tritanopia

6-7   *Describe research by Hubel and Wiesel on the role of neurons in the primary sensory cortex in vision.*

Read pages 195-197 and then answer the following questions:

1. Study the overview of the visual system in Figure 6.24 in your text. Trace the flow of visual information by adding numbers to the following terms:

   _____ primary visual cortex

   _____ thalamus

   _____ optic nerves

   _____ visual association cortex

   _____ visual stimulus

2. a. Briefly explain how perception can be seen as a hierarchy of information processing.

   b. List two findings that tend to contradict this model.

3. Summarize research by Hubel and Wiesel (1977, 1979) on the earliest stages of visual analysis.

   a. Study Figure 6.25 in your text and describe the preparations.

   b. How did Hubel and Wiesel begin to locate a particular neuron's receptive field?

   c. What indicated that they had found the receptive field?

d. Describe what happened when the stimulus was moved just outside its receptive field.

4. a. According the Hubel and Wiesel, what is the relation between the geography of the primary visual cortex and the location of receptive fields of neurons?

   b. Explain why the map is compared to a mosaic.

5. Begin a list of the characteristics of these "tiles."

   a. Where are the neurons that receive information directly from the thalamus located in the layers of the primary visual cortex? (See Figure 6.26 in your text.)

   b. Where do these neurons send information?

   c. Describe the response characteristics of *simple cells* and *complex cells*. (See Figure 6.27 in your text.)

   d. How do the response characteristics of neurons within adjacent clusters of a given tile differ from each other? Use the term *feature detectors* in your answer.

6. a. Explain why the primary visual cortex is not capable of analyzing an entire scene.

   b. Where does such an analysis take place?

Lesson I Self Test

1. All sensory systems use rate of firing to encode _____ of stimulation.

   a. presence
   b. type
   c. source
   d. intensity

2. A stimulus with a value of 1 jnd is just above the

   a. difference threshold.
   b. absolute threshold.
   c. receiver-operating characteristic.
   d. response bias.

3. Receiver-operating characteristic curves

   a. can be used to detect the presence of response bias.
   b. indicate the detectability of stimuli.
   c. are composed of jnds.
   d. were invented by Fechner.

4. Visual information passes to the brain according to the following sequence.

   a. cornea, retina, fovea, brain
   b. photoreceptor, bipolar cell, ganglion cell, brain
   c. lens, ganglion cell, bipolar cell, brain
   d. photoreceptor, optic nerve, optic disk, brain

5. What is the role of photopigment in the transduction of light?

   a. It reflects light onto the retina.
   b. It splits apart when struck by a photon and begins the process of transduction.
   c. It stimulates the production of a molecule derived from vitamin A.
   d. It recombines to maintain visual acuity.

6. When driving at night, it is more difficult to see if the driver of an oncoming car does not "dim" his high beams because

   a. bright light directed at the fovea reduces visual acuity.
   b. the number of intact rods is reduced in the dark.
   c. bright light bleaches the photopigments in the rods.
   d. there are too few intact rhodopsin molecules for your eyes to respond immediately to bright light.

7. Wavelength is a _____ dimension of light and hue is the corresponding _____ dimension.

   a. perceptual; physical
   b. physical; perceptual
   c. perceptual; psychological
   d. psychological; perceptual

8. When red and green light are combined,

   a. the process is called pigment mixing.
   b. only people without tritanopia can detect the two wavelengths.
   c. the result is a darker color.
   d. the result is yellow light.

9. Thomas Young was essentially correct when he hypothesized that the eye contains _____ types of color receptors that respond to _____ .

   a. three; red, green, and blue
   b. three; black, white, and gray
   c. six; the spectral colors.
   d. two; red/green and yellow/blue

10. From their experiments with microelectrodes, Hubel and Wiesel concluded that

a. the primary visual cortex is the place where perceptual analysis takes place.
b. simple cells detect simple features of a scene and complex cells detect all-over form.
c. the primary visual cortex contains neurons that serve as feature detectors.
d. the information received by the primary visual cortex comes from the visual association cortex.

Lesson II

Read the interim summary on pages 204-205 of your text to reacquaint yourself with the material in this section.

6-8   *Describe the structure and functions of the auditory system.*

Read pages 198-204 and then answer the following questions:

1. For the following phases of vibration, indicate the corresponding changes in air pressure and movement of the eardrum. (See Figure 6.28 in your text.)

    Direction of Vibration   *Air Pressure*   *Eardrum*

    moving toward you

    moving away from you

2. Sound is measured in frequency units of cycles per second called _____.

3. Study Figure 6.29 in your text and list the corresponding perceptual dimensions of sound that accompany changes in

    a. intensity

    b. frequency

    c. complexity

4. Study Figure 6.30 in your text and then draw the anatomy of the ear. Label the following parts: pinna, ear canal, eardrum, hammer, anvil, stirrup, cochlea, oval window, round window.

5. Indicate the function of each of the parts of the ear in your drawing.

6. a. Study Figure 6.31 in your text and indicate which regions of the basilar membrane vibrate in response to high-, middle-, and low-frequency sounds.

b. Describe how the liquid inside the cochlea moves in response to sound vibrations. (Mention the round window.)

c. Explain the importance of the surgical procedure called fenestration.

7. a. What is the name of the cells of the auditory system that perform the same function as the photoreceptors of the visual system ?

b. Where are they located? (See Figure 6.32 in your text.)

8. Describe how high-frequency and medium-frequency sounds are encoded:

a. Cite evidence that makes it unlikely that the brain encodes pitch through synchronous firing of axons.

b. By what means does the brain receive information about the high- and medium-frequency sounds?

c. Summarize supporting research:

1. What were the observations by von Békésy (1960)?

2. Describe how Stebbins et al. (1969) used antibiotics to study the anatomical coding of pitch.

9. Describe how low-frequency sounds are encoded:

a. State the results of research by Kiang (1965).

b. Describe how the basilar membrane encodes low-frequency sounds.

c. Summarize supporting research by Miller and Taylor (1948).

10. a. What is the most effective means to identify the location of

1. high-frequency sounds? (See Figure 6.33 in your text.)

2. sound frequencies below 3000 Hz?

b. Explain how differences in arrival time establish the location of a sound:

    1. Study Figure 6.34 in your text and compare the vibrations of the eardrums when the sound source is located

        a. to the side of the head.

        b. in front of the head.

    2. Explain why the alarm calls of birds start and end slowly.

11. a. Use your own words to define:

    1. *complex tone*

    2. *overtone*

    3. *fundamental frequency*

    4. and now *timbre*

b. Use these terms to explain how the ear identifies a sound such as a clarinet. (See Figure 6.35 in your text.)

Read the interim summary on page 209 of your text to reacquaint yourself with the material in this section.

6-9   *Describe receptor cells on the tongue, their role in transducing gustatory stimuli, and the four qualities of taste.*

Read pages 205-207 and then answer the following questions:

1. a. What is the name of the bumps on the tongue?

   b. Where are receptor cells on the tongue located?

   c. Describe the *microvilli* and their function.

2. Study Figure 6.36 in your text and draw or describe the location of the papillae, taste buds, receptors cells, microvilli and axons to the brain.

3. Explain how gustatory information is relayed to the brain. Begin with the effects of chemical molecules dissolved in the saliva.

4. a. List the four qualities of taste.

    1.   2.

    3.   4.

    b. Study Figure 6.37 in your text and draw or describe the regions of the tongue that respond best to each of the qualities of taste.

5. a. What characteristics of the stimulus determine the kind of taste we experience?

    b. List the types of molecules that produce the following tastes:

       1. salty

       2. bitter and sweet

       3. sour

    c. What is the probable biological significance of our ability to detect the following tastes?

       1. salty

       2. bitter

       3. sweet

       4. sour

6-10 *Describe the anatomy of the olfactory system and some of the problems of studying the dimensions of odor.*

Read pages 207-209 and then answer the following questions:

1. a. Study Figure 6.38 your text and notice the location of the olfactory mucosa, receptor cells and their axons, and olfactory bulbs.

    b. All other sensory modalities send information to the _____ , but olfactory information is sent to the _____ _____.

    c. List two other ways that the olfactory system differs from the other senses.

       1.

       2.

2. Summarize Amoore's research on identifying "odor primaries" and the types of receptors that might be responsible for detecting each of them.

Read the interim summary on page 213 of your text to reacquaint yourself with the material in this section.

6-11 *Describe the somatosenses, the internal senses, and the vestibular senses.*

Read pages 209-213 and then answer the following questions:

1. All somatosensory information is detected by the _____ of neurons rather than by separate _____ _____.

2. Some dendrites have specialized endings. List and describe the function of two of these endings. (See Figure 6.39 in your text.)

    1.

    2.

3. a. Warmth and coolness are probably detected by _____ kinds of detectors.

   b. Temperature detectors respond best to _____ in temperature, but they eventually _____ to changes in the temperature of the environment.

4. a. Distinguish between *touch* and *pressure*.

   b. Describe the sensations you would feel when a small weight is first placed on your arm and what you would feel a few minutes later.

   c. Explain the reason for this difference.

5. Describe the method for determining the *two-point discrimination threshold*. (See Figure 6.40 in your text.)

6. a. List the two components of pain.

    1.

    2.

   b. Give an example of drugs that affect the

    1. physical reaction to pain.

2. emotional reaction to pain.

c. List the two types of pain sensation and give an example of stimuli that would cause each of them.

1.

2.

d. What is the biological significance of the ability to experience pain? (Refer to the opening vignette as well.)

7. Describe the types of stimuli detected by the two types of stretch receptors found near or in muscles and their functions.

1.

2.

8. a. Name the two organs that contribute to our sense of balance.

b. Study Figure 6.41 in your text and notice the vestibular apparatus of the inner ear.

c. Describe how the *semicircular canals* detect head rotation.

d. Describe how the *vestibular sacs* detect head tilt.

e. Describe another useful function of the vestibular sacs.

Lesson II Self Test

1. The frequency of sound waves corresponds to the perception of

a. loudness.
b. pitch.
c. timbre.
d. fundamental tones.

2. The basilar membrane

a. divides the cochlea into two parts.
b. protects the eardrum from damage from high-frequency sounds.
c. surrounds the ossicles.
d. lines the ear canal.

3. We perceive the location of sounds by using

a. rate and range.
b. sound thresholds.
c. orienting responses and arrival time.
d. relative loudness and arrival time.

4. A complex tone is

a. a combination of the fundamental frequency and its overtones.
b. a multiple of the basic pitch of a sound.
c. a combination of two or more simple tones of a single frequency.
d. perceived as louder than a simple one.

5. Foods do not taste as good when you have a head cold because

a. fluid intake must be increased and the diminished taste of food has evolved as an important signal in regulating body fluids..
b. congestion makes it difficult for food odors to reach receptors for your sense of smell.
c. your saliva becomes thicker and blocks some receptor cells.
d. fever impairs the functioning of receptor cells.

6. Most poisonous foods are alkaloid and taste

a. sour.
b. sweet.
c. salty.
d. bitter.

7. Research on olfaction

a. has shown that we possess a very large number of receptors for specific odors.
b. indicates the existence of four primary odors.
c. has found that the olfactory bulbs send information directly to the limbic system.
d. has shown that the human olfactory system is relatively insensitive.

8. Pacinian corpuscles detect

a. warmth.
b. coolness.
c. pain.
d. vibration.

9. If a small weight is placed on your motionless arm, you will eventually stop feeling its presence because sensory endings

a. experience fatigue.
b. only respond to movement.
c. are self-inhibiting.

    d. require muscular contraction.

10. The _____ detect changes in the rotation of the head.

    a. semicircular canals
    b. vestibular sacs
    c. free nerve endings
    d. cilia

Answers for Self Tests

Lesson I			**Lesson II**	
1.	d	Obj. 6-1	1.	b	Obj. 6-8
2.	b	Obj. 6-2	2.	a	Obj. 6-8
3.	b	Obj. 6-2	3.	d	Obj. 6-8
4.	b	Obj. 6-3	4.	a	Obj. 6-8
5.	b	Obj. 6-4	5.	b	Obj. 6-9
6.	c	Obj. 6-4	6.	d	Obj. 6-9
7.	b	Obj. 6-5	7.	c	Obj. 6-10
8.	d	Obj. 6-5	8.	d	Obj. 6-11
9.	a	Obj. 6-6	9.	b	Obj. 6-11
10.	c	Obj. 6-7	10.	a	Obj. 6-11

6.1 absolute threshold	6.10 color mixing
6.2 accommodation	6.11 complementary
6.3 anatomical coding	6.12 cone
6.4 aqueous humor	6.13 conjugate movement
6.5 auditory hair cell	6.14 cornea
6.6 basilar membrane	6.15 correct negative
6.7 bipolar cell	6.16 dark adaptation
6.8 cilia	6.17 deuteranopia
6.9 cochlea	6.18 difference threshold

6.10

The addition of two or more lights of different wavelengths.

6.11

Colors that make white or shades of gray when added together; a negative afterimage is complementary to the color to which the eye was exposed.

6.12

One of the photoreceptors in the retina; responsible for acute daytime vision and for color perception.

6.13

A cooperative movement of the eyes that ensures that an image falls on corresponding parts of the two retinas.

6.14

The transparent tissue covering the front of the eye.

6.15

From signal-detection theory; accurately reporting the absence of a stimulus.

6.16

The process involving chemical changes in the photoreceptors of the retina that enables the eye to see dimly illuminated objects after moving from an area of high illumination.

6.17

A hereditary form of color blindness in which green cones are filled with red photopigment.

6.18

The minimum detectable difference between two stimuli.

6.1

The minimum value of a stimulus that can be detected.

6.2

Changes in the shape of the lens to adjust for distance.

6.3

A means of representing information in the nervous system by location; different neurons represent different types of information..

6.4

A fluid that nourishes the cornea and other portions of the front of the eye; produced by tissue behind the cornea that filters it from the blood.

6.5

The receptive cell for audition; specialized neuron that transduces mechanical energy caused by movements of the basilar membrane into neural activity.

6.6

A membrane that divides the cochlea of the inner ear into two compartments; contains the receptive organ for audition.

6.7

A type of neuron in the retina that receives information from photoreceptors and passes it on to the ganglion cells.

6.8

Hairlike projections of auditory hair cells that are stretched by the flexing of basilar membrane.

6.9

A snail-shaped chamber in the inner ear where audition takes place; the basilar membrane is located there.

6.19 false alarm	6.28 just-noticeable difference (jnd)
6.20 feature detector	6.29 lens
6.21 fovea	6.30 microvilli
6.22 free nerve ending	6.31 miss
6.23 fundamental frequency	6.32 muscle spindle
6.24 ganglion cell	6.33 nanometer (nm)
6.25 hertz (Hz)	6.34 negative afterimage
6.26 hit	6.35 olfactory mucosa
6.27 hue	6.36 optic disk

6.28

The smallest difference between two stimuli that is consistently perceived.

6.29

A transparent convex-shaped tissue that helps focus images on the retina.

6.30

Hairlike appendages of the receptor cells of taste buds that project into the saliva.

6.31

From signal-detection theory; reporting the absence of a stimulus that was actually present.

6.32

Stretch receptors found throughout a muscle that send information about changes in muscle length to the brain.

6.33

A billionth of a meter.

6.34

The image that is seen after a portion of the retina is exposed to visual stimulus for a period of time; consists of colors complementary to those of the stimulus.

6.35

A patch of mucous membrane on the roof of the nasal sinuses that contains dendrites of receptor cells for olfaction, located in the olfactory bulbs.

6.36

The blind spot; the location on the retina where the axons of the ganglion cells gather and exit the eye, forming the optic nerve.

6.19

From signal-detection theory; reporting the presence of a stimulus that actually did not occur.

6.20

A neuron in a sensory system that is connected to other neurons in such a way that it responds when a stimulus containing a particular characteristic is detected.

6.21

A small pit near the center of the retina, containing densely packed cones; responsible for the most acute and detailed vision.

6.22

The most common type of sensory receptors found in the middle layers of both smooth and hairy skin; responds primarily to noxious stimuli.

6.23

The basic frequency of a complex sound.

6.24

A neuron in the retina that receives information from photoreceptors by means of the bipolar cells and sends axons across the retina and through the optic nerves to the brain.

6.25

The measurement of the frequency of vibration of sound waves, measured in cycles per second.

6.26

From signal-detection theory, accurately reporting the presence of a stimulus.

6.27

A perceptual dimension of color that is closely related to the physical dimension of wavelength.

6.37 ossicle	6.46 receiver operating characteristic curve (ROC)
6.38 oval window	6.47 receptive field
6.39 overtone	6.48 response bias
6.40 Pacinian corpuscle	6.49 retina
6.41 papilla	6.50 rhodopsin
6.42 photon	6.51 rod-cone break
6.43 photopigment	6.52 rod
6.44 protanopia	6.53 round window
6.45 pursuit movement	6.54 saccadic movement

6.46	6.37
From signal-detection theory; a graph of hits versus false alarms plotted over a range of response biases; indicates the detectability of a stimulus.	One of the three bones of the middle ear, the hammer, anvil and stirrup, that transmit sound vibrations from the eardrum to the membrane behind the oval window of the cochlea
6.47	6.38
A portion of the visual field in which stimuli elicit responses in a particular neuron in the nervous system.	One of two openings in the vestibule next to the cochlea; the stirrup presses against the membrane of the oval window and transmits sound waves through it into the fluid inside the cochlea.
6.48	6.39
From signal-detection theory; a person's tendency to be cautious or liberal in reporting the presence of a weak stimulus.	Part of a complex sound; a multiple of the fundamental frequency.
6.49	6.40
The lining of most of the inner surface of the eye that contains the photoreceptors and associated neural circuitry.	A specialized ending of a dendrite of a somatosensory neuron; detects vibration.
6.50	6.41
The photopigment contained in rods.	A bump on the surface of the tongue that contains the taste buds.
6.51	6.42
A discontinuity in the dark-adaptation curve caused by the transition between vision mediated by cones and that mediated by rods.	A particle of light.
6.52	6.43
One of the photoreceptors in the retina; very sensitive to light but plays no role in color vision.	The substance inside photoreceptors that is responsible for transduction; composed of a protein molecule (opsin) and a molecule of retinal, derived from vitamin A.
6.53	6.44
One of the two openings in the vestibule in the inner ear; a membrane behind it moves in and out in response to pressure changes in the fluid induced by vibrations of the stirrup.	A hereditary form of color blindness in which red cones are filled with green photopigment.
6.54	6.45
Jerky movements of the eyes from one point to another.	A movement that the eyes make to maintain the image of a moving object on the fovea.

6.55	6.64
sclera	vestibular apparatus
6.56	6.65
semicircular canal	vestibular sac
6.57	6.66
spectral color	wavelength
6.58	6.67
taste bud	Weber fraction
6.59	6.68
tectorial membrane	white noise
6.60	
temporal coding	
6.61	
timbre	
6.62	
transduction	
6.63	
tritanopia	

6.64 The receptive organs of the inner ear that contribute to balance and perception of head movement.	6.55 Tough, white membrane of the eye.
6.65 Organs of the inner ear that detect head tilt through the movement of calcium carbonate crystals.	6.56 Liquid filled organs that detect rotation of the head.
6.66 A physical dimension of light closely associated with the perceptual dimension of hue.	6.57 A color that can be found in the visual spectrum; the colors we see in the rainbow.
6.67 The ratio of the magnitude of a jnd to the absolute magnitude of a stimulus; varies for different sensory systems.	6.58 Found in the papilla of the tongue; contains the receptor cells for taste.
6.68 A mixture of all the perceptible frequencies of sound.	6.59 A membrane that overhangs the basilar membrane; the tips of the cilia of the hair cells are embedded there.
	6.60 A means of representing information in the nervous system in terms of time; the most common temporal code is rate.
	6.61 A perceptual dimension of a sound that corresponds to its complexity.
	6.62 The conversion of physical energy from environmental stimuli into neural activity.
	6.63 A hereditary form of color blindness caused by a defect in blue cones.

Chapter 7
Perception

Lesson I

Read the interim summary on pages 236-238 of your text to reacquaint yourself with the material in this section.

7-1 *Describe the distinction between figure and ground and the Gestalt laws of grouping.*

Read pages 219-222 and then answer the following questions:

1. What is a boundary? What role does it play in distinguishing figure from ground. (See Figure 7.2 in your text.)

2. See Figures 7.3 and 7.4 in your text and explain the following statement: "The presence of a boundary is not necessary for the perception of form." Be sure to use the term *illusory contours* in your answer.

3. a. State and briefly explain the principle tenet of *Gestalt psychology*.

   b. Why does our visual system group elements together?

4. a. List the five Gestalt laws of grouping. (See Figures 7.5-7.9 in your text.)

      1.

      2.

      3.

      4.

      5.

   b. Now make sketches that illustrate each of the laws (or provide a brief verbal description).

7-2 *Outline the brain mechanisms of visual perception, describe the effects of brain damage on perception, and discuss current models of pattern perception.*

Read pages 222-228 and then answer the following questions:

1. Review how clusters of neurons in the retina respond to environmental stimulation. (You may wish to look back at Chapter 6.)

   a. What does the gridwork of squares superimposed on the drawing in Figure 7.10 in your text represent?

   b. What kind of information is analyzed in each "tile?"

   c. Does perception take place in the primary visual cortex? Explain your answer.

2. Summarize what Zeki (1978) discovered about the organization of the visual association cortex.

3. Where is information from all subregions of visual association cortex finally combined? (See Figure 7.11 in your text.)

4. Try the demonstration with the roll of paper described in your text and then explain why a person who is partially blind can still perceive objects and backgrounds.

5. Damage to visual association cortex affects perception. Describe the problems shown by patients with

   a. visual agnosia.

   b. prosopagnosia.

6. a. Models of pattern perception have been developed by _____ psychologists.

   b. Explain the term *template* in your own words.

   c. Briefly describe the template model of perception.

   d. What facts make it difficult to accept this theory?

7. a. Explain the term *prototype* in your own words.

   b. Briefly describe the prototype model of perception.

   c. Cite research by Standing (1973) that demonstrated the capacity of the brain to retain images.

   d. What do these results suggest about the capacity of the brain to form and retain visual prototypes?

8. a. Explain the term *distinctive features* in your own words.

   b. Briefly describe the distinctive-features model of perception.

   c. Study Figure 7.15 in your text and then explain how Gibson and Levin (1975) account for the ability to recognize a capital letter N.

9. Discuss some of the difficulties with the distinctive-features model of perception:

   a. Look at Figures 7.16 and 7.17 in your text and summarize two difficulties with incorporating the role of context into this model.

      1.

      2.

   b. How long does it take to recognize a triangle versus a pair of scissors? Which figure is more complex? What do these answers say about the distinctive-features model of perception?

7-3   *Discuss serial- and parallel- processing models of mental functions.*

Read pages 228-232 and then answer the following questions:

1. List the four major parts of a general-purpose computer and describe their functions. (See Figure 7.18 in your text.)

   1.

   2.

   3.

   4.

2. a. Define *artificial intelligence* in your own words.

   b. Describe several advantages and disadvantage to this approach to understanding the way the brain works.

      1. advantages

2. disadvantages (Be sure to use the term *constrained* as you answer this question.)

3. Study Figure 7.19 in your text and explain why computers are referred to as *serial devices*.

4. In what way is a computer serial analysis similar to human perception? In what way are they dissimilar?

5. Does the brain work fast enough to function efficiently as serial device? Explain.

6. Identify and describe a better model for understanding how the human brain works.

7. The effects of brain damage have provided information about the intact human brain. Describe the general effects of moderate brain damage and what they indicate about how the brain functions:

   a. How does widespread, moderate brain damage affect person's ability to go about daily activities?

   b. What, then, can we conclude about the way information is processed in the brain?

   c. What do the effects of severe damage to specific parts of the brain suggest about the way information is coordinated by the brain?

8. a. If you were to identify a letter of the alphabet through a process of elimination using the table in Figure 7.15, what kind of process would you be following?

   b. What alternative was suggested by Selfridge and Neisser (1963)?

7-4 *Describe neural network models, compare them with serial models, and describe research on top-down and bottom-up perceptual processing.*

Read pages 232-236 and then answer the following questions:

1. Define *neural network* in your own words.

2. a. Describe the properties of the simple elements of a neural network.

   b. Relate these properties to what you already know about neurons.

3. What have investigators who have written computer programs to simulate neural networks observed about the way these programs

   a. "learn" to recognize particular patterns?

b. respond when some of the connections are cut?

4. List some of the differences between models using neural networks and models using serial processing.

5. a. If the brain is composed of parallel neural networks, describe the likely relationship among networks.

    b. Describe the kind of neural networks that may exist at each of the following levels of visual perception:

       1. primary visual cortex

       2. subregions of visual association cortex of the occipital lobe

       3. visual association cortex of the temporal lobe

6. Summarize research by Palmer (1975) on the role of context in perception:

    a. After showing subjects familiar scenes, what did Palmer then show them? (See Figure 7.23 in your text.)

    b. Name and explain the use of the device he used to present the stimuli.

    c. How accurately did subjects identify objects that fit the context of the original scene? did not fit the context? (See Figure 7.24 in your text.)

    d. What do these results suggest about the role of context in object identification?

7. Describe the following:

    a. bottom-up processing.

    b. top-down processing.

8. a. Study Figure 7.25 in your text and explain why serial models would have difficulty accounting for your ability to identify each obscured letter.

    b. Now explain why a parallel processing model is a better choice.

9. Study Figure 7.26 in your text and explain how a parallel model might account for our ability to determine that the third item in Figure 7.25 is SPOT.

Lesson I Self Test

1. We classify what we see into two broad categories:

   a. animate and inanimate.
   b. foreground and background.
   c. figure and ground.
   d. relevant and irrelevant.

2. Our perception of wind currents in a field of wheat illustrates the Gestalt law of

   a. proximity.
   b. similarity.
   c. closure
   d. common fate.

3. What is the name of the brain region where all the information about a visual scene is combined?

   a. primary visual cortex
   b. visual association cortex of the occipital lobe
   c. visual association cortex of the temporal lobe
   d. thalamus

4. Most psychologists prefer the prototype model of perception to the template model of perception because

   a. prototypes are not idealized representations of objects.
   b. prototypes are more flexible.
   c. each object would be represented by only one prototype.
   d. it has face validity.

5. An important difficulty with the distinctive features model of perception is

   a. the need for an almost limitless number of special circuits for feature detection.
   b. that the effects of context receive too much weight.
   c. the lack of an acceptable operational definition of "distinctive feature."
   d. that the perception of simple and complex features occurs at about the same speed.

6. The modern computer has been a useful model for understanding the human brain because it

   a. contain four major parts that correspond with particular regions in the brain.
   b. operates as quickly as the brain.
   c. allows us to think concretely about something that is difficult to observe.
   d. responds to damage in the same way the brain does.

7. Parallel processors work

a. simultaneously at several different tasks.
b. one step at a time.
c. slowly.
d. the way neural synapses do.

8. Unlike serial processors, neural networks

a. contain a central processor.
b. are limited only by the skill of the programmer.
c. depend on a memory bank based on templates.
d. can "learn" to recognize particular stimuli.

9. Using a tachistoscope, Palmer (1975) demonstrated that correct responses were

a. related to the appropriateness of the context.
b. examples of problem solving.
c. carefully reasoned.
d. related to visual acuity.

10. The use of context in perception is an example of

a. trial and error.
b. bottom-up processing.
c. top-down processing.
d. serial processing.

Lesson II

Read the interim summary on pages 249-250 of your text to reacquaint yourself with the material in this section.

7-5   *Describe the binocular and monocular cues for the perception of distance.*

Read pages 238-243 and then answer the following questions:

1. a. Animals with eyes in the front of the head can obtain both _____ and _____ cues, but animals with eyes on the side of the head can obtain only _____ cues.

b. Summarize Figure 7.27 in your text:

1. List the monocular and binocular cues for depth perception.

Monocular   Binocular

1.   1.

2.   2.

3.

4.

5.

6.

7.

8.

2. Under what circumstances do we make use of movement cues?

3. Study Figure 7.28 in your text. When the eyes converge on a distant object the angle between them is _____ than when they converge on a _____ object.

4. a. Try the demonstration in your text of holding your fingers in front of your eyes and explain why you can judge the distance of each finger. Be sure to use the terms *retinal disparity* and *stereopsis* in your answer.

   b. Summarize research by Julesz (1965) that demonstrated the role of retinal disparity in depth perception.

   c. Cite research recording activity of individual neurons that further supports your explanation.

5. Discuss monocular cues that can be illustrated in a painting or photograph:

   a. Explain how we judge the distance of objects using *interposition*.

   b. Almost everyone who sees Figure 7.30 in your text sees two objects with the left-hand object being closer. Use the concept of *good form* to explain why we do not usually see a complex figure and how we judge the location of each object.

   c. While you are hiking you see a church steeple in the distance. Explain how familiarity with *sizes* helps you determine how far away you are from the town.

   d. Study Figures 7.31 and 7.32 in your text and explain why we rely on *perspective* and ignore the size of retinal images to determine the size of an object.

   e. Study Figures 7.33 and 7.34 in your text and describe how cues provided by *texture* and *haze* influence distance perception.

   f. Study Figure 7.35 in your text and explain how cues provided by *shading* help us judge the distance of parts of an object.

g. Study Figure 7.36 in your text and draw a simple scene with objects above and below the horizon. Then explain how *elevation* in relation to the horizon influences distance perception.

6. Discuss how monocular cues from head and body movements influence distance perception:

a. If you gaze at a scene while moving your head from side to side, what is the location of objects that change the most in relation to head movements?

b. Study Figure 7.37 in your text and using the phenomenon of *motion parallax* explain how the size of features in the environment change as we change our location.

7-6   *Describe and discuss the phenomena of brightness and form constancy.*

Read pages 243-246 and then answer the following questions:

1. Explain the concept of *brightness constancy* in your own words.

2. Summarize how Katz (1935) demonstrated this phenomenon:

a. Study Figure 7.38 in your text and describe the procedure.

b. How accurately did subjects match squares of different shades of gray on the right with the gray square in shadow?

c. If subjects had compared color shades based strictly on the amount of light reflected by the two squares, how would their accuracy rate have changed?

3. a. Study Figure 7.39 in your text and explain the concept of *form constancy* in your own words.

b. According to von Helmholtz, why does our perception of an object's size remain relatively constant? Be sure to use the term *unconscious inference* in your answer.

c. Study Figure 7.40 in your text and explain why we perceive the shape of the window as rectangular.

d. Try the demonstration with the light source and book that is described in your text. Obviously, the size of the afterimage on your retina remains constant. Why, then, does your perception of its size change as you look around your room?

7-7 *Discuss research on the perception of motion and the combining of information from successive fixations.*

Read pages 246-249 and then answer the following questions:

1. Summarize research by Ball and Sekuler (1982) on how practice can affect motion detection:

   a. Describe how they trained subjects to detect the motion of a series of dots.

   b. Explain why each subject was trained to detect movement in a different direction.

   c. What were the results of training? How long did the effects of training persist?

   d. What can we conclude?

2. a. Try the three demonstrations of eye movements and retinal images described in your text and then explain how the brain interprets the meaning of moving retinal images.

   b. State the general rule for determining how objects of different sizes appear to move in relationship to each other. (See Figure 7.41 in your text for a laboratory application of this rule.)

   c. Describe how Johansson (1973) demonstrated the kinds of information that can be obtained from movement and list some of the features that the subjects could detect.

3. a. After each rapid steplike eye movement, or _____, the eye stops briefly to rest and gather information. These stops are called _____.

   b. Study Figures 7.42 and 7.43 in your text and using the concept of fixation explain why one of the figures is more difficult to evaluate.

4. a. Explain the phenomenon of *backward masking* in your own words.

   b. Summarize Breitmeyer's (1980) explanation of the role this phenomenon plays in perception.

   c. Study Figure 7.44 in your text and explain what would happen if backward masking did not take place.

5. Describe the *phi phenomenon* and give an example of an important application of it.

Lesson II Self Test

1. Convergence as a cue about distance depends on information

   a. about the angle between the eyes.
   b. about the amount of disparity produced by images of the objects on both retinas.
   c. obtained from monocular vision.
   d. about the size of objects midway between the target object and the eyes.

2. A stereoscope can be used to demonstrate the role of

   a. backward masking.
   b. retinal disparity.
   c. negative afterimages.
   d. motion parallax.

3. Which monocular cue cannot be represented realistically in a drawing?

   a. texture.
   b. haze.
   c. elevation.
   d. movement.

4. We perceive telephone poles stretched out for miles along the highway as all being the same size because of

   a. elevation.
   b. good form.
   c. interposition.
   d. perspective.

5. When we perceive distance by observing the location of an object in relation to the horizon, we are using cues about

   a. interposition.
   b. perspective.
   c. elevation.
   d. shading.

6. A gray card in sunlight looks darker than a white card in the shade. This is an example of

   a. brightness constancy.
   b. form constancy.
   c. unconscious inference.
   d. counterbalancing.

7. When we approach an object or when it approaches us, we perceive its size

   a. as getting bigger.
   b. as constant.
   c. in proportion to the size of the retinal image it produces.
   d. from the size of the afterimage.

8. Our ability to distinguish between movements of a retinal image caused by eye movements and those caused by the movements of objects depends on

   a. feedback from the eye muscles.
   b. perception of relative motion.
   c. top-down processing.
   d. the brain's "knowledge" that it has moved the eyes.

9. Rapid steplike movements of the eyes are called

   a. conjugate movements.
   b. saccades.
   c. fixations.
   d. sweeps.

10. We would have difficulty reading if it were not for

   a. backward masking.
   b. phi phenomenon.
   c. motion parallax.
   d. binocular vision.

Answers for Self Tests

Lesson I			Lesson II		
1.	c	Obj. 7-1	1.	a	Obj. 7-5
2.	d	Obj. 7-1	2.	b	Obj. 7-5
3.	c	Obj. 7-2	3.	d	Obj. 7-5
4.	b	Obj. 7-2	4.	d	Obj. 7-5
5.	d	Obj. 7-2	5.	c	Obj. 7-5
6.	c	Obj. 7-3	6.	a	Obj. 7-6
7.	a	Obj. 7-3	7.	b	Obj. 7-6
8.	d	Obj. 7-4	8.	d	Obj. 7-7
9.	a	Obj. 7-4	9.	b	Obj. 7-7
10.	c	Obj. 7-4	10.	a	Obj. 7-7

7.1 artificial intelligence	7.10 haze
7.2 backward masking	7.11 interposition
7.3 bottom-up processing	7.12 law of closure
7.4 brightness constancy	7.13 law of common fate
7.5 convergence	7.14 law of good continuation
7.6 elevation	7.15 law of proximity
7.7 figure and ground	7.16 law of similarity
7.8 form constancy	7.17 motion parallax
7.9 Gestalt psychology	7.18 neural network

7.10 A monocular distance cue; parts of a landscape that are farthest away will be less distinct because of haze in the earth's atmosphere.	7.1 A field in which researchers construct computer programs to simulate human skills such as visual pattern perception in an effort to better understand human brain mechanisms.
7.11 A monocular distance cue; if one object is placed between us and another object in such a way as to partially block our view of the more distant one we can immediately determine which is closer.	7.2 A phenomena in which the second of two visual stimuli presented in succession erases the image of the first.
7.12 A Gestalt law of grouping; our visual system "closes" or fills-in the outline of an incomplete figure.	7.3 A model of pattern recognition asserting that raw material of perception is an analysis of the details of a stimulus; also called data-driven processing.
7.13 A Gestalt law of grouping; elements moving in the same direction will be perceived as belonging together and forming a figure.	7.4 A perceptional phenomenon in which shades of color are perceived in relation to the surrounding environment and not simply by the amount of reflected light.
7.14 A Gestalt law of grouping; the path of a line or group of objects will be perceived as the simplest or most predictable.	7.5 A distance cue; when the eyes gaze at an object the angle between them is related to the object's distance; the brain uses this information to compute the distance.
7.15 A Gestalt law of grouping; elements closest to each other will perceived as belonging to the same figure.	7.6 A monocular distance cue; when the horizon is visible we perceive objects just above or below it as being farther from us.
7.16 A Gestalt law of grouping; elements that physically resemble each other will be perceived as belonging to the same figure.	7.7 A tendency to classify what we see as either objects (figures) or background (ground)
7.17 A monocular distance cue; changes in the relative location of objects as an observer moves provides cues to their distance.	7.8 A perception phenomena in which an object's size and shape remain constant regardless of its movements relative to us; inaccurately called size constancy because size is only an aspect of form.
7.18 A mathematical model based on the properties of networks of neurons in the human brain; able to "learn" to perceive particular patterns.	7.9 A theory of perception asserting that in order to understand visual perception it is not enough to analyze individual elements of a scene; the relationships between the elements must also be considered.

7.19	7.28
perspective	template
7.20	7.29
phi phenomenon	texture
7.21	7.30
prosopagnosia	top-down processing
7.22	7.31
prototype	unconscious inference
7.23	7.32
retinal disparity	visual agnosia
7.24	
serial device	
7.25	
shading	
7.26	
stereopsis	
7.27	
tachistoscope	

7.28 In psychology, special kinds of visual memories that may be used to recognize categories of forms; stimuli are compared to templates and a match results in a perception; similar to prototypes but less flexible.	7.19 A monocular distance cue; the tendency for parallel lines that recede from us to converge at a single point.
7.29 A monocular distance cue; a coarser texture appears closer and a fine texture appears more distant.	7.20 The perceived movement caused by turning on two or more lights in sequence, one at a time.
7.30 A model of pattern recognition asserting that perception is strongly influenced by the context in which it occurs; thus, perceptions depend on existing memories.	7.21 Visual perception deficit caused by damage to visual association cortex; inability to recognize faces.
7.31 An explanation of form constancy suggested by von Helmholtz; the perceived size of an object is computed from the size of its retinal image and its perceived distance from us.	7.22 In psychology, special kinds of visual memories that may be used to recognize categories of forms; stimuli are compared to prototypes and a resemblance results in a perception; similar to templates but more flexible.
7.32 Visual perception deficit caused by damage to visual association cortex; inability to recognize familiar objects.	7.23 A binocular distance cue that provides the basis for stereopsis; caused by the fact that the images of objects at different distances fall on different locations of the two retinas.
	7.24 A machine such as a general-purpose digital computer that processes information in a step-by-step manner.
	7.25 A monocular distance cue; if an object is illuminated from above a convex object will be light on top and dark on the bottom.
	7.26 The perception of depth using retinal disparity; can be demonstrated using a stereoscope, which shows two slightly different pictures one to each eye.
	7.27 A machine that can present visual stimuli very briefly.

Chapter 8
Memory

Lesson I

Read the interim summary on pages 257-258 of your text to reacquaint yourself with the material in this section.

8-1   *Explain the difference between the behavioral and cognitive approaches to learning and memory, outline the learning process, and describe research on sensory memory.*

Read pages 254-257 and then answer the following questions:

1. Explain the difference between the behavioral, physiological, and cognitive approaches to the study of memory.

2. Compare the characteristics of the following three kinds of memory:

   a. Sensory memory

      1. duration

      2. capacity

   b. Short-term memory

      1. duration

      2. capacity

   c. Long-term memory

      1. duration

      2. capacity

3. Why do psychologists object to the model of memory presented in Figure 8.1 in your text?

4. What kind of memory do each of the following situations illustrate?

   a. You recall nursery rhymes you learned as a child.

b. You look up an address and remember it long enough to write it on the envelope.

c. You think you just saw a shooting star, but you are not really sure.

d. Although you haven't played Gin Rummy in years, you agree to play with your younger cousin. You're surprised at how easily you can remember the rules.

5. Visual sensory memory is referred to as _____ memory and auditory sensory memory is referred to as _____ memory.

6. Summarize results of research by Sperling (1960) on iconic memory:

a. Describe the stimulus and explain how Sperling presented it to subjects.

b. Describe the *whole-report* procedure.

c. How many letters did subjects usually recall?

d. What did Sperling think might account for their responses?

e. Describe the *partial-report* procedure. Why did he present the tone *after* the letters were flashed?

f. How accurately were subjects able to recall a specific line now?

g. How accurately were subjects able to recall a specific line when the time between the flash and the tone was extended?

h. What do these results suggest

a. about the duration of iconic memory?

b. as the reason that subjects could not recall more than four or five letters?

7. Summarize research by Eriksen and Collins (1967) that confirmed Sperling's conclusions:

a. Study Figure 8.2 in your text and describe the stimuli and how it was presented to subjects.

b. In general, how did the length of the delay between the two flashes effect the ability of subjects to perceive the letters?

c. What do the results suggest about the capacity and duration of iconic memory?

8. Summarize research on the physical appearance of sensory data in iconic memory.

a. Study Figure 8.3 in your text and then explain how Banks and Barber (1977) demonstrated that color information is present in iconic memory.

b. Explain how Sperling (1960) demonstrated that names of objects could not be retrieved from iconic memory.

9. Briefly explain the role of echoic memory in speech comprehension.

10. Summarize research Darwin et al. (1972) on the duration of echoic memory:

a. Describe the stimuli and say how they were presented to subjects.

b. In general, how did the length of the delay between the stimulus and the tone effect the accuracy of responses?

c. What do these results suggest about the duration of echoic memory?

Read the interim summary on page 269 of your text to reacquaint yourself with the material in this section.

8-2   *Describe research on the encoding of information in short-term/working memory and on the process of proactive inhibition.*

Read pages 258-260 and then answer the following questions:

1. Study Figure 8.4 in your text and explain why it may be a more accurate than the model in Figure 8.1.

2. Some psychologists prefer to refer to short-term memory as _____ _____ because it contains both _____ information and information retrieved from _____-_____ memory.

3. a. How many items of information can be retained in short-term memory? (Miller, 1956)

b. Explain the concept of *chunking* in your own words.

c. Why is it advantageous to be able to combine information into "chunks?"

4. Now use this information to explain why few people can accurately repeat the fifteen seemingly random words and why these words can easily be remembered when arranged differently.

5. Explain the concept of *proactive inhibition* in your own words.

6. Summarize research to determine whether the cause of proactive inhibition was a storage problem or a retrieval problem:

a. How well did subjects recall successive lists of numbers? (Wickens, 1972) How well did they do when lists of letters were presented instead?

b. What is this phenomenon called?

c. Describe how Gardiner et al. (1972) modified Wicken's technique.

d. Explain the significance of the fact that informed subjects showed release from inhibition regardless of whether they were informed of the difference in the categories before being presented with the words or afterwards. (See Figure 8.5 in your text.)

8-3   *Describe evidence for the existence of phonological and visual short-term memory.*

Read pages 261-266 and then answer the following questions:

1. Use one word to describe the primary form of coding of verbal information in short-term memory.

2. a. What results did Conrad (1964) obtain when he asked subjects to write down letters from lists they had been shown?

   b. What did the nature of their errors suggest about the way visual information is encoded?

3. a. However, Hintzman (1967) suggested that the errors could also reflect a form of _____ coding.

   b. What observation was the basis of his alternative explanation?

   c. Explain the process of *subvocal articulation* in your own words.

4. Explain why

   a. Conrad chose deaf children as subjects when he replicated his experiment.

   b. some children still made "acoustical" errors.

   c. these results confirm the presence of articulatory coding in short-term memory.

5. a. Salame and Baddeley (1982) showed all subjects sequences of digits on a computer terminal and then asked them to write down what they saw. Describe the testing conditions for

      1. control subjects.

      2. experimental subjects.

   b. What kind of interference was the most disruptive?

c. What do the results suggest about acoustical coding in short-term memory?

6. a. Study Figure 8.6 in your text and draw the loop of the hypothesized relationship between the two components of phonological memory: the auditory system and the articulatory system in the brain. (Baddeley (1986)

b. Carefully summarize Baddeley's explanation of the cooperation between the auditory system and the articulatory system of the brain. (Study Figure 8.6 in your text.)

7. Summarize research on chunking of familiar and unfamiliar information in visual short-term memory:

a. Explain why it was easier for chess experts to recall the position of pieces in a real game than for novices. (deGroot, 1965)

b. Study Figure 8.7 in your text and describe the results that Phillips (1974) obtained when he tested subjects' ability to recognize small differences in patterns that were presented at different delay intervals.

c. What do these results suggest about the ability to store visual information in short-term memory and its capacity?

8. a. Study Figure 8.8 in your text and describe the pairs of shapes that subjects were asked to compare in a study by Shepard and Metzler (1971).

b. Study Figure 8.9 in your text and describe the variable that affects a person's decision time.

c. When asked to describe how they made a particular comparison, what did subjects report?

d. What is the possible utility of this ability?

9. a. If expert abacus users do not have a better immediate memory for letters or words than other people, how do they perform long strings of calculations unaided?

b. Describe how Hatano and Osawa (1983) tested this hypothesis.

8-4   *Describe research on the physiological basis of phonological and visual short-term memory and on the loss of information from short-term memory.*

Read pages 266-268 and then answer the following questions:

1. a. Conduction aphasia is a profound deficit in _____ _____ _____ caused by damage to a region of the _____ _____ _____:

    b. How does conduction aphasia affect speech

       1. comprehension?

       2. production?

       3. repetition?

    c. Study Figure 8.10 in your text and carefully explain the presumed reason why the lesion that causes conduction aphasia disrupts the ability to repeat words.

2. Summarize research by Kovner and Stamm (1972) that demonstrated that some neural circuits involved in visual short-term memory are located in visual association cortex.

    a. Why did the Kovner and Stamm operate on the monkeys before the experiment?

    b. Describe the *delayed matching-to-sample* task that the monkeys learned and the role of short-term memory in its performance. (See Figure 8.11 in your text.)

    c. What was the effect of brief electrical stimulation to

       1. visual association cortex?

       2. locations other than visual association cortex?

3. Waugh and Norman (1965) conducted research on the disappearance of information in short-term memory.

    a. Explain the task they taught to subjects. (Be sure to use the term the *probe*.)

    b. How many items separated the probe and the target?

    c. Describe the two ways the lists were presented and explain why the researchers followed this procedure.

    d. Study Figure 8.12 in your text. Which factor influenced performance the most--rate or number of items?

    e. What do the results suggest about the reason why information in short-term memory disappears?

Lesson I Self Test

1. Sperling used a tachistoscope to show subjects a set of nine letters. They could not recall more than four or five of them correctly because

   a. the set of letters was greater than the capacity of iconic memory.
   b. the visual stimulus fades quickly.
   c. there was no basis to chunk the information.
   d. stimuli are not accurately represented in sensory memory.

2. Echoic memory is important for

   a. spelling.
   b. comprehension of words.
   c. sound location.
   d. reading.

3. Short-term memory

   a. stores information is an unencoded manner.
   b. has a capacity of from seven to eleven items.
   c. is difficult to distinguish from perception.
   d. receives both new information and information from long-term-memory.

4. Alberto is learning English as a second language. He has noticed that he sometimes confuses word order in English with word order in Spanish. His experience resembles the phenomenon of

   a. retrieval errors.
   b. displacement.
   c. proactive inhibition.
   d. decay.

5. Gardner, Craik, and Birtwistle studied the causes of release from proactive inhibition. Their study, which used the names of wildflowers and garden flowers, concluded that

   a. proactive inhibition is caused by displacement.
   b. proactive inhibition affects retrieval of information.
   c. proactive inhibition affects storage of information.
   d. the consolidation hyppothesis cannot be correct.

6. When Conrad repeated a study in which subjects saw lists of letters and then wrote down what they saw, why did he choose deaf subjects?

   a. to eliminate distractions from background noise
   b. to prevent transmitting information through tone of voice or inflection
   c. to eliminate any confusion of letters on the basis of their sounds
   d. to reduce subvocal articulation as much as possible

7. The ability of expert chess players to remember actual chessboards underscores

   a. the advantages of chunking information.
   b. the power of encoding verbal information in working memory.
   c. the fact that information coding is negatively affected by complexity.

   d. the ability to manipulate information in long-term memory.

8. Expert abacus users successfully performed calculations without an abacus by using

   a. almost imperceptible finger motions.
   b. mental images.
   c. chunking.
   d. subvocal articulation.

9. Mr. Barton talks easily and understands what is being said, but he has difficulty repeating what he hears. He has a disorder called

   a. prosopagnosia.
   b. agnosia.
   c. conduction aphasia.
   d. dyslexia.

10. The most important reason information in short-term memory is lost is

   a. decay.
   b. displacement.
   c. our inability to retrieve it.
   d. disruption.

Lesson II

Read the interim summary on pages 287-288 of your text to reacquaint yourself with the material in this section.

8-5   *Discuss the consolidation hypothesis of learning and the effects of deep and shallow processing on remembering.*

Read pages 269-274 and then answer the following questions:

1. Identify the two major types of learning.

   a.

   b.

2. Give your own examples of learning as a(n)

   a. active process.

   b. passive process.

3. Explain the concept of *consolidation* in your own words.

4. a. Define the term *retrograde amnesia* in your own words.

   b. Describe how a blow to the head can cause retrograde amnesia. Refer to the disruption of short-term memory.

5. State two conclusions about the consolidation process drawn from the effects of head injury.

   1.

   2.

6. a. What clinical observation suggested that violent electrical activity in the brain might be beneficial?

   b. What procedure did Cerletti devise as a substitute for Meduna's drug induced seizures?

   c. What side effect of treatment was noticed almost immediately? How did Zubin and Barrera (1941) confirm this observation?

   d. How does a single treatment affect

      1. short-term memory?

      2. long-term memory?

   e. What does this difference suggest about the way the brain stores old and new information?

7. State two assumptions of consolidation theory that have been challenged by recent research.

   1.

   2.

8. Describe the two kinds of rehearsal suggested by Craik and Lockhart (1972).

   a. maintenance rehearsal

   b. elaborative rehearsal

9. Summarize research on the effectiveness of elaboration by Craik and Tulving (1975):

   a. Describe the task subjects were asked to perform. Mention the complexity of the sentences.

b. What were the subjects asked to do next?

c. Study Figure 8.13 in your text and describe the circumstances in which subjects had the best recall of words they had used.

d. What do these results suggest about the way to organize material to facilitate memorization?

10. Craik and Lockhart (1972) suggested a useful framework for understanding how information enters long-term memory. Explain what they meant by:

a. *shallow processing* and *surface features*.

b. *deep processing* and *semantic features*.

11. Cite research by Hyde and Jenkins (1969) that supports their framework:

a. Describe the tasks and the two different sets of directions given to subjects.

b. Study Figure 8.14 in your text and describe the circumstance in which subjects had the best recall of words.

12. a. Explain two criticisms of the depth of processing model of memory:

1.

2.

b. What is the status of this framework today and what did it contribute to an understanding of memory?

8-6   *Discuss research on the distinction between episodic and semantic memory and the distinction between explicit and implicit memory.*

Read pages 274-278 and then answer the following questions:

1. Summarize research by Sachs (1967) on the relative importance of specific words and meaning in long-term memory:

a. Describe the task that the subjects were asked to perform. Explain the ways that the test and comparison sentences could differ from each other.

b. Study Figure 8.15 in your text and describe the results.

2. a. Define the terms *episodic memory* and *semantic memory* proposed by Tulving in your own words and give your own example of each.

b. Explain why it is inaccurate to conclude that these types of memories represent different memory systems.

c. How has Tulving revised his model?

3. Define *explicit memory* and *implicit memory* in your own words and give several examples of each.

4. Cite *behavioral evidence* obtained by Graf and Mandler (1984) that supports this distinction:

a. Describe the task and the two sets of directions that were given to subjects.

b. Describe how the subjects' implicit and explicit memory was tested using the same cue but different instructions.

c. Study Figure 8.16 in your text and state how deliberate processing affected explicit and implicit memory.

8-7   *Describe anterograde amnesia in humans and laboratory animals and discuss the implications for the organization of long-term memory.*

Read pages 278-281 and then answer the following questions:

1. a. Define *anterograde amnesia* in your own words.

b. What was the cause of anterograde amnesia of

1. Korsakoff's syndrome patients?

2. Patient H.M.?

2. a. Describe the nature of following types of memory in patients with anterograde amnesia:

1. short- and long-term memory.

2. explicit and implicit memory.

b. Describe the study by Graf, Squire, and Mandler (1984). (Study Figure 8.18 in your text.)

c. Describe, in general, the types of tasks that people with anterograde amnesia can do.

3. a. What is the name of the part of the brain that seems to be involved in the formation of new explicit memories and where is it located? (See Figure 8.19 in your text.)

b. Name other brain regions that may play a role.

4. Why is the word <u>context</u> underlined in your text?

5. Summarize research using a radial arm maze to test for explicit memory in animals. (See Figure 8.20 in your text.)

a. Explain the task and describe the performance of normal rats.

b. Describe the performance of rats with hippocampal damage.

c. Study Figure 8.21 in your text and describe the design and results of research by Olton and Papas (1979) using a seventeen-arm radial maze.

d. What can we conclude from this study?

8-8 *Explain how long-term memories may alter the structures of the brain, how information is remembered, and how information can be remembered more efficiently.*

Read pages 281-287 and then answer the following questions:

1. Describe some of the possible physical changes that could occur in real neural circuits in the brain as a result of learning.

2. Refering to the rowboat story, explain how existing long-term memories influence the organization of information entering long-term memory.

3. a. Explain the difference between *learning* and *remembering*.

b. Summarize what we know about remembering in two sentences.

1.   2.

c. If remembering is automatic, how can you explain the fact that we often make a deliberate effort to remember something? What is it that we are doing?

4. a. Study Figure 8.22 in your text and if you have not already done so, try the exercise.

b. How does the Stroop effect support the statement "Remembering is automatic."?

c. Explain why even information that is difficult to recall is still retrieved automatically.

d. Define *recollection* in your own words.

5. After listening to subjects retell a story or draw a picture they had previously seen, what did Bartlett (1932) conclude about memory formation?

6. Summarize research by Spiro (1977, 1980) on the interplay between reality and personal conceptions of reality:

a. Describe how the story that subjects remembered was influenced by a

1. contradictory ending.

2. consistent ending.

b. What was the apparent reason for the "extra facts"?

c. How much weight, then, should we give to a person's confidence in the accuracy of his or her remembrances?

d. Explain how the form of a question can affect the way details of an event are recalled.

7. a. Describe *mnemonic systems* in your own words.

b. Mnemonic systems make use of two long recognized facts about memory. List them.

1.

2.

8. Briefly describe how information is organized using the *method of loci*.

9. a. Describe the task Bower and Clark (1969) asked subjects to perform. Explain the directions thay gave to the two groups of subjects.

   b. Study Figure 8.23 in your text and describe the circumstances in which subjects had the best recall.

   c. What do the results suggest about the usefulness of narrative stories?

10. Identify the concepts (listed below) illustrated in the following situations.

    1. Tai found it especially difficult to learn Hamlet's Soliloquy, but by repeating the words again and again he finally succeeded.

    2. "I was surprised that he could not remember more of what happened," Susie said to her mother after visiting her friend in the hospital. "He doesn't even remember the bus hitting the tree."

    3. "I can't remember the name of the travel agency, but the ad is in the yellow pages near the bottom on the left."

    4. "It was so easy to learn our new telephone number," Bobby said to his grandmother. "It's almost the same as our old ZIP code."

    5. "Dad is recovering very well from his stroke," Suzanne told her cousin. "He talks so easily, you might not think anything is wrong until you realize he hasn't remembered anything from your last visit--or even that you visited!"

    6. "That's your fourth strike in six frames," Andy said. "How do you keep the ball so straight?" "I really don't know," Alison replied a little self-consciously.

    7. "I don't think I can give you any more help," Grandpa told Alex, who was trying to draw a family tree for his social studies class. "Oh please, Grandpa," Alex said. "You can remember this name. Do you think he was named after a relative? Would it seem like an unusual name today?"

    choices: implicit memory, retrograde amnesia, elaborative rehearsal, memorization, anterograde amnesia, recollection, shallow processing

Lesson II Self Test

1. The consolidation hypothesis assumes that

   a. short-term and long-term memory are physiologically different.
   b. the transfer of information from short-term to long-term memory is an unconscious act.
   c. the transfer of information from short-term to long-term memory is rapid.
   d. the distinction between short-term and long-term memory are only apparent, not real.

2. Electroshock therapy is a common treatment for

a. epilepsy.
b. amnesia.
c. severe depression
d. schizophrenia.

3. _____ processing depends on the analysis of _____ features.

a. shallow; semantic
b. deep; semantic
c. surface; shallow
d. deep; linguistic

4. Evidence suggests that episodic memory and semantic memory

a. are independent memory systems.
b. depend on elaborative rehearsal.
c. exist for each sensory modality.
d. are parts of the same memory system.

5. The best way to reveal implicit memory is to ask the subject

a. a series of oral questions.
b. a series of implicit questions.
c. to demonstrate a skill.
d. to demonstrate a skill and describe each action.

6. Research using word recall suggests that deliberate processing has

a. a strong effect on explicit memory.
b. a strong effect on implicit memory.
c. no effect on either explicit or implicit memory.
d. an effect on semantic memory but not episodic memory.

7. Patients like H.M.

a. can never learn any new information.
b. are quickly bored by repetitive tasks.
c. cannot recall explicit memories formed before the brain damage occurred.
d. have relatively normal short-term memory.

8. Anterograde amnesia results from damage to the

a. pons.
b. hippocampus.
c. amygdala.
d. occipital lobes.

9. The Stroop effect demonstrates that remembering is

a. creative.
b. compulsive.
c. automatic.
d. transient.

10. Mnemonic systems do not

    a. simplify information; they make it more elaborate.
    b. make it easier to learn information; they make it possible.
    c. depend on rehearsal; they depend on organization.
    d. depend on recollection; they depend on retrieval.

Answers for Self Tests

Lesson I			Lesson II		
1.	b	Obj. 8-1	1.	a	Obj. 8-5
2.	b	Obj. 8-1	2.	c	Obj. 8-5
3.	d	Obj. 8-2	3.	b	Obj. 8-5
4.	c	Obj. 8-2	4.	d	Obj. 8-6
5.	b	Obj. 8-2	5.	c	Obj. 8-6
6.	c	Obj. 8-3	6.	a	Obj. 8-6
7.	d	Obj. 8-3	7.	d	Obj. 8-7
8.	b	Obj. 8-3	8.	b	Obj. 8-7
9.	c	Obj. 8-4	9.	c	Obj. 8-8
10.	b	Obj. 8-4	10.	a	Obj. 8-8

8.1 anterograde amnesia	8.10 electroshock treatment
8.2 chunking	8.11 episodic memory
8.3 conduction aphasia	8.12 explicit memory
8.4 consolidation	8.13 hippocampus
8.5 context	8.14 iconic memory
8.6 deep processing	8.15 implicit memory
8.7 delayed matching-to-sample task	8.16 Korsakoff's syndrome
8.8 echoic memory	8.17 long-term memory
8.9 elaborative rehearsal	8.18 maintenance rehearsal

8.10 A treatment for severe depression in which a brief surge of electricity is passed through a person's head, inducing a seizure; causes retrograde amnesia.	**8.1** The inability to learn new information permanently, caused by brain damage; short-term memory and recall of events learned before the injury are relatively normal.
8.11 Memory about specific events tied to the contexts in which they occurred.	**8.2** Use of information already present in long-term memory to organize and simplify incoming information in short-term memory; the capacity of short-term memory is seven plus or minus two chunks.
8.12 A memory that a person is able to describe in words.	**8.3** A severe deficit in phonological working memory caused by damage to the left parietal lobe; patients can talk and understand but have great difficulty repeating precisely what has been said to them.
8.13 An component of the limbic system located in the temporal lobe of the brain; plays an important role in learning.	**8.4** The hypothetical basis of short- and long-term memory; short-term memory consists of neural activity and long-term memory consists of structural changes in neurons induced by this activity.
8.14 A form of sensory memory that holds a brief visual image of a scene that has just been perceived.	**8.5** The system or structure in which information is presented; serves to organize and clarify information and make it easier to remember.
8.15 A memory that cannot be described in words; must be demonstrated through the performance of a behavior.	**8.6** The analysis of information based on the meaning or semantic features of a stimulus; such analysis often leads to better retention.
8.16 Anterograde amnesia caused by brain damage produced by chronic alcoholism or severe amnesia.	**8.7** A test of short-term memory in which subjects are shown a visual pattern and are then required, after a delay of several seconds, to identify from a choice of two or more, the one they had previously seen.
8.17 Relatively permanent memory of apparently unlimited capacity.	**8.8** Sensory memory for sounds that have just been perceived.
8.18 Simple repetition of verbal information; less effective than other rehearsal means in producing lasting changes in long-term memory.	**8.9** A way of thinking about recently learned information that relates it to information already in long-term memory.

8.19

method of loci

8.20

mnemonic system

8.21

phonological short-term memory

8.22

proactive inhibition

8.23

release from proactive inhibition

8.24

retrograde amnesia

8.25

semantic memory

8.26

sensory memory

8.27

shallow processing

8.28

short-term memory

8.29

subvocal articulation

8.30

working memory

8.28	8.19
Immediate memory for stimuli that have just been perceived; conceptually similar to working memory, which also includes information that has just been retrieved from long-term memory.	A memory aid that consists of thinking about elements of new information in specific locations within a memorized building and then recalling it by mentally walking through the building, stopping at each location.
8.29	8.20
"Talking to oneself" without actually engaging in speech.	Systematic ways of organizing new information to facilitate memorization; examples include method of loci and narrative stories.
8.30	8.21
Memory that contains information that has just been perceived as well as information that has just been retrieved from long-term memory; some forms of "thinking" take place here.	A coding system for the short-term storage of words based on their sounds and the movements made to pronounce them.
	8.22
	A phenomena in which previously learned information interferes with attempts to learn new information.
	8.23
	A phenomena in which proactive inhibition diminishes after the category of information being memorized suddenly switches.
	8.24
	A lack of memory for events that occurred before an injury to the brain.
	8.25
	Long-term memory for facts that does not include the context in which the facts were learned.
	8.26
	A very short-lived, but fairly accurate, representation of information that has just been perceived.
	8.27
	The analysis of information based on physical characteristics or surface features of a stimulus; such analysis often leads to relatively poor retention.

Chapter 9
Language

Lesson I

Read the interim summary on pages 301-303 of your text to reacquaint yourself with the material in this section.

9-1   *Explain the functions of language and describe the recognition of individual speech sounds.*

Read pages 292-295 and then answer the following questions:

1. Describe the field of *psycholinguistics*.

2. a. What are some of the significant advantages we humans enjoy because we can engage in verbal behavior?

   b. Describe how we can use language to increase the amount of information stored in short-term and long-term memory.

3. a. List some of the functions of verbal communication and provide an example to illustrate each function.

   b. A considerate speaker will help the listener to use and understand new information by placing it in the correct _____.

   c. What information does the speaker expect the listener to already know in the following situations?

      1. I saw her again last night.

      2. The Browns were able to come after all.

   d. Speakers and listeners use the _____-_____ _____ to identify information and signal understanding.

   e. Name two techniques a speaker can use to signal new information.

      1.   2.

123

   f. Define *stress* in your own words and underline the word that the speaker should stress to indicate new information in the following situations.

     1. Dianne should pick the ripe tomatoes. (Dianne, not Mark.)

     2. Dianne should pick the ripe tomatoes. (There are also some green ones on the vine.)

     3. Dianne should pick the ripe tomatoes. (Not the ripe cucumbers.)

   g. Which article indicates old or given information? new information?

   h. If someone said to you "I saw the snake," what would your response be? Why?

   i. Suppose, instead, the person said "I saw a snake." Why would you react differently?

4. a. List three factors that influence our perception of speech sounds.

   b. Define the term *phoneme* in your own words.

   c. Carefully explain why we can distinguish between *pa* and *ba*. Be sure to use the terms *voice-onset time* and *voicing* in your answer.

5. Lisker and Abramson (1970) asked subjects to listen to computer-generated sounds of a puff followed by *ah*.

   a. What two phonemes did subjects report hearing?

   b. Study Figure 9.1 in your text and explain how subjects used voice-onset time to distinguish between them.

6. Summarize research that suggests that psychologically the fundamental unit of speech is not an individual phoneme but groups of phonemes:

   a. How easily did Liberman et al. (1967) isolate the phoneme /d/ from the syllables *doo* and *dee?*

   b. Which speech sound did subjects in Savin and Bever's (1970) experiment report hearing first? Why?

   c. How did Ganong (1980) demonstrate that the sounds that follow a phoneme are important for speech perception?

9-2   *Describe research on recognition and comprehension of words in continuous speech.*

Read pages 295-299 and then answer the following questions:

1. Summarize research on the importance of context in word recognition:

    a. Study Figure 9.2 in your text and describe the accuracy of subjects attempting to identify individual words isolated from normal conversation or presented in the original context. (Pollack and Pickett, 1964)

    b. How accurately did subjects recognize meaningful strings of words? these same words in a jumbled order (random order)? (Miller et al., 1951)

    c. The effect of content on the perception of words is an example of _____-_____ processing.

    d. Cite research that demonstrated the importance of contexts on word recognition: the environment, nonverbal behavior such as tone of voice, and lip movements.

2. a. Speakers automatically understand and follow _____ _____ for combining words into phrases, clauses, and sentences.

    b. Briefly describe how subjects in research by Reber and Allen (1978) acquired the grammar rules for the letters M, V, R, T, and X.

    c. How accurately did subjects later identify "grammatical" strings of these letters and how clearly did they explain the reasons for their choices?

    d. What do these results suggest about the automatic acquisition and use of syntactical rules? (Be sure to use the term *implicit* in your answer.)

3. List the six *syntactical cues* that speakers and listeners rely on for accurate communication.

    1.   4.

    2.   5.

    3.   6.

4. What kinds of information do *word order* and *word class* provide?

5. a. Define these terms in your own words and give several examples of each type.

    1. *function words*

2. *content words*

3. *affixes*

b. Explain why subjects more easily remembered a longer word string with affixes than a shorter string without them.

c. Describe how word meaning and function words help make the syntax of a sentence clear.

d. Explain what changes occur in short-term memory when we hear meaningful words.

e. Refer to changes in short-term memory to explain why some subjects in an experiment by Blank and Foss (1978) recognized the phoneme /p/ more quickly than others.

f. Define *prosody* in your own words and give two examples of the use of prosody in speech.

g. Prosody is indicated in writing by _____ _____.

6. a. Explain what Chomsky means by the *deep structure* and the *surface structure* of a sentence.

b. Study Figure 9.3 in your text and explain what the sentence "Rosa always date shranks" reveals about some of the steps in the transformation of deep structure to surface structure.

9-3   *Describe evidence about the nature of speech comprehension and production from the study of aphasia.*

Read pages 299-301 and then answer the following questions:

1. a. Define *aphasia* in your own words.

b. Study Figure 9.4 in your text and describe the site of brain damage that results in *Wernicke's aphasia* and then describe some of the most important symptoms of this disorder.

c. What do most researchers believe is the primary deficit in Wernicke's aphasia?

d. Describe the site of brain damage that results in *pure word deafness* and then describe some of the most important symptoms of this disorder.

e. Compare the different symptoms of Wernicke's aphasia and pure word deafness to explain the importance of Wernicke's area in speech production.

2. a. Return to Figure 9.4 and describe the site of brain damage that results in *Broca's aphasia* and then describe some of the most important symptoms of this disorder.

b. What do most investigators believe is the primary deficit in Broca's aphasia?

c. Describe *agrammatism* that sometimes results from damage to Broca's area.

d. Describe two experiments in which agrammatic subjects were shown pictures to assess their speech comprehension and use of syntactical rules.

e. Explain why difficulty with syntactical rules is characteristic of Broca's, but not Wernicke's, aphasia and why both disorders disrupt speech comprehension.

3. Study Figure 9.5 in your text and trace the flow of information in the brain in answering an orally-phrased question:

a. Which brain region receives the auditory input?

b. What is the relationship between Wernicke's area and the stimulation of perceptions and memories?

c. What roles are played by Broca's area?

Read the interim summary on pages 310-311 of your text to reacquaint yourself with the material in this section.

9-4   *Describe the role of eye-tracking experiments in the study of reading and discuss research on the distinction between phonetic and whole-word recognition.*

Read pages 303-308 and then answer the following questions:

1. What is similar about the way people learn to pronounce words and the way the NETtalk model does?

2. a. The rapid jumps or _____ that your eyes are making as you read this sentence can be followed using a device called an _____ _____. You do not perceive the letters and words while your eyes are moving, but only during the brief pauses or _____ between jumps.

b. Study Figure 9.8 and describe two ways that the fixations of good readers differ from those of poor readers.

c. College students reading for meaning fixate on a higher percentage of content words than function words. Can we attribute this pattern to the fact that function words are usually shorter than content words?

d. Cite research on the effects of familiarity and word length on duration of fixation. (See Figure 9.9 in your text.)

3. a. What is the difference between word recognition through whole word reading and phonetic reading? (Be sure to use the term *phonological decoding* in your answer.)

b. What is the first step in word recognition?

c. What factor determines which reading method will prevail?

d. Why is whole-word recognition an essential skill for English speakers?

4. Explain why subjects were quicker to say that *tie* and *pie* rhymed than *tie* and *rye*.

5. Summarize research by Margolin et al. (1985) on the effects of brain damage on word recognition through whole-word and phonetic reading:

a. What effect did the woman's head injury have on her ability to read phonetically? by whole-words?

b. What event occurred that indicated she could still *recognize* words using the whole-word method?

c. What do the results suggest about the mechanisms of word recognition through whole-word and phonetic reading?

6. a. Define the concept of *lexical recognition* in your own words.

b. Explain why phonetic reading is a *prelexical* process and reading aloud is a *postlexical* process.

7. Summarize research on the factors that affect reading:

a. How do tasks that interfere with subvocal articulation affect reading comprehension?

b. How did the sight of previous words affect the recognition of later words? Use the concept of *priming* to explain why.

c. How does the amount of subvocal articulation affect reading rate?

8. Describe two ways that subvocal articulation may be useful.

9-5 *Describe research on the way that readers comprehend the meaning of words and sentences.*

Read pages 308-310 and then answer the following questions:

1. Explain how we learn the meaning of content words, abstract content words, and function words.

2. a. Define the concept of *semantic priming* in your own words.

   b. Now use this concept to explain how memories may be evoked by the perception of words and cite research to support your answer.

   c. Draw possible networks, based on the one in Figure 9.10 in your text, for the concepts linked to these sentences:

   The bed was moved.   The bed was made.

3. Describe research by Swinney (1979) using semantic priming.

   a. Explain the experimental procedure. (Be sure to use the term *lexical decision task* in your answer.)

   b. What factor influenced the speed with which subjects recognized whether the letters did or did not spell a word?

   c. Study Figure 9.11 in your text and then carefully explain how semantic priming leads to the selection of the correct response.

4. Describe research by Sharkey and Mitchell (1985) on the duration of priming effects.

Lesson I Self Test

1. Speakers can effectively communicate new and old information through

   a. the given-new contract.
   b. stress and choice of articles.
   c. choice of verb tense.
   d. observation and practice.

2. The smallest unit of speech that contributes to the meaning of a word is a

a. vowel.
b. consonant.
c. phoneme.
d. syllable.

3. Subjects, who learned the rules combining M, X, R, T, and X,

a. forgot almost all of them when retested later.
b. demonstrated the automatic nature of the use of syntax.
c. had clear insight into their own behavior.
d. later explained how they had solved the task.

4. The different meanings of "The boy hit the ball" and "The ball hit the boy" are examples of

a. a semantic rule.
b. a syntactic rule.
c. differences in word class.
d. the distinction between function words and content words.

5. Content words help us to determine the _____ of a sentence and function words help us determine its _____.

a. meaning; syntax.
b. structure; semantics
c. clarity; intent
d. meaning; implications

6. Most investigators believe the primary deficit of Wernicke's aphasia is

a. loss of speech comprehension.
b. an inability to speak fluently
c. pure word deafness.
d. loss of whole-word reading skills.

7. Mr. N. described a picture of a bird building a nest by saying "Bird...builds...twigs and eggs...builds...eggs hatch." Mr. N. probably has

a. Wernicke's aphasia.
b. pure word deafness.
c. conduction aphasia.
d. agrammatism.

8. By using eye movements to study the reading process, researchers have learned that

a. college students reading for meaning spend less time fixating on function words because they are shorter.
b. poor readers spend less time examining each word.
c. word shape is the most important correlate of reading speed.
d. we recognize words during the brief fixations between saccades.

9. Phonological word recognition is a(n) _____ process.

a. prelexical
b. postlexical

c. essential

d. semantic

10. When we read a word in a context that makes its meaning clear,

a. only the appropriate meaning is unconsciously evoked.

b. all meanings of the word are consciously evoked.

c. all meanings of the word are unconsciously evoked.

d. only the appropriate meaning is unconsciously evoked until the topic has changed.

Lesson II

Read the interim summary on pages 320-321 of your text to reacquaint yourself with the material in this section.

9-6 *Describe the stages of language acquisition, the acquisition of adult rules of grammar, and the acquisition of the meanings of words.*

Read pages 311-316 and then answer the following questions:

1. What is the response of

a. newborns in the delivery room to a sound in the room?

b. two- or three-week-old infants to the sound of a voice or a nonspeech sound?

c. infants a few months old to the sound of an angry or pleasant voice?

d. What is your response to the question, "How well developed is the infant auditory system?"

2. Summarize research on the auditory perception of infants:

a. Describe the procedure Trehub (1976) used to determine what kind of sound very young infants perceive. (See Figure 9.12 in your text.)

b. Study Figure 9.13 in your text and describe or draw the response curve of infants to familiar and novel sounds. Explain why the rate of response to familiar sounds declined.

c. What do these results suggest about the ability of infants to discriminate between speech sounds?

d. Describe how Eimas et al. (1971) demonstrated that even very young infants can make fine discriminations.

3. Trace the progression of the development of speech sounds in infants:

a. What sounds do infants make at birth? one month? six months?

    b. What did Mowrer (1960) suggest about babbling? Why do others reject this assertion? (Oller et al., 1976)

    c. How do we know that adult speech influences babbling?

    d. Describe the first sounds and speech features of one-year-olds across all languages and cultures.

    e. Which skill develops first--the ability to produce a sound or the ability to recognize it? Give an example.

4. a. Make a general statement about the grammar of children everywhere.

    b. Explain why young children cannot form complex sentences.

    c. Describe a difficulty in determining the

       1. rules of children's grammar.

       2. complexity of a particular grammar rule.

5. a. What kind of words do children tend to use first? Why?

    b. Continue to describe how children increase the length and complexity of their sentences.

    c. Describe *inflections* in your own words and explain why they are difficult to learn to use properly.

    d. According to Slobin (1966), what must happen before a child begins to use a particular syntactical rule?

    e. Refer to the way children learn a language to explain why some English verbs have two acceptable forms.

6. a. Define the terms *overextension* and *underextension* in your own words and give an example of each. Explain why children make these errors when they are learning the meaning of words.

    b. Explain why it is difficult to teach the meaning of abstract words to children and say what must precede an understanding of them.

9-7   *Explain the controversy over the reasons that children learn language, describe research on the way that adults talk to children, and discuss the role of reinforcement.*

Read pages 316-320 and then answer the following questions:

1. Summarize the arguments surrounding the assertion that language acquisition is an innate ability:

   a. How does Chomsky describe adult speech? How does his description support the assertion?

   b. According to McNeill (1970), how is the human brain specialized for language acquisition?

   c. Describe the concept of *language universals* in your own words and give some examples.

   d. Explain how their existence has been interpreted as support for the assertion.

   e. Now describe an alternate explanation for the existence of language universals.

   f. Explain how the ease with which children learn a language has been interpreted by people on both sides of the debate.

2. a. When adults speak to children, they use _____-_____ _____ which is marked by short, simple, repetitive sentences.

   b. What are some of the characteristics of child-directed speech that were identified by the deVilliers (1978)? Can you think of some examples from your own experience with young children?

   c. What is the frequent topic of child-directed speech? (Snow et al., 1976) How do caregivers teach children the meaning of words? (Snow, 1977)

   d. Where in a sentence do adults tend to place a new word when talking to children? Why? Give examples of the importance of this location.

   e. Describe two ways that adults teach children more complex forms of speech.

3. How do adults and child adjust their speech to allow for the age of the child to whom they are speaking? Cite research to support your answer.

4. a. When a child shows signs of _____ , adults _____ their speech.

    b. What is the best strategy to follow in order to improve language and other skills?

5. a. According to Skinner (1957) what shapes a child's use of language?

    b. What do many linguists say about Skinner's assertion?

    c. Explain the role of reinforcement in language acquisition:

        1. Describe two ways adults signal a child that a sentence was grammatically correct.

        2. Describe some of the obvious and less obvious ways that the effects of speech are reinforcing.

Read the interim summary on page 324 of your text to reacquaint yourself with the material in this section.

9-8   *Describe research on the abilities of other primates to communicate verbally.*

Read pages 321-324 and then answer the following questions:

1. a. Why did early attempts to teach chimpanzees to communicate with humans fail? How did the Gardners overcome this limitation?

    b. Briefly compare Washoe's language acquisition and that of children and evaluate her progress.

    c. Why do Terrace et al. (1979) challenge the assertion that the skills these animals have learned is verbal behavior? How have these criticisms been answered?

    d. Explain why research such as Project Washoe is useful.

2. a. Briefly describe some of the skills that Premack (1976) taught Sarah.

    b. What two important abilities did Sarah demonstrate by learning to work with plastic disks?

    c. See Figure 9.14 in your text and describe how Woodruff et al. (1978) used Sarah's "language" skills to demonstrate cognitive abilities.

3. Under what conditions are attempts to teach animals language most successful?

4. a. Explain how researchers made certain that Washoe, and not humans, taught Loulis to sign.

b. Describe Washoe's attempts to teach signs to Loulis.

Lesson II Self Test

1. Research using a pacifier with a pressure-sensitive switch demonstrated that infants

   a. suck vigorously when startled by a novel sound.
   b. suck more slowly as habituation occurs.
   c. can perceive an angry voice from a pleasant one.
   d. cannot make fine distinctions between speech sounds.

2. Babbling

   a. is the first sound an infant makes.
   b. contains all the sounds that occur in all world languages.
   c. is influenced by the adult speech the infant hears.
   d. is the first attempt at verbal communication.

3. In acquiring adult grammar rules, children

   a. learn the simplest rules first.
   b. depend on adults to explain them.
   c. learn irregular verbs first.
   d. confuse the use of function and content words.

4. Jenny pointed to the moon and said "Look at the big ball in the sky." Jenny's comment is an example of

   a. abstraction.
   b. overextension.
   c. underextension.
   d. symbolic reasoning.

5. Critics of the assertion that language acquisition is an innate ability point out that

   a. adults speak differently to children than to other adults.
   b. children learn a language more easily than adults.
   c. language universals are the product of innate brain mechanisms.
   d. the language centers in an adult's brain are similar to those in a child's brain.

6. When adults speak to children, they

   a. rarely make allowances for the age of the child.
   b. place the name of the object they are describing at the beginning of the sentence.
   c. use modifiers to convey subtle distinctions.
   d. pronounce words clearly and exaggerate intonation.

7. The most important factor controlling adult's speech to children is the child's

    a. attentiveness.
    b. age.
    c. relationship to adult.
    d. speech level.

8. Reinforcement appears to play a role in language acquisition because

    a. parents are quick to praise their child's success.
    b. like language acquisition, reinforcement cannot occur without the intervention of another.
    c. parents repeat "cute" things their children say.
    d. the effects of speech are themselves reinforcing.

9. The Gardeners chose to teach Washoe Ameslan because

    a. it had already been used successfully in early pioneering studies.
    b. they were already skilled in its use and would not waste research time.
    c. it is a manual language and chimps' hand and finger dexterity is almost as good as our own.
    d. they wanted to avoid proactive interference from any chimpanzee verbalizations.

10. Research such as Project Washoe are useful because of what they can teach us about

    a. Darwin's theory of evolution and language acquisition.
    b. our own language and cognitive abilities.
    c. the wisdom of teaching other primates to communicate with us.
    d. animals' perception of human beings.

Answers for Self Tests

Lesson I			Lesson II		
1.	b	Obj. 9-1	1.	b	Obj. 9-6
2.	c	Obj. 9-1	2.	c	Obj. 9-6
3.	b	Obj. 9-2	3.	c	Obj. 9-6
4.	b	Obj. 9-2	4.	b	Obj. 9-6
5.	a	Obj. 9-2	5.	d	Obj. 9-7
6.	a	Obj. 9-3	6.	d	Obj. 9-7
7.	d	Obj. 9-3	7.	a	Obj. 9-7
8.	d	Obj. 9-4	8.	d	Obj. 9-7
9.	a	Obj. 9-4	9.	c	Obj. 9-8
10.	c	Obj. 9-5	10.	b	Obj. 9-8

9.1 affix	9.10 given-new contract
9.2 agrammatism	9.11 inflection
9.3 Broca's aphasia	9.12 language universal
9.4 child-directed speech	9.13 lexical decision task
9.5 content word	9.14 lexical recognition
9.6 deep structure	9.15 overextention
9.7 eye tracker	9.16 phoneme
9.8 fixation	9.17 priming
9.9 function word	9.18 prosody

9.10	9.1
The cooperation between speaker and listener that assures that the listener understands which information is familiar and which is new; the speaker emphasizes new information through stress or choice of articles.	A sound added to the beginning (prefix) or end (suffix) of words to change their grammatical function.
9.11	9.2
Special affixes and other changes to words that alter their syntactical or semantic function; for example, adding -ed changes a verb to the past tense.	A language disturbance caused by damage to the left frontal lobe; loss of the ability to comprehend or produce grammatical elements of speech.
9.12	9.3
Characteristics found in all languages, include the presence of noun and verb phrases, grammatical categories of words such as nouns, and rules that establish the relation between subject, verb, and object.	A language disturbance caused by damage to Broca's area in the left frontal lobe; labored, ungrammatical, but meaningful speech almost devoid of function words.
9.13	9.4
A procedure in which subjects see strings of letters briefly and must decide whether they spell out words.	The speech of adults directed toward children who are learning to talk; short, simple, well-formed, repetitive sentences; clear pronunciation, exaggerated intonation, and few abstract or function words.
9.14	9.5
The process by which we recognize a written word.	A noun, verb, adjective, or adverb that expresses meaning.
9.15	9.6
The use of a word to indicate a larger class of items than is appropriate; occurs while a child is learning the meanings of words.	According to Chomsky, the essential meaning of a sentence, independent of its actual form.
9.16	9.7
The smallest units of speech that express meaning, such as /s/.	Device that follows the movements of a subject's pupils to determine where a subject directs the eyes while reading.
9.17	9.8
The facilitatory effect that the perception of one word has on the recognition of one that occurs later.	A pause in eye movements that occurs between saccades.
9.18	9.9
Changes in the stress, rhythm, and pitch of speech.	Short words such as prepositions and articles that express little meaning but help give grammatical structure to the sentence.

9.19

psycholinguistics

9.20

pure word deafness

9.21

stress

9.22

surface structure

9.23

syntactical rule

9.24

underextension

9.25

voice-onset time

9.26

Wernicke's aphasia

9.19

A branch of cognitive psychology concerned with the study of language-related behavior.

9.20

Ability to recognize nonspeech sounds, to speak, read, and write; inability to understand speech; caused by brain damage that disconnects primary auditory cortex bilaterally from the auditory association cortex.

9.21

Emphasis placed on a syllable or word in spoken speech; provides a cue that the information being presented is new.

9.22

According to Chomsky, the particular grammatical form a sentence takes.

9.23

A Rule that specifies the way that words are combined to form phrases and sentences in a particular language.

9.24

The use of a word in a more limited way than is appropriate; occurs while a child is learning the meanings of words.

9.25

The delay between the initial sound of a voiced consonant and the onset of vibration of the vocal cords; serves as a perceptual cue.

9.26

A language disorder; poor speech comprehension and fluent but meaningless speech; caused by damage to Wernicke's area, a region of auditory association cortex on the upper part of the left temporal lobe.

Chapter 10
Thinking and Intelligence

Lesson I

Read the interim summary on pages 343-344 of your text to reacquaint yourself with the material in this section.

10-1 *Describe the basic approaches to the study of intelligence and discuss attempts to understand verbal ability and deductive reasoning through an information-processing analysis.*

Read pages 328-334 and then answer the following questions:

1. Summarize these widely-used approaches to the study of intelligence.

   a. *differential approach*

   b. *developmental approach*

   c. *information-processing approach*

2. a. The correlation between school success and a test of _____ _____ ranges between _____ and _____.

   b. Explain why tests alone cannot adequately explain the nature of intelligence.

3. Summarize how Hunt (1985) is using the information-processing approach to study intelligence:

   a. List the four components of reading comprehension that he has identified.

      1.

      2.

      3.

      4.

   b. Lexical recognition, or the ability to recognize a group of _____ as a _____, consists of two major components: _____ _____ and _____ of _____.

1. What is the correlation between vocabulary size and total verbal ability as measured by a well-known intelligence test?

2. Explain the usual test of speed of lexical recognition and why the speed of the response reveals more than the accuracy of the response.

3. In general, what is the correlation between speed of response and school success?

c. Why is the comprehension of isolated sentences and expressions more difficult than recognition of individual words? (You may want to review the meaning of "syntax" and "semantics" in Chapter 9.)

1. Describe a *sentence verification task*. (See Figure 10.1 in your text.) How do literate people differ on the accuracy and speed of their responses? What other task do the quickest subjects also perform well?

2. Cite research that speed of sentence verification is different from speed of lexical recognition. (Palmer et al., 1985).

3. What did Carpenter and Just (1985) suggest as an explanation for the correlation between sentence verification and verbal comprehension?

4. What is an even better predictor of verbal ability than verbal comprehension? Describe how to test this skill and usual results.

5. What did this task reveal about speech comprehension?

4. Describe the abilities that are needed to comprehend connected discourse:

a. Why are we able to understand someone else even when the speaker does not describe every detail? (Schank and Abelson, 1977)

b. What are the important components in comprehending connected discourse and how do they differ among individuals?

5. Describe a test to determine the relationship between allocation of attention and reading comprehension. (Wagner and Sternberg, 1983) How well do good and poor readers perform?

6. How does skill in deductive reasoning correlate with school success? Why?

7. Describe the three parts of a *syllogism*.

8. Summarize research on why skill in deductive reasoning correlates highly with spatial ability:

   a. Describe the skills that comprise spatial ability.

   b. Define the concept of *mental models* and then describe one hypothesized kind of mental model. (See Figure 10.2 in your text.)

   c. See Figure 10.3 in your text and describe a mental model solution to questions about the height of four brothers.

9. a. People with damage to the _____ _____ lobes) have deficits in spatial ability. (Luria, 1973)

   b. Describe some anecdotal evidence of mental models. (Feynman, 1985)

10-2 *Describe research on the characteristics of concepts and the process of concept formation.*

Read pages 334-337 and then answer the following questions:

1. Define the term *concept* in your own words.

2. Why is the ability to *generalize* a useful one?

3. a. See Figure 10.4 in your text and describe the Collins and Quillian (1969) model of the organization of concepts.

   b. Why, according to them, did subjects quickly answer questions about a specific concept but take longer to answer questions about the general concept?

   c. Cite two studies that suggest people do not store concepts in an organized hierarchy. (Rips et al., 1973; Roth and Mervis, 1983)

d. Our concepts are based on our _____ and _____ with our environment. Rosch has suggested that our concepts are memories of particular examples, or _____.

e. Define the concept of organization at the *basic-level* in your own words and describe research on how we appear to use this system of organization.

4. a. Describe the procedure and the stimulus Hull (1920) used to demonstrate that people can learn to recognize visual similarities without explicit awareness. (See Figure 10.5 in your text.)

b. What response indicated subjects were not aware they had learned to recognize particular radicals?

c. Review research from Chapter 4 that demonstrated pigeons can also form concepts implicitly (that is, learn to recognize photographs containing a human).

5. a. See Figure 10.6 in your text and briefly describe an experimental procedure for studying hypothesis-testing and explain why it is no longer widely used.

b. Explain the emphasis of an influential approach to the study of concept formation proposed by Rosch.

c. Describe Mervis' (1987) observations of children learning the meaning of words.

d. See Figure 10.7 in your text and describe additional research on the association between exemplars and concepts. (Mervis and Long (1987)

10-3 *Explain how heuristics affect decision making.*

Read pages 337-340 and then answer the following questions:

1. a. Define *heuristics* in your own words.

b. When these shortcuts fail, what do we call the failures?

c. What are the two most important categories of heuristics?

1.   2.

2. Carefully explain the *representativeness heuristic* and the associated failure called the *base-rate fallacy*.

3. a. Reread the example of the athletic psychology professor and then make up an example of your own that might fool other people.

b. Use the concepts of the representativeness heuristic and base-rate fallacy to explain why people would tend to be fooled.

4. Explain the *availability heuristic*.

5. Summarize research on how this heuristic can negatively effect decision making:

a. Explain how Tversky and Kahneman (1982) demonstrated the influence of this heuristic on the answer to a question about the position of the letter *k* in English words.

b. Review the priming phenomenon and then describe how priming affected the availability of adjectives subjects used to describe a stranger. (Higgins et al., 1977)

c. Explain why personal encounters are given disproportionate weight in decision making and cite research to support your answer. (Borgida and Nisbett, 1977)

d. Explain why flight instructors were reluctant to praise their students (Kahneman and Tversky, 1973). (Be sure to use the term *regression fallacy* in your answer.)

10-4 *Discuss Sternberg's information-processing theory of intelligence and Gardner's neuropsychological theory of intelligence.*

Read pages 340-343 and then answer the following questions:

1. List the three elements of Sternberg's triarchic theory.

1.

2.

3.

2. Define *componential intelligence* and its three components in your own words.

1. *metacomponents*

2. *performance components*

3. *knowledge acquisition components*

3. a. Define *experiential intelligence* in your own words.

   b. Describe two advantages of good experiential intelligence

4. a. Define *contextual intelligence* and its three components in your own words.

   1. *adaptation*

   2. *selection*

   3. *shaping*

   b. Evaluate the importance of selection by describing the results of a study of child prodigies as adults.

5. a. Describe the behavior of the physician after he suffered extensive damage to his frontal lobes.

   b. What does his behavior suggest about the importance of considering the practical uses of intelligence? the use of modern intelligence tests as a measure of overall intelligence?

6. a. Briefly describe the seven categories of intelligence proposed by Gardener and the basis for his selection.

   b. Offer an explanation why not all of the seven categories have traditionally been recognized as aspects of intelligence.

   c. Explain two advantages of Gardner's approach.

Read the interim summary on page 348 of your text to reacquaint yourself with the material in this section.

<hr>

10-5 *Describe Spearman's two-factory theory of intelligence and the results of intelligence research using factor analysis.*

<hr>

Read pages 344-347 and then answer the following questions:

1. a. State the basic assumption of the differential approach to the study of the nature of intelligence.

    b. State two different positions concerning the global nature of intelligence.

2. a. Spearman proposed that performance on a test of intellectual ability is determined by _____ factors: the _____ or _____ factor and the _____ or _____ factor.

    b. What, according to Spearman, are the three "qualitative principles of cognition" that comprise the *g* factor?

    c. Explain how analogy questions incorporate all three principles of cognition.

    d. Intercorrelations among various tests of mental ability usually range from .30 to .70. Use this information and support Spearman's two-factor theory.

    e. According to Spearman, what determines a person's score on a particular test?

3. If a researcher performs a factor analysis what kind of information will be obtained?

4. a. What correlations did Birren and Morrison (1961) subject to factor analysis and how did they obtain their data?

    b. Study Table 10.2 in your text. What are the numbers in the three columns called? Define this term in your own words.

    c. Explain how an analysis of these factor loadings is useful in determining which abilities are represented by factors A, B, and C.

5. Does a factor analysis guarantee that the results will explain all aspects of human intelligence? Explain your answer.

6. a. What data did Thurstone (1938) submit to factor analysis and how did he obtain the original data?

    b. What factors did he obtain from the analysis?

    c. Why was revealed by a second factor analysis of Thurstone's data by Horn and Cattell (1966)?

    d. What names did they give to these factors? Briefly describe them.

    e. Study Figure 10.8 in your text and give three reasons why these load heavily on the fluid intelligence factor.

    f. Study Table 10.3 in your text and describe the kind of tests that load heavily on crystallized intelligence.

Lesson I Self Test

1. Scientists who study intelligence by trying to assess the kinds of cognitive abilities people use to think and solve problems are proponents of the

    a. differential approach.
    b. developmental approach.
    c. informational-processing approach.
    d. intuitive approach.

2. Sentence verification tasks measure subjects' ability to recognize

    a. whether individual words form a sentence.
    b. if the sentence is grammatical.
    c. which sentence describes the display.
    d. whether the sentence fits the context.

3. Concepts are

    a. expressed in complete sentences.
    b. logically organized into formal systems.
    c. based on our own perceptions and interactions.
    d. cultural inventions.

4. Subjects learned to associate Chinese characters with nonsense syllable names through

    a. simplification--pairing the radical with the name.
    b. an automatic, implicit process.
    c. a conscious process.
    d. organization based on base-level concepts.

5. We observe that some characteristics tend to go together. When we see some of these characteristics and then conclude that others are also present, we are using the

    a. representativeness heuristic.
    b. availability heuristic.
    c. regression fallacy.
    d. base-rate fallacy.

6. Flight instructors were reluctant to praise students for good performances because they observed that students usually did worse after they had been praised. Their experience illustrates

    a. the base-rate fallacy.
    b. the regression fallacy.
    c. that criticism is more effective than praise.
    d. that praise makes people feel uncomfortable.

7. _____ is to componential intelligence as _____ is to contextual intelligence.

    a. metacomponent; performance component
    b. adaptation; performance component
    c. selection; shaping
    d. metacomponent; adaptation

8. An advantage of Gardner's neuropsychological theory of intelligence is that

    a. none of his types of intelligence have been previously identified.
    b. it is based on evidence rather than heuristics.
    c. it provides for non-Western views of intelligence.
    d. seven categories allow for greater distinction than three.

9. A factor analysis can identify

    a. the best types of question to use to measure intelligence.
    b. the number of tests necessary to accurately measure intelligence.
    c. which questions relate to particular abilities.
    d. the best type of test for a particular age group.

10. Fluid intelligence

    a. represents a person's overall capacity for intellectual performance.
    b. is culturally determined.
    c. represents what a person has actually learned to do.
    d. depends on crystallized intelligence.

Lesson II

Read the interim summary on page 355 of your text to reacquaint yourself with the material in this section.

10-6 *Describe Galton's contributions to intelligence testing, the Binet-Simon Scale, the Stanford-Binet Scale, and Wechsler's tests and discuss the reliability and validity of intelligence tests.*

Read pages 348-353 and then answer the following questions:

1. a. Describe how Charles Darwin influenced the work of his cousin Sir Francis Galton.

   b. Describe Galton's contributions in the following areas:

      1. modern statistical tests

      2. distribution pattern of human traits (See Figure 10.9 in your text.)

      3. assessing the relationship between variables

      4. assessing the heritability of human traits

2. a. What did Binet and Henri (1896) say about Galton's simple sensory tests?

   b. What was the original purpose of the Binet-Simon Scale?

   c. Define *norm* in your own words and explain its importance to intelligence testing.

   d. Why are standardized testing procedures important?

   e. Why did Binet revise the original test?

   f. Describe the concept of *mental age* in your own words.

3. a. Briefly explain the kinds, levels, and grouping of tests on the Stanford-Binet Scale.

   b. Explain the rationale of the *intelligence quotient (IQ)*.

   c. State the formula for computing IQ. What is name of the result?

   d. Explain how the *deviation IQ* differs from the *ratio IQ*. What is the standard deviation of the IQ, and how is the deviation IQ expressed?

   e. Calculate the ratio or deviation IQs for these students who recently took the Binet Scale. (See Figure 10.10 in your text.)

      1. I.L., 11 years old, mental age of 13.

2. S.M., 12 years old, mental age of 9.

3. J.L-T., 12 years old, score of 0.5 standard deviations above the mean.

4. a. See Table 10.4 in your text and describe the subtests and sample items from the WAIS-R. How are scores obtained on this test expressed?

b. What is an important advantage of the WAIS-R?

c. Describe two groups of people whose intelligence can be measured accurately using this test.

5. a. What steps do test givers take to maintain the reliability of modern intelligence tests?

b. Define *criterion* in your own words and explain how it is related to the concept of validity.

c. See Table 10.5 in your text and summarize the relationship between SAT verbal subtest scores and freshman grades.

10-7 *Discuss the use and abuse of intelligence tests.*

Read pages 353-355 and then answer the following questions:

1. a. Explain how cultural bias affects test construction and cultural differences affect test performance.

b. Explain how low scores on an intelligence test can affect both future educational opportunities and self-image.

c. Finally, explain how the use of intelligence tests may affect curriculum and teaching methods.

2. Identify several groups of children that may benefit from the general use of intelligence tests.

3. a. Define *mental retardation* in your own words.

b. Name and briefly describe the degrees of mental retardation.

Read the interim summary on pages 361-362 of your text to reacquaint yourself with the material in this section.

10-8   *Discuss the meaning of heritability and describe the sources of genetic and environmental effects during development.*

Read pages 355-358 and then answer the following questions:

1. Define the concept of *heritability* in your own words and explain how this concept is often misinterpreted.

2. Keep your definition in mind and explain this statement: Even if hereditary factors do influence intelligence, the heritability of intellectual abilities is considerably less than 1.0.

3. Carefully explain how ancestral origin, the amount of environmental variability in the population, and the degree of interaction between genetic inheritance and the environment affect any assessment of the heritability of intellectual abilities.

4. Summarize genetic and/or environmental factors that can adversely affect intellectual development at or during

   a. conception

   b. prenatal development

   c. birth

   d. infancy

   e. later life

5. a. Mental deterioration is referred to as _____. Two common causes late in life are
      _____ _____ and _____.

   b. What is one of the first observable symptoms of Alzheimer's disease?

   c. Which circuits of neurons are affected first? What happens next? Study Figure 10.11 in your text and describe how the progressive degeneration affects the physical appearance of the brain.

   d. What are some of the common causes of depression in the elderly?

10-9 *Discuss the results and implications of heritability studies of general intelligence and specific abilities.*

Read pages 358-361 and then answer the following questions:

1. a. Explain why comparisons of identical twins reared together is an important source of information on the degree to which heredity influences intelligence.

   b. Studies of identical twins reared apart is an important source of information on the effects of _____ on heredity.

   c. What can researchers estimate by comparing the differences in the correlations of test scores of identical twins and fraternal twins?

2. a. Study the top of Table 10.6 in your text. What is the correlation in intelligence between parent and child? identical twins? fraternal twins? and adoptive parent and child?

   b. In general, how is the correlation in intelligence related to the percentage of genetic similarity?

   c. Study the bottom of Table 10.6. What is the range of the estimates of the effect of heredity? environment?

   d. In general, to what extent is intelligence influenced by heredity? environment?

3. a. What is an important consideration when interpreting the meaning of estimates of the importance of genetic and environmental factors such as those presented in Table 10.6?

   b. According to Plomin (1988), why are some estimates of the contribution of environmental factors to the intelligence of siblings raised together very low?

   c. Estimates of the contribution of environment to the intelligence of siblings decline when the measurements are made during adulthood. What may account for the decline? Cite research to support your answer.

4. a. Describe how Scarr and Weinberg (1978) compared specific intellectual abilities of parents with their biological and adoptive children and that of children with their biological and adoptive siblings.

   b. Study Table 10.7 in your text and summarize the effect of kinship on specific abilities.

c. Explain why vocabulary scores were an exception to the general pattern.

Lesson II Self Test

1. Which one of the following is a contribution Galton made to the field of intelligence?

    a. the adoption of the use of the normal curve
    b. the concept of correlation
    c. a single criterion to measure overall intelligence
    d. coining the word "intelligence"

2. _____ is to the Binet-Simon Scale as _____ is to the Stanford-Binet Scale.

    a. ratio IQ; deviation IQ
    b. standard deviation; norms
    c. mental age; intelligence quotient
    d. sensory testing; verbal testing

3. Because the WAIS-R tests verbal and performance abilities separately it is useful in estimating the intelligence of people who

    a. have had few educational and cultural opportunities.
    b. are physically handicapped.
    c. have had little experience taking intelligence tests.
    d. experience test anxiety.

4. Modern intelligence tests

    a. indicate that school curricula must be changed so that children will obtain higher scores in the future.
    b. are no longer culturally biased.
    c. can identify children with learning disabilities.
    d. should not be given to children from disadvantaged backgrounds.

5. Heritability is a statistical measure that expresses the extent to which

    a. observed variability in a trait results from genetic variability.
    b. inherited genes are responsible for producing a particular trait.
    c. gender and age are responsible for a particular trait.
    d. observed variability in a trait results from environmental factors.

6. The heritability of a trait is affected by

    a. the number of genes involved in the trait.
    b. the number of ancestors a person has.
    c. the genetic variability in the population
    d. the degree to which a person perceives the influence of environmental factors.

7. In which situation would environmental factors account for much of the variability in intelligence?

    a. an isolated tribal society

150

b. a medieval society in which only the rich or religious received any formal education

c. an orphanage where all children receive the same care

d. a North American suburb

8. Dr. J. is treating a boy who has suffered brain damage as a result of eating lead paint. His condition is an example of

a. a harmful prenatal environmental influence on intelligence.

b. a harmful postnatal environmental influence on intelligence.

c. familial, hereditary mental retardation.

d. familial, nonhereditary mental retardation.

9. Twins who share the same sets of chromosomes, prenatal environment, and postnatal environment are

a. identical twins raised together.

b. identical twins raised apart.

c. fraternal twins raised together.

d. fraternal twins raised apart.

10. Estimates of the contribution of environmental variability to the intelligence of children in the same family that are based on measurements made during adulthood rather than during childhood are

a. lower because fluid intelligence has stabilized.

b. higher because the need to achieve is stronger in adults.

c. lower because during adulthood environments are less similar.

d. higher because crystallized intelligence is growing more rapidly.

Answers for Self Tests

Lesson I			Lesson II		
1.	c	Obj. 10-1	1.	b	Obj. 10-6
2.	c	Obj. 10-1	2.	c	Obj. 10-6
3.	c	Obj. 10-2	3.	a	Obj. 10-6
4.	b	Obj. 10-2	4.	c	Obj. 10-7
5.	a	Obj. 10-3	5.	a	Obj. 10-8
6.	b	Obj. 10-3	6.	a	Obj. 10-8
7.	d	Obj. 10-4	7.	b	Obj. 10-8
8.	c	Obj. 10-4	8.	b	Obj. 10-9
9.	c	Obj. 10-5	9.	a	Obj. 10-9
10.	a	Obj. 10-5	10.	c	Obj. 10-9

10.1 Alzheimer's disease	10.10 developmental approach
10.2 availability heuristic	10.11 deviation IQ
10.3 base-rate fallacy	10.12 differential approach
10.4 Binet-Simon Scale	10.13 exemplar
10.5 componential intelligence	10.14 experiential intelligence
10.6 concept formation	10.15 factor loading
10.7 concept	10.16 g factor/s factor
10.8 contextual intelligence	10.17 heritability
10.9 criterion	10.18 heuristics

10.10 An approach to the study of the nature of intelligence; study of how infants learn to perceive, manipulate, and think about the world.	**10.1** A form of dementia in the elderly characterized by profound and widespread brain degeneration, starting with neurons that secrete acetylcholine.
10.11 An IQ score invented by Wechsler; the person's score is compared to norms for people of the same chronological age and expressed in terms of the number of standard deviations from the mean.	**10.2** A category of heuristics; decisions regarding the importance or frequency of an event are influenced by the related examples that come to mind most quickly and easily.
10.12 An approach to the study of the nature of intelligence; creation and analysis of tests to identify and measure individual differences in the problem-solving abilities.	**10.3** An error in judgment resulting from misuse of the representativeness heuristic; paying too much attention to some distinctive characteristics of a person or situation while ignoring evidence about probabilities.
10.13 According to Rosch, a typical example derived from experience that is used to judge the membership of a particular object to a particular concept.	**10.4** An early intelligence test assembled by Binet and Henri to identify children with special needs, revised in 1905 to test normal children as well; included norms and ability to determine mental age.
10.14 One of the three components of Sternberg's triarchic theory of intelligence; the ability to classify situations quickly and to solve certain categories of problems "automatically," based on experience.	**10.5** One of the three components of Sternberg's triarchic theory of intelligence; the mental mechanisms people use to plan and execute tasks.
10.15 In intelligence testing, the degree to which a particular subtest is related to a group of other subtests, the group constituting a component of intellectual ability.	**10.6** A mental process by which we learn to organize our perceptions and experiences with the things around us into useful categories.
10.16 Terms proposed by Spearman to account for performance on an intelligence test; g represents general reasoning ability, s represents a specific ability	**10.7** A kind of mental image or category for objects, actions, or states of being that share important characteristics.
10.17 A statistical measure that expresses the extent to which the observed variability in a trait in a given population is a result of genetic variability.	**10.8** One of the three components of Sternberg's triarchic theory of intelligence; acquired through the behaviors (adaptation, selection, and shaping) that were selected for during evolutionary process.
10.18 Principles or rules that guide and facilitate decision making; usually, but not always, reliable.	**10.9** An independent measure of the variable being assessed; in intelligence testing no single criterion exists because there is no single definition of intelligence.

10.19

information-processing approach

10.20

mental age

10.21

mental model

10.22

mental retardation

10.23

norm

10.24

ratio IQ

10.25

regression fallacy

10.26

representativeness heuristic

10.27

Stanford-Binet Scale

10.28

syllogism

10.29

Wechsler Adult Intelligence Scale (WAIS)
Wechsler Intelligence Scale for Children (WISC)

10.28

A form of deductive reasoning consisting of a major and minor premise that are assumed to be true and a conclusion, whose truth is to be evaluated.

10.29

WAIS, WAIS-R: original, revised versions of Wechsler's intelligence tests for adults; 11 subtests in two categories--verbal and performance. WISC, WISC-R: intelligence test for children resembling the WAIS.

10.19

An approach to the study of the nature of intelligence based on research methods that have been developed by cognitive psychologists to study the types of skills people use to think and solve various types of problems.

10.20

The level of intellectual performance observed from the average child at a particular age.

10.21

Special mental images representing information that people devise to help them solve problems; a possible explanation why spatial ability correlates highly with skill at syllogistic reasoning.

10.22

A deficiency in intellectual abilities, often accompanied by deficits in physical and social skills; most often caused by brain damage or abnormal brain development.

10.23

In intelligence testing, data from comparison groups that permits an individual's score on an intelligence test to be compared with scores obtained by peers; introduced with the 1905 Binet-Simon Scale.

10.24

Mental age divided by chronological age, multiplied by 100.

10.25

An error in judgment; failure to consider the concept of regression toward the mean--the tendency for an extreme event to be followed by an event closer to the mean.

10.26

A category of heuristics; the tendency to conclude from past experiences that when some characteristics of a concept are present others will also be.

10.27

An intelligence test translated by Terman, first published in 1916, containing a formula for computing the intelligence quotient (IQ) as a ratio IQ; the 1960 version replaced it with the deviation IQ.

Chapter 11
Consciousness

Lesson I

Read the interim summary on page 369 of your text to reacquaint yourself with the material in this section.

11-1 *Define consciousness and explain how it is a social behavior.*

Read pages 367-369 and then answer the following questions:

1. a. What is the most common and most important meaning of the word *consciousness?*

   b. We directly experience our own consciousness, but what is the only way to verify someone else's consciousness?

2. a. Explain the two conditions that must be met in order to obtain someone's assistance through verbal communication. Be sure to use the terms *verbal access* and *verbal control* in your answer.

   b. Give several examples of events in our bodies to which we do and do not have verbal access. What is the selective advantage of having verbal access to some of these events?

   c. Give several examples of behaviors under verbal control.

   d. Give an example of communication that is not necessarily conscious. (Noirot, 1972)

3. Decide whether each of the following situations illustrates verbal access or verbal control.

   _____ telling ourselves that there is something in our eye

   _____ saying we are sleepy

   _____ hearing "Please pass the bread," and doing so

   _____ telling someone about a dream

_____ closing the window after someone complains about the cold.

4. a. State three social benefits of the ability to communicate.

   b. Cite research that supports the hypothesis that we use the same brain mechanisms whether we are communicating with others or with ourselves.

   c. What kind of observation suggests that other animals possess varying degrees of consciousness?

   d. Although verbal activity is usually conscious, give an example of verbal activity that is not.

Read the interim summary on page 375 of your text to reacquaint yourself with the material in this section.

11-2 *Describe attention, discuss its importance, and describe research on the factors that affect auditory and visual attention.*

Read pages 369-375 and then answer the following questions:

1. a. Define *attention* in your own words.

   b. Describe three ways that attention may be controlled and give an example of each. What is the purpose of attentional mechanisms?

   c. Explain how attention affects both short-term and explicit long-term memory. (You may wish to review the concepts of explicit and implicit memory in Chapter 8.)

2. a. Study Figure 11.1 in your text and describe how information in a *dichotic listening* test is presented to subjects, what kind of message is presented to each ear, and how subjects are asked to respond to one of the messages.

   b. What effect did *shadowing* one of the messages have on subjects' tone of voice? Why?

   c. What effect did *shadowing* have on subjects' ability to recall information from the unattended ear?

   d. Cite two experiments that refute the suggestion that information from the unattended ear is lost because that channel is simply shut down.

e. Because subjects responded to particular kinds of information presented to the unattended ear, what is happening to the information?

3. Summarize research on the behavioral effects of information from the unattended ear:

a. How did subjects respond when they heard words that had previously been presented along with an electric shock?

b. The results suggest that the unattended information produced an _____ memory.

c. Describe the task McKay (1973) used to demonstrate the effects of information to the unattended ear.

d. Describe and explain the results.

4. a. Study Figure 11.2 in your text and describe how Treisman (1960) tested subjects' skill at shadowing a message.

b. Describe and explain the results.

c. Explain the practical value of selective attention by referring to the *cocktail-party phenomenon*. (See Figure 11.3 in your text.)

5. a. Explain or draw what subjects saw on the video-display screen during the experiment by Posner et al., 1980.

b. Study Figure 11.4 in your text and explain how advance warning affected response time.

c. Now explain what the differences in response times indicated about selective attention. Be sure to explain why subjects were asked to gaze at the fixation point.

6. a. Study Figure 11.5 in your text and describe how Neisser and Becklen (1975) studied the way subjects

allocate attention to events occurring in close proximity.

b. How successfully did subjects follow both actions?

c. When subjects were asked if they recognized a series of shapes that had originally been presented as overlapping colored pairs, how did they respond (Rock and Gutman, 1981)? (See Figure 11.6 in your text.)

d. Describe research that demonstrated what happens to unattended visual information. (Neisser, 1969)

7. a. Briefly review the cause and effects of *sensory neglect*.

b. Explain the cause and symptom of *simultanagnosia* characteristic of *Balint's syndrome*.

c. Study Figure 11.7 in your text and explain what people with Balint's syndrome report seeing. Explain what their response indicates about brain mechanisms of selective attention.

Read the interim summary on pages 379-380 of your text to reacquaint yourself with the material in this section.

11-3 *Explain the significance of the symptoms of isolation aphasia, visual agnosia, and the split-brain syndrome to our understanding of consciousness.*

Read pages 375-379 and then answer the following questions:

1. a. As a result of carbon monoxide poisoning, a woman suffered severe brain damage. Describe the damage.

b. Explain why this condition is called *isolation* aphasia.

c. How did the brain damage affect her voluntary movements, speech, learning, and consciousness?

d. What does this case contribute to our understanding of consciousness?

2. a. How did brain damage from blood vessel inflammation affect the man's ability to recognize objects or pictures of them? What did the man often do when he was shown a picture of a particular object?

b. Study Figure 11.9 in your text and carefully explain how visual information was processed by the man's brain.

c. What does this case contribute to our understanding of consciousness?

3. a. Why is a *split-brain operation* performed and what brain connection is severed? (Study Figure 11.10 in your text.)

b. How does surgery affect the functioning of the two hemispheres of the brain and the behavior of the patient?

c. Although surgery profoundly alters the brain, why are behavioral changes often difficult to detect?

d. Study Figure 11.11 in your text and explain why olfaction is an exception to the crossed representation of sensory information in the brain. Describe research on the behavior of split-brain patients when odors are presented to the left and right nostril.

e. What does this case contribute to our understanding of consciousness?

Read the interim summary on pages 386-387 of your text to reacquaint yourself with the material in this section.

11-4 *Describe the history of hypnosis, its induction, and its characteristics.*

Read pages 380-382 and then answer the following questions:

1. a. Hypnosis, previously called _____ , is an unusual form of _____ _____ .

b. Hypnosis is a fascinating phenomenon, but why is it important to the study of psychology?

c. Briefly explain the discovery and first uses of hypnosis. (See Figure 11.12 in your text.)

2. The only necessary condition for successful hypnosis is the subject's _____ that he or she will be hypnotized.

3. Briefly explain the following characteristics of hypnosis:

a. positive hallucinations

    b. negative hallucinations

    c. posthypnotic suggestibility

    d. posthypnotic amnesia

4. a. What does research indicate is the cause of changes in perception that hypnotized people experience?

    b. Study Figure 11.12 in your text and describe how Pattie (1937) demonstrated a difference between hypnosis-induced anesthesia and drug-induced anesthesia.

    c. Study Figure 11.13 in your text and describe how Miller et al. (1973) demonstrated differences in hypnosis-induced blindness and physical blindness. Be sure to use the term *Ponzo illusion* in your answer.

    d. What do the contradictory actions and explanations of subjects in each of these studies indicate about consciousness?

5. a. State Barber's conclusions (1969) concerning the association between hypnosis and antisocial acts.

    b. Describe how Milgram (1963, 1974) demonstrated the extent to which unhypnotized subjects would commit antisocial acts.

    c. Explain why research on hypnosis and antisocial behavior must include appropriate control groups.

11-5 *Describe and evaluate current theories of hypnosis, discuss people's susceptibility to hypnosis, and describe its uses and limitations.*

Read pages 382-386 and then answer the following questions:

1. a. Why does Hilgard refer to his explanation of hypnosis as a *neodissociation* theory?

    b. List and describe the two kinds of dissociations Hilgard describes.

       1.

2.

c. How does Hilgard define the *hidden observer*?

d. According to Hilgard, why did the hidden observer report more pain?

2. a. Explain why Barber (1979) argues that hypnosis is a social behavior, not a special state of consciousness.

b. Summarize research by Orne (1959) on one aspect of Barber's argument--subject expectations:

1. What false information did Orne present in lecture and how did it later affect hypnotized subject who had heard that lecture?

2. Use the results from this research to explain why subjects who have been hypnotized willingly perform silly behaviors.

3. a. Explain why Barber (1975) argues that hypnosis is a form of role playing.

b. Explain how Barber's theory contributes to a functional explanation of hypnosis.

4. Are there some behaviors that can be seen only when a person is hypnotized? Explain the significance of your answer.

5. a. Describe the three sets of instructions that were given to hypnotized subjects who had one of their arms in a bucket of ice water. (Spanos et al., 1983)

b. Study Figure 11.14 in your text and describe how each set of instructions affected the report of pain.

c. Explain why these results challenge Hilgard's suggestion that the hidden observer is always aware of reality.

6. a. What are some personal characteristics that appear to affect susceptibility to hypnosis?

   b. Describe evidence that suggests that the right hemisphere may play a special role in hypnosis.

7. a. State two reasons why the use of hypnosis to induce analgesia is not more widespread.

   1.

   2.

   b. Describe two other beneficial uses of hypnosis.

   c. Explain how hypnosis is used in criminal investigations and why this particular use of hypnosis has been severely criticized. Be sure to use the term *television technique* in your answer.

   d. Describe how Laurence and Perry (1983) demonstrated hypnosis can induce false memories that people sincerely believe.

8. What concept do each of the following situations illustrate?

_____ You are trying to talk on the phone at the same time your young niece is trying to persuade you to take her out to play.

_____ "You are beginning to get sleepy."

_____ "I have a headache."

_____ Mrs. L., who was recovering from a recent brain injury, agreed to take part in an experiment. When she was asked to identify some objects that had been placed on a table in front of her without touching them, she could not do so.

_____ Following hypnosis, Marcy bent over and untied her shoe when the hypnotist coughed.

_____ During hypnosis, the hypnotist asked Mark if he would look at the clock on the wall and tell him the time. Mark replied that there was no clock on the wall.

_____ "Will you please return my library book too?"

_____ The subject's understanding that he or she is going to be hypnotized.

choices: essential feature of hypnosis, visual agnosia, cocktail party phenomenon, verbal access, nonessential feature of hypnosis, negative hallucination, verbal control, posthypnotic suggestibility

Lesson I Self Test

1. Which is the most accurate statement about consciousness?

   a. All instances of communication involve consciousness.
   b. We have verbal access to all the physiological processes of our bodies.
   c. Verbal behavior defines consciousness.
   d. Consciousness is a uniquely human trait.

2. It is useless to tell a one-year-old child to put the toys away because

   a. we do not have verbal access to the child.
   b. the child does not have verbal access to this behavior.
   c. we do not have verbal control of this behavior.
   d. the child has no sense of consciousness.

3. In a dichotic listening test, information presented to the unattended ear

   a. cannot affect our behavior.
   b. is soon lost.
   c. does not affect verbal processing.
   d. is transferred unconsciously to long-term memory.

4. Subjects were asked to gaze at a fixation point while waiting for directional arrows to appear because researchers wanted to

   a. be sure that movement of attention was independent of eye movement.
   b. track eye movements with an eye tracker.
   c. reduce the visual field.
   d. reduce the possibility of distraction.

5. The case of the woman with isolation aphasia suggests that consciousness

   a. is simply an activity of the brain's speech mechanism.
   b. is synonymous with the ability to talk about perceptions and memories.
   c. and self-awareness are different phenomena.
   d. is necessary for learning.

6. Research with people who have had a split-brain operation suggest that

   a. the corpus callosum is the center of consciousness.
   b. consciousness of events in the left hemisphere depends on communication with the right hemisphere.
   c. the speech dominant left hemisphere is more important.
   d. they no longer have verbal access to events controlled by the right hemisphere.

7. In order for a person to be hypnotized he or she must

   a. be completely relaxed.
   b. become drowsy as the hypnotist speaks.
   c. fixate the eyes on a slowly moving object.
   d. understand that he or she is to be hypnotized.

8. Most studies of the effects of hypnosis on antisocial behavior have failed to

   a. operationally define an antisocial act.
   b. measure how deeply the subject is hypnotized.
   c. use a representative group of subjects.
   d. use control groups to determine the limits of the antisocial behavior of unhypnotized subjects.

9. Hilgard believes the hidden observer is the result of _____, but Barber believes the hidden observer is a result of _____.

   a. dissociation; role-playing
   b. role-playing; dissociation
   c. the ability to empathize; hypnotic suggestion
   d. hypnotic suggestion; the ability to empathize

10. Which is the most accurate statement about hypnosis?

   a. Hypnosis may be related to the functions of the left hemisphere.
   b. The ability to be hypnotized is strongly related to personality type.
   c. All hypnotic phenomena have been demonstrated with nonhypnotized subjects.
   d. Hypnosis cannot induce people to recall events that never happened.

Lesson II

Read the interim summary on pages 399-400 of your text to reacquaint yourself with the material in this section.

11-6 *Name and describe the stages of sleep, indicate how they are measured, and describe dreams and their possible symbolism.*

Read pages 387-392 and then answer the following questions:

1. Sleep is a state of _____ _____.

2. a. Describe the purpose of the following items:

   1. *polygraph*

   2. *electroencephalogram (EEG)*

   3. *electromyogram (EMG)*

   4. *electrocardiogram (EKG)*

   5. *electro-oculogram (EOG)*

   b. Describe the sleep laboratory, how a subject is prepared to spend the night there, and how data are recorded. (See Figure 11.15 in your text.)

    c. Describe the stages of alert wakefulness and drowsy wakefulness. Study Figure 11.16 in your text and draw this activity as it appears on the EEG record. Label your drawing with the correct terms.

    d. Study Figure 11.17 in your text and describe how some of the physiological functions monitored in the sleep laboratory change during the four stages of sleep:

      1. EEG during Stages 1, 2, 3, and 4

      2. the name of the EEG activity of Stage 4

      3. EMG and EOG during Stages 1, 2, and 3

      4. the name of the sleep of Stages 3 and 4

      5. the EEG and EOG record change during REM sleep. Although the EMG is quiet, what movements does the subject sometimes make?

      6. the length of episodes of REM sleep and the interval between them. (Study Figure 11.18 in your text.)

      7. changes in the ability to move and genital changes during REM sleep.

3. a. Compare the dream reports of subjects awakened during REM sleep and slow-wave sleep.

    b. Why do some people claim they have not dreamed for years?

4. Summarize research on the content and symbolism of dreams:

    a. Compare the content of dreams during REM sleep (Hall, 1966) and slow-wave sleep. Why do we tend to remember the unusual ones?

    b. Describe Freud's concepts of the *latent content* and *manifest content* of dreams.

    c. According to Hall (1966), why is the meaning of the symbols in a dream usually clear to the dreamer?

    d. When experimenters attempted to insert material into subjects' dreams, how did subjects respond?

    e. How do psychotherapists use dreams to help their clients?

11-7 *Discuss and evaluate the hypotheses that sleep is a period of repair and that sleep is a useful behavioral response.*

Read pages 392-395 and then answer the following questions:

1. a. Describe the hypothesis that sleep is a period of repair.

    b. How did the sleep of people who ran a 92 kilometer race change on the two nights following the race?

    c. How did the sleep of healthy people who spent six weeks resting in bed change?

    d. What conclusions can we make from these observations?

2. a. Offer two contradictory explanations for the increased rate of protein synthesis during sleep (Drucker-Colín and Spanis, 1976).

    b. What is the status of the search for toxic chemicals produced during wakefulness?

3. a. In general, what happens to people who have been kept awake for long periods of time?

    b. How do feelings of sleepiness change during extended wakefulness?

    c. How long do the subjects sleep when they finally do sleep?

4. Carefully summarize what the results of the research you have just describe indicates about the hypothesis of sleep as a period of repair.

5. a. Describe how researchers selectively deprive subjects in the sleep laboratory of REM sleep. How do researchers treat control subjects in the same experiment?

    b. Study Figure 11.20 in your text and then describe the *flowerpot technique* used to selectively deprive animal subjects of REM sleep.

    c. Describe the REM sleep patterns of subjects following REM sleep deprivation.

d. How well did REM sleep-deprived mice learn to run through a maze? (Rideout, 1979)

e. Compare the reactions to the second viewing of a particularly gruesome film of subjects who slept normally the next night with those of subjects who were deprived of REM sleep.

f. What do these results suggest about a possible function of REM sleep?

g. Offer two explanations why the sleep of infants is mostly REM sleep.

6. a. Briefly describe Webb's (1975) view of sleep.

b. Summarize research by Magni et al., 1959 on sleep circuits in the brain:

1. Study Figure 11.21 in your text and describe which two blood supplies were isolated from each other.

2. What effect did anesthesia injected into the brain stem have on the sleeping cat?

3. What do the results suggest about the location of sleep circuits in the brain?

7. a. What are some of the factors that influence the sleep patterns of small and large animals?

b. How do their sleep patterns correspond to their ecological niche?

c. Evaluate the hypothesis that sleep is a useful behavioral response.

11-8 *Describe the nature, causes, and treatment of sleep disorders.*

Read pages 395-399 and then answer the following questions:

1. a. Define *iatrogenic disorder* in your own words.

b. Explain why insomnia is one of these disorders.

c. What are some other causes of insomnia?

2. a. Describe how sleeping medications disrupt REM sleep patterns to produce a kind of sleep that is not normal.

    b. How do disruptions of REM sleep make it difficult to stop taking sleeping medication?

    c. How may the use of sleeping medications lead to other forms of drug dependency?

3. a. What are some of the reasons people sometimes think they are insomniacs when they are not?

    b. Describe *sleep apnea* and explain how it disrupts sleep and causes insomnia. How are some types of sleep apnea treated?

    c. According to some investigators, how may sleep apnea be related to *sudden infant death syndrome*?

4. a. Describe the immediate cause and symptoms of *cataplexy*.

    b. Describe *hypnagogic hallucinations*.

    c. What appears to be the underlying cause of cataplexy?

    d. Cite evidence that cataplexy involves inherited brain abnormalities. (See Figure 11.23 in your text.)

    e. How is cataplexy treated? Be sure to refer to *serotonin* in your answer.

    f. What evidence suggests there may be a connection between dreams and LSD-induced hallucinations?

    g. Describe the onset, symptoms, duration, and treatment of *sleep attacks*.

    h. List the three symptoms of *narcolepsy*.

5. a. Why can we be sure that sleepwalkers are not acting out a dream?

b. What are some of the popular misconceptions about sleepwalking?

c. What is the best treatment for sleepwalking?

d. Cite evidence that sleepwalking may be hereditary.

6. a. When does most sleeptalking occur?

b. What are "truth serums?" Are they effective?

7. a. Explain the difference between *night terrors* and *nightmares*.

b. When do night terrors occur?

8. a. _____, or bed-wetting, is sometimes but not always caused by _____
_____.

b. Why is this condition sometimes unnecessarily prolonged?

c. Describe a successful treatment procedure. What may account for its success?

Lesson II Self Test

1. Which is the most accurate statement about sleep?

   a. Sleep is a state of unconsciousness.
   b. Sleep is a state of altered consciousness.
   c. Sleep is uniform.
   d. Sleep is the lack of behavior.

2. _____ is to alertness as _____ is to Stage 4 sleep.

   a. delta activity; beta activity
   b. delta activity; alpha activity
   c. alpha activity; delta activity
   d. beta activity; delta activity

3. Bouts of REM sleep

   a. occur during all stages of sleep.
   b. are accompanied by muscular paralysis.

   c. occur at irregular intervals throughout the night.

   c. are accompanied by unpleasant frightening sensations.

4. According to Hall, the symbols of dreams

   a. are universal

   b. divert attention from the manifest content of dreams.

   c. are the private property of the dreamer.

   d. are not symbols at all but represent what the object seems to be.

5. People who have been kept awake for long periods

   a. become psychotic.

   b. have high blood levels of toxic chemicals.

   c. when permitted to sleep make up all of their lost sleep.

   d. suffer no apparent harm.

6. REM sleep deprivation

   a. leads to more frequent bouts of REM sleep when subjects are allowed uninterrupted sleep.

   b. facilitates learning.

   c. reduces anxiety and tension.

   d. reduces appetite so mice do not learn to run through a maze quickly.

7. The neural mechanisms of sleep may have evolved to

   a. facilitate storage of information in short-term memory.

   b. permit dreaming as a means of problem-solving.

   c. ensure safety and energy conservation.

   d. promote protein synthesis.

8. The principal cause of insomnia is

   a. personal problems.

   b. insufficient exercise.

   c. daytime napping.

   d. sleeping medications.

9. Which of the following disorders involves loss of control of REM sleep mechanisms?

   a. cataplexy

   b. sleepwalking

   c. sleep talking

   d. night terrors

10. The best treatment for sleepwalking is

   a. drugs that increase the activity of neurons that use serotonin.

   b. drugs that decrease the activity of neurons that use serotonin.

   c. to establish a regular pattern of sleep and wakefulness.

   d. to allow the child to outgrow this behavior.

Answers for Self Tests

<table>
<tr><td>

Lesson I

1. c Obj. 11-1
2. c Obj. 11-1
3. b Obj. 11-2
4. a Obj. 11-2
5. b Obj. 11-3
6. d Obj. 11-3
7. d Obj. 11-4
8. d Obj. 11-4
9. a Obj. 11-5
10. c Obj. 11-5

</td><td>

Lesson II

1. b Obj. 11-6
2. d Obj. 11-6
3. b Obj. 11-6
4. c Obj. 11-6
5. d Obj. 11-7
6. a Obj. 11-7
7. c Obj. 11-7
8. d Obj. 11-8
9. a Obj. 11-8
10. d Obj. 11-8

</td></tr>
</table>

11.1 alpha activity	11.10 electroencephalogram (EEG)
11.2 attention	11.11 electromyogram (EMG)
11.3 Balint's syndrome	11.12 electro-oculogram (EOG)
11.4 beta activity	11.13 enuresis
11.5 cataplexy	11.14 flowerpot technique
11.6 corpus callosum	11.15 hidden observer
11.7 delta activity	11.16 hypnagogic hallucination
11.8 dichotic listening	11.17 iatrogenic disorder
11.9 electrocardiogram (EKG)	11.18 isolation aphasia

11.10

The record of the electrical activity of the brain, recorded through small metal disks attached to the scalp.

11.11

The record of the electrical activity of the muscles, recorded through small metal disks attached to the skin.

11.12

The record of eye movements, recorded through small metal disks attached to the skin near the eyes.

11.13

Bed-wetting; a disorder of slow-wave sleep that is usually outgrown or may be treated through a simple training procedure.

11.14

A technique used to deprive laboratory animals of REM sleep; the animal is placed on an inverted flower pot surrounded by water; when REM sleep occurs its head hits the water and it wakes.

11.15

A phenomenon of hypnosis; according to Hilgard, special instructions cause a part of the hypnotized person's consciousness to become dissociated from the rest.

11.16

A symptom of narcolepsy; paralysis and the occurrence of a premature dream just as the person is falling asleep.

11.17

Any mental or physical disorder that is caused by attempts to treat a disorder.

11.18

A speech disturbance; inability to understand or produce speech; can repeat words and learn new sequences of words; results from isolation of speech mechanisms from other parts of the brain.

11.1

Rhythmical activity of the electroencephalogram characterized by medium-amplitude, medium-frequency electrical activity that occurs when a person is relaxed.

11.2

The selective process that controls our awareness of particular events around us, according to their location or characteristics.

11.3

A deficit resulting from damage to the parietal lobe on both sides of the brain; person has difficulty controlling eye movements and cannot simultaneously perceive two objects placed in the line of sight (simultanagnosia).

11.4

Rhythmical activity of the electroencephalogram characterized by high-frequency, low-amplitude electrical activity that occurs when the person is alert.

11.5

A symptom of narcolepsy in which the person falls to the ground, paralyzed but conscious; usually triggered by strong emotional states such as anger; related to the paralysis that accompanies REM sleep.

11.6

A band of axons that connects the cerebral cortex of the two hemispheres of the brain.

11.7

Rhythmical activity of the electroencephalogram characterized by low-frequency, high-amplitude electrical activity that occurs in Stage 4 slow-wave sleep.

11.8

An experimental task that requires subjects to listen to one of two different messages presented simultaneously to each ear through headphones.

11.9

The record of the electrical activity of the heart, recorded through small metal disks attached to the skin.

11.19

latent content/manifest content

11.20

narcolepsy

11.21

positive hallucination/negative hallucination

11.22

polygraph

11.23

posthypnotic suggestibility

11.24

rapid eye movement (REM) sleep

11.25

shadow

11.26

simultanagnosia

11.27

sleep apnea

11.28

sleep attack

11.29

slow-wave sleep

11.30

split-brain operation

11.31

verbal access

11.32

verbal control

11.28 A symptom of narcolepsy; sudden, irresistible urge to sleep, lasting only a few minutes; person awakens refreshed and often reports a dream.	11.19 According to Freud, latent content is the hidden part of a dream stemming from unfulfilled sexual desires, disguised in the manifest content (plot) of the dream.
11.29 The deepest stages of sleep, characterized by regular, slow EEG waves.	11.20 Disorder that includes the symptoms of cataplexy, hypnagogic hallucinations, and sleep attacks.
11.30 A surgical procedure to treat severe epilepsy; the corpus callosum is severed, disconnecting neural communication between the right and left hemispheres of the brain.	11.21 Phenomena of hypnosis; the conviction that one perceives things that are not present (positive hallucination) or that one does not perceive things that are present (negative hallucination).
11.31 The ability to describe verbally an event such as a perception, thought, memory, or feeling.	11.22 A machine that monitors and makes a permanent record of the EEG, EKM, EMG, EOG, and other physiological events.
11.32 The ability to initiate, stop, or control a behavior of another person through verbal communication.	11.23 The tendency of a person to perform a behavior suggested by the hypnotist some time after hypnosis is over.
	11.24 A state of sleep; irregular, low-voltage electrical activity, irregular heartbeat and respiration, muscular relaxation, narrative storylike dreams; alternates with slow-wave sleep in a 90-minute cycle.
	11.25 An experimental task in which subjects are asked to continuously repeat a message to which they are listening.
	11.26 One of the symptoms of Balint's syndrome; inability simultaneously to perceive two objects placed in the line of sight (simultanagnosia).
	11.27 Inability to breathe while asleep.

Chapter 12
Motivation

Lesson I

Read the interim summary on pages 419-420 of your text to reacquaint yourself with the material in this section.

12-1 *Explain the terms motivation and drive and describe and evaluate the drive reduction theory and the optimum-level hypothesis.*

Read pages 405-409 and then answer the following questions:

1. a. Define *motivation* in your own words.

   b. Motivation can affect the _____, the _____, and the _____ of an organism's behavior.

   c. Explain the two types of phenomena characteristic of motivation and give an original example of each.

   d. Motivation cannot be separated from _____. Explain this statement.

2. a. Define *drive* in your own words and give an example of a biological need and a nonbiological drive.

   b. Study Figure 12.1 in your text and explain the drive hypothesis of motivation and the drive reduction hypothesis of reinforcement.

3. a. According to Hull, what is a *habit*?

   b. Write Hull's equation and define each term.

   c. If a hungry animal in search of food has a high drive strength and a high habit strength the excitatory potential of its behavior will also be high. Now estimate the values of D and H (high, medium, low or zero) to predict the excitatory potential of the behavior of an animal that is

1. hungry, but has little experience obtaining food by running through a maze.

2. hungry, but has no experience obtaining food by running through a maze.

3. not hungry and has learned how to obtain food by running through a maze.

d. According to Hull, how do events in the environment come to stimulate new drives?

4. a. According to Spence, what is *incentive*?

b. How did he believe incentive affected behavior?

5. Describe the logical problems inherent in theories based on drive.

6. Explain why many psychologists believe that reinforcement is caused by events that actually *increase* rather than decrease drive.

7. a. Study Figure 12.2 in your text and describe the experimental procedure in classic research by Sheffield et al. (1951).

b. Why were male rats prevented from ejaculating?

c. Although sexual activity was interrupted, how did the male rats respond?

d. Why is the Spence theory inadequate to explain the results of this experiment?

8. a. Study Figure 12.3 in your text and describe the experimental procedure for producing electrical brain stimulation.

b. Explain why the effects of this stimulation contradict the drive reduction hypothesis.

9. a. The _____-_____ hypothesis is an attempt to find a common explanation for both _____ and _____ reinforcement.

b. Explain the *optimum-level hypothesis* of reinforcement and punishment.

c. According to this hypothesis, what kind of activity will the organism engage in if understimulated? overstimulated?

d. What problem applies to the optimum-level hypothesis as well as the drive-reduction hypothesis?

10. Match the term with the correct definition.

_____ a response to understimulation

_____ gives direction to behavior

_____ energizes behavior, increases as the goal is approached

_____ a response to overstimulation

_____ physiological change that energizes behavior

_____ effect of a stimulus that increases the probability of a behavior

_____ a collective term for the factors that influence the nature, strength, and persistence of a behavior

Choices:
a. diversive exploration
b. drive
c. specific exploration
d. reinforcement
e. habit
f. motivation
g. incentive

12-2 *Describe Murray's social needs and the results of research based on them.*

Read pages 409-413 and then answer the following questions:

1. a. According to Murray, what is the *need for achievement?*

b. List and define the three variables that, according to McClelland and his colleagues, determine the motivation to perform a particular task

1.

2.

3.

2. Describe the *Thematic Apperception Test (TAT)* devised by Murray and explain how it measures social needs.

3. a. How does the *need to avoid failure* affect people's behavior?

   b. How is this need measured?

4. a. According to McClelland and his colleagues, how is the aversiveness of failing a task related to the probability of succeeding at the task? Why?

   b. What kind of task(s) does the theory of achievement motivation predict will be attempted by a person with a

      1. moderate amount of the need to achieve?

      2. high need to avoid failure?

   c. What results did Isaacson (1964) obtain when he tested groups of male college students with either a high need to achieve or a high need to avoid failure? (Study Figure 12.4 in your text.)

5. a. Define the *need for power* in your own words.

   b. Summarize research on the need for power:

      1. What kind of positions, friends, and behaviors do people with a high need for power seek? (Winter, 1973)

      2. Describe the control and experimental conditions Fodor (1984) created to assess the arousal of subjects with a high need for power.

      3. How was arousal level measured after the industrial simulation?

      4. Study Figure 12.5 in your text and describe and explain the results.

6. a. Define the *need for affiliation* in your own words.

b. How do people with a high need for affiliation interact with other people, how do they regard their own social skills, and how do they feel in situations in which they perceive their social skills are being judged?

c. Constantian (1981) measured motivation strength by studying the relationship between two variables. Name them and describe the task she used to measure them.

d. Study Figure 12.6 in your text and describe and explain the results.

12-3 *Discuss how intermittent reinforcement, conditioned reinforcement, intrinsic motivation, and learned helplessness affect perseverance.*

Read pages 413-417 and then answer the following questions:

1. a. Define *perseverance* in your own words.

   b. How quickly does extinction occur if a behavior has previously been

      1. reinforced regularly?

      2. reinforced intermittently?

   c. In other words, intermittent reinforcement leads to _____.

   d. Cite research that supports the suggestion that early experience can affect perseverance.

2. Explain how conditioned reinforcers provided by the action of others or by a person's own actions can affect the tendency to persevere. Give an example of each kind of reinforcer.

3. a. Define *intrinsic motivation* in your own words.

   b. Now define *extrinsic reinforcer* in your own words.

4. Summarize research by Lepper et al., 1973 on the *undermining of intrinsic motivation*:

   a. Briefly describe the experimental procedure, including the treatment of the three groups of children.

   b. Study Figure 12.7 in your text. How did receiving an unexpected award and being "bribed" affect later decisions on how to spend free-choice time? Why?

5. a. Subsequent research has shown that extrinsic reinforcers can either _____ or _____ intrinsic motivation. The most important characteristic of an extrinsic reinforcer is that it is based on a person's _____.

   b. What effects do extrinsic reinforcers have on behavior if they are given for

   1. a job well-done?

   2. any job, regardless of how it is done?

   c. Describe Deci's (1971) observations and conclusions.

   d. Describe a situation in which intrinsic motivation is undermined.

6. a. People value activities they _____ themselves more highly than activities _____ choose for them.

   b. Describe how Swann and Pittman (1977) demonstrated that even the illusion of free choice increases the value of an activity.

7. a. What is the general basis for explanations of human preference for free choice?

   b. Describe research by Catania and Sagvolden (1980) on the importance of cognitive process to preference for free choice:

   1. Study the left side of Figure 12.8 in your text and describe the first step of the task pigeons were trained to perform.

   2. Now study the right side of the figure and describe how the pigeons could exercise "free choice."

   3. Describe and explain the results of the experiment.

8. What concepts are illustrated in the following situations?

   _____ Mark is telling a story based on some cards that the psychologist has given him.

   _____ When Jackie heard about the tryouts for the play she decided to audition for one of the minor parts even though she really wanted to play the leading role

   _____ "She spends all of her spare time talking with friends on the phone or writing to friends who live out of town," Natalie's mother commented to a friend.

_____The moderator introduced the guest speaker as a man with a long career in government beginning as student body president in college and culminating with election to Congress, where he serves as chairman of three important and influential subcommittees.

_____When he learned that he had not been accepted by the team, he decided to spend more time practicing by himself after school and try again next semester.

_____John likes woodworking so much that he has filled his house with furniture, and now makes things as presents for his friends.

Choices:
a. need for power
b. perseverance
c. need to avoid failure
d. intrinsic motivation
e. taking the TAT
f. need for affiliation

9. Define *learned helpless* in your own words and explain how it differs from other forms of learning.

10. Explain how Overmeier and Seligman (1967) demonstrated learned helplessness in dogs.

11. a. According to Seligman (1975), how does experience with situations that lead to learned helplessness affect subsequent behavior?

    b. What issue has been raised by his critics?

    c. According to McReynolds (1980) what factors controls whether people will respond in a new situation after having failed at a task?

12-4 *Discuss evidence concerning the physiology of reinforcement, including the reinforcing effects of opiates.*

Read pages 417-419 and then answer the following questions:

1. a. What kind of behaviors are elicited through electrical stimulation of the lateral hypothalamus?

    b. Study Figure 12.9 in your text and explain how electrical stimulation reinforces behaviors. Be sure to use the term *dopamine* in your answer.

2. a. What more natural stimuli activate neurons in the lateral hypothalamus? (Rolls, 1982)

    b. Explain the significance of the finding that some neurons respond only when the animal is hungry.

3. a. Explain how stimulants such as amphetamine and cocaine produce their reinforcing effect.

    b. What effect do these stimulants have on electrical brain stimulation?

4. Explain how opiates produce their effects on the mechanisms of analgesia, reinforcement, and arousal. Be sure to use the term *endorphin* in your answer.

Lesson I Self Test

1. Drive

    a. energizes an organism's behavior.
    b. give direction to behavior.
    c. accounts for inconsistent behavior.
    d. is a learned behavior controlled by discriminative stimuli.

2. Using Hull's equation $E = D \times H$, calculate the excitatory potential of a response for a hungry animal that has not learned how to run through a maze toward food. The value of E is

    a. low
    b. medium
    c. high
    d. zero

3. Drive reduction and optimum-level hypotheses share the common problem that researchers do not

    a. agree whether reinforcement is caused by events that decreases or increases drive.
    b. agree on how many drives there are.
    c. know how to detect and measure a specific drive.
    d. agree that all drives are unpleasant, aversive conditions.

4. According to the theory of achievement motivation, people with a _____ need to achieve choose _____ tasks with a _____ incentive value of succeeding.

    a. low; easy; low
    b. moderate; easy; high
    c. high; moderately difficult; moderate
    d. moderate; moderately difficult; moderate

5. People with a high need for power prefer

    a. friends like themselves.
    b. friends who are not very popular.
    c. to avoid emotional commitments to others.
    d. one-to-one relationships.

6. What is the best way to encourage a person to persevere at a long, difficult task?

    a. Reinforce work on all components of the task.
    b. Never reinforce work on any of the components of the task.
    c. Intermittently reinforce work on components of the task.
    d. Reinforce work on any component of the task if the person stops working.

7. To prevent extrinsic reinforcers from undermining intrinsic motivation, the extrinsic reinforcer should be given only if the person's performance

    a. is consistently high.
    b. is consistently low..
    c. improves.
    d. declines.

8. Rita's mother has found that her young daughter is more cooperative if she is asked, "Would you like to clean your room before or after lunch?" Rita cooperates because

    a. she has a free choice.
    b. even the illusion of free choice increases the value of an activity.
    c. young children prefer to be treated politely.
    d. even young children resist being in a subordinate position.

9. The unresolved issue surrounding learned helplessness is whether or not

    a. it is a stable personality trait.
    b. it is inversely related to preference for free choice.
    c. adverse consequences for physical and emotional health are reversible.
    d. some people are more vulnerable than others to the effects of experiences with learned helplessness.

10. Stimulants such as amphetamine and cocaine produce their reinforcing effect by

    a. mimicking the effect of endorphins.
    b. decreasing sensitivity to pain.
    c. slowing the re-uptake of dopamine.
    d. increasing dopamine synthesis.

Lesson II

Read the interim summary on pages 428-429 of your text to reacquaint yourself with the material in this section.

12-5 Discuss social and cultural influences on eating and the physiological mechanisms that begin a meal.

Read pages 420-424 and then answer the following questions:

1. a. Define *regulatory behavior* in your own words and give several examples.

   b. Define *homeostasis* in your own words.

   c. Now explain the role of regulatory behaviors in the process of homeostasis.

2. In general, cultural and social factors influence _____ and _____ we eat.

3. Briefly explain the empty stomach theory of hunger and cite research that refutes this theory. (Inglefinger, 1944)

4. Study Figure 12.10 in your text.

   a. Name an important fuel for the body. What is its source?

   b. Name the two forms in which nutrients are stored in the body.

   c. What products does the body break these stored nutrients into?

   d. When the digestive system is empty, what kind of fuel is used primarily by the brain? by the rest of the body?

5. a. Study Figure 12.11 in your text and explain the *glucostatic hypothesis* proposed by Mayer (1955a). Be sure to use the term *glucostat* in your answer.

   b. Describe the first evidence discovered by Russek (1971) that glucostats were not located in the brain, as Mayer had assumed.

   c. What anatomical facts suggested that the liver might be the site of glucostats? (See Figure 12.12 in your text.)

   d. Study Figure 12.13 in your text and describe the procedure Russek used to search for glucostats in the liver.

   e. What was the effect on eating of glucose injections to the liver? nonnutritive solutions to the liver?

   f. Why do these results confirm the location of glucostats in the liver?

   g. What is the unresolved issue concerning the nature of these detectors?

12-6 *Discuss the physiological mechanisms that end a meal and the possible causes of obesity and anorexia nervosa.*

Read pages 424-428 and then answer the following questions:

1. Explain why a meal does not stop when the body's supply of nutrients is replenished.

2. a. The primary cause of satiety seems to be a _____ _____.

    b. Cite research demonstrating that the stomach contains receptors that respond to food *quantity* to support your last answer.

    c. Cite research demonstrating the stomach also contains receptors that respond to food *quality*.

3. a. How did Booth et al., 1982 alter the caloric content of the lunch served to the subjects?

    b. Study Figure 12.14 in your text and describe how the calorie content of the soup affected the number of sandwiches subjects ate. How quickly did calorie content effect sandwich consumption?

    c. What do the results suggest about the role of learning on normal food intake?

4. a. How do mealtime experiences early in life influence later eating habits?

    b. Summarize research on the relationship between metabolism and obesity:

        1. What did Rose and Williams (1961) conclude about the effects of metabolic rate after studying paired subjects?

        2. How quickly did thin subjects who volunteered to eat a high calorie diet return to their normal weight when permitted to chose their own food? Why?

        3. Cite research that suggests body weight (and presumably metabolic rate) are influenced by genetics.

        4. Describe how Brownell et al., 1986 demonstrated that gaining and losing large amounts of weight can affect metabolic rate.

5. a. Is childhood obesity related to adult obesity? (Stunkard and Burt, 1967) Discuss a possible explanation.

    b. Explain how fattening diets fed to young rats and adult rats affected their total number of fat cells.

c. How does early prenatal malnutrition appear to affect adult body weight? Cite research to support your answer.

6. Study Figure 12.15 in your text and describe how well a group of active Indian men and a group of sedentary Indian men matched their food intake to their activity level.

7. a. Describe the symptoms of *anorexia nervosa*.

b. Describe *bulimia* and some of its subsequent affects on behavior and emotion.

c. What group of people has the highest incidence of this condition?

d. Briefly describe some of the possible explanations for this condition.

Read the interim summary on page 434 of your text to reacquaint yourself with the material in this section.

12-7 *Compare the responses of males and females to erotic imagery and describe the effects of sex hormones on sexual behavior.*

Read pages 429-433 and then answer the following questions:

1. a. Compare the responses of men and women to pictures of romantic situations and of explicit sexual situations.

b. How do men and women respond to a picture of a woman? a naked man?

c. How does sexual orientation influence the nature of sexual fantasies?

2. Explain the *organizational effects* and the *activational effects* of sex hormones in your own words.

3. a. Describe how Davidson et al., 1979 demonstrated the activational effects of testosterone on male sexual behavior.

b. Describe patterns of change in the sexual response of castrated men. What may account for the difference?

c. What environmental factors effect testosterone production?

d. Does testosterone level affect sexual orientation?

4. a. What is the effect on a woman's sex drive of the removal of her adrenal glands? her pituitary gland? (See Figure 12.16 in your text.)

   b. What physiological factor had the strongest influence on the sexual activity of married couples? (Persky et al., 1978)

5. a. What is the difference between the menstrual cycle of primates and the *estrous cycle* of other mammals?

   b. At what time during the estrous cycle do females of nonprimate species permit copulation? Why? How does their sexual receptivity differ from that of female primates?

   c. What change occurs in the ovaries at menopause? What effect does it have on sexual receptivity?

   d. Study Figure 12.17 in your text and describe the hormonal changes during the menstrual cycle. Be sure to note periods of peak sexuality.

   e. How do birth control pills effect peak sexuality? Why?

12-8 *Describe and discuss paraphilias, transvestism, and transsexualism.*

Read pages 433-434 and then answer the following questions:

1. Explain *paraphilias*, *transvestism*, and *transsexualism* in your own words.

2. Outline one explanation why males develop paraphilias more often than females. What other explanations for their occurrence have been proposed?

3. What is the usual sexual orientation of true transvestites? Outline a superficial explanation for this behavior.

4. a. Compare the reasons why transvestites and transsexuals dress in clothes of the opposite sex.

   b. According the Money, what may be the cause of transsexualism?.

Read the interim summary on pages 439-440 of your text to reacquaint yourself with the material in this section.

12-9 *Discuss the biological significance of aggressive behavior and their physiological basis.*

Read pages 435-436 and then answer the following questions:

1. a. Define *intraspecific aggression* in your own words.

    b. Discuss two ways that intraspecific aggression may maintain the vigor of an animal species.

2. a. Describe typical *threat gestures* and *appeasement gestures* in your own words. (See Figure 12.17 in your text.)

    b. Discuss how these behaviors promote the survival of a species of animals.

3. a. How does electrical brain stimulation of the hypothalamus and structures in the limbic system affect aggressive behavior? How does destruction of certain other brain structures affect aggressive behavior?

    b. Define *psychosurgery* in your own words.

    c. Explain why the surgery performed on the woman who was thrown from her horse is not considered to be psychosurgery.

    d. Why has it been difficult to evaluate the usefulness of psychosurgery to alleviate aggressive behavior in humans?

    e. In general, what is the prevailing attitude toward psychosurgery in humans?

4. a. Study Figure 12.19 in your text and summarize the effects of early castration on the adult aggressive behavior of male mice. How do these mice respond to injections of testosterone?

    b. What do these results suggest about the organizational and activational effects of testosterone on aggressive behavior?

c. Describe the conclusions of the few studies on the relationship between testosterone and male human aggression.

12-10 *Describe the variables that affect human aggression.*

Read pages 436-439 and then answer the following questions:

1. a. List two important sources of aggressive behavior that young children may observe.

    b. How do victims of child abuse frequently treat their own children? Cite research to support your answer. (Parke and Collmer, 1975)

    c. What was the conclusion of research on the effects of watching violent television shows on the amount of aggressive behavior of eight-year-old boys and the same boys ten year later? (Lefkowitz et al., 1977)

    d. Explain why we cannot conclude from research on the television viewing of boys in private boarding schools that violent television programs may encourage pacifism.

2. a. Carefully explain the frustration-aggression theory proposed by Dollard and his colleagues, especially their operational definition of *frustration*.

    b. List two causes of aggressive behavior that Berkowitz cited to refute the frustration-aggression theory.

    c. In research by Berkowitz (1978) on the role of frustration, which group of angry subjects "punished" their partners the most? Why? How did he suggest the frustration-aggression theory be altered?

    d. What is the biological advantage of pain-induced aggression? Cite research to support your answer.

3. a. Explain emotional *catharsis* in your own words.

    b. Geen et al., (1975) made some subjects angry at a confederate. Some of the angry subjects were permitted to shock the confederate twice and others only once. How did the two angry groups respond?

c. What inconsistent behavior was observed? What may account for it?

Lesson II Self Test

1. A likely cause of hunger is

   a. a drop in metabolic rate.
   b. an empty stomach.
   c. depletion of the body's store of nutrients.
   d. contractions of the stomach.

2. Hunger detectors appear to be located in the

   a. stomach.
   b. liver.
   c. gall bladder.
   d. pancreas.

3. A likely cause of satiety is

   a. an increase in metabolic rate.
   b. a full stomach.
   c. replenished stores of nutrients.
   d. the cessation of stomach contractions.

4. Which is the most accurate statement about obesity?

   a. Overweight children will "outgrow" their obesity.
   b. People with an inefficient metabolism must eat less food in order to control their weight.
   c. Extremely meager diets alter the number of fat cells.
   d. Gaining and losing large amounts of weight alters metabolic rate.

5. The organizational effects of testosterone

   a. affect the development of male sex organs and the brain.
   b. initiate the male sexual response.
   c. slowly decline following castration.
   d. affect the intensity of sexual desire.

6. A female's blood level of estradiol peaks

   a. just before menstruation.
   b. during intercourse.
   c. just before ovulation.
   d. during menstruation.

7. Most transvestites dress in clothes of the opposite sex because

   a. they are homosexual.

b. they despise their gender.
c. the clothes are a source of sexual stimulation.
d. they wish they were women.

8. Threat gestures

a. are a form of intraspecific aggression.
b. help prevent fighting.
c. are a response to appeasement gestures.
d. are invariably followed by an attack.

9. Psychosurgery

a. is the removal of brain tissue to alter behavior in the absence of evidence that the tissue is abnormal.
b. is the removal of abnormal brain tissue to alter behavior.
c. should only be performed after all other attempts to control violent behavior have failed.
d. should be considered successful if the person is easier to control.

10. Field studies of long-term viewing of violence on television suggest that

a. children who watch television violence should engage in physical activities to discharge their feelings.
b. the more closely violent television situations reassemble the child's environment the greater their effect will be.
c. young children are more vulnerable than older children to the effects of television violence.
d. long-term viewing appears to increase aggressive behavior, but the evidence is not definitive.

Answers for Self Tests

Lesson I

1. a Obj. 12-1
2. d Obj. 12-1
3. c Obj. 12-1
4. c Obj. 12-2
5. b Obj. 12-2
6. c Obj. 12-3
7. c Obj. 12-3
8. b Obj. 12-3
9. a Obj. 12-3
10. c Obj. 12-4

Lesson II

1. c Obj. 12-5
2. b Obj. 12-5
3. b Obj. 12-6
4. d Obj. 12-6
5. a Obj. 12-7
6. c Obj. 12-7
7. c Obj. 12-8
8. d Obj. 12-9
9. a Obj. 12-9
10. d Obj. 12-10

12.1 activational effect	12.10 estrous cycle
12.2 anorexia nervosa	12.11 frustration
12.3 appeasement gesture	12.12 glucostatic hypothesis
12.4 bulimia	12.13 glycogen
12.5 catharsis	12.14 homeostasis
12.6 diversive exploration	12.15 incentive
12.7 dopamine.	12.16 intraspecific aggression
12.8 drive	12.17 intrinsic motivation
12.9 drive reduction hypothesis	12.18 learned helplessness

12.10	12.1
The hormonal cycle of females of nonprimate species; the lining of the uterus does not slough off as it does during the menstrual cycle.	An effect of a hormone that occurs after the organism is fully developed; lasts only as long as the hormone is present.
12.11	12.2
An event that interferes with the occurrence of an expected goal; hypothesized to result in aggressive behavior.	An eating disorder usually seen in young women; severe decrease in eating without loss of appetite or interest in food; intense fear of becoming obese even when dangerously thin.
12.12	12.3
Mayer's hypothesis that hunger occurs when the blood level of glucose becomes low; he thought this drop was detected by special neurons located in the brain which he called glucostats.	A gesture made by a submissive animal in response to a threat gesture by a dominant animal; tends to inhibit an attack.
12.13	12.4
Animal "starch"; insoluble form of carbohydrate stored in the liver and muscles; can be converted into glucose when needed.	A phenomenon associated with anorexia nervosa; binges of overeating, usually followed by self-induced vomiting and use of laxatives, usually with feelings of guilt and depression.
12.14	12.5
The process of detection and correction that maintains physiological systems at their optimum levels.	A Greek term adopted by Freud to describe the release of tension that results from the actual or symbolic acting out of an aggressive drive.
12.15	12.6
The energizing effect on behavior that occurs as an organism approaches a goal and anticipates performing a particular behavior and receiving a reinforcer.	A form of exploration hypothesized by Berlyne; a response to understimulation (boredom) that will increase the kinds of stimuli the animal encounters.
12.16	12.7
An attack by one animal on another member of the same species.	A transmitter substance involved in brain mechanisms of reinforcement; drugs that prevent its release or block its effect prevent electrical brain stimulation from being reinforcing.
12.17	12.8
The ability of a particular activity to produce its own reinforcing effects; for example, games or hobbies.	An unpleasant state usually, but not always, resulting from biological need or deprivation; energizes an organism's behavior.
12.18	12.9
Learning that an aversive event cannot be avoided or escaped; supposedly results in the reduced ability to recognize aversive situations that can be avoided.	An explanation for reinforcement; behaviors that reduce drive are reinforced through the process of negative reinforcement.

12.19 motivation	12.28 psychosurgery
12.20 need for achievement (nAch)	12.29 regulatory behavior
12.21 need for affiliation	12.30 specific exploration
12.22 need for power	12.31 Test Anxiety Questionnaire (TAQ)
12.23 need to avoid failure	12.32 Thematic Apperception Test (TAT)
12.24 optimum-level hypothesis	12.33 threat gesture
12.25 organizational effect	12.34 transsexualism
12.26 paraphilia	12.35 transvestism
12.27 perseverance	12.36 undermining of intrinsic motivation

12.28

The removal of brain tissue in an attempt to alter a person's behavior in the absence of evidence that the tissue is abnormal.

12.29

Physiological mechanisms of complex organisms that detect deficits or imbalances in the body and control behaviors that will return them to normal levels.

12.30

One of two forms of exploration hypothesized by Berlyne; a response to overstimulation that leads to the needed item, decreasing the organism's drive level.

12.31

A test devised to measure people's anxiety about taking tests as a way of determining their need to avoid failure.

12.32

A test used to determine the strength of various social needs; subjects examine a set of cards showing drawings of ambiguous social situations and then tell a story.

12.33

A response by an animal that communicates aggressive intent to another animal before violence actually occurs.

12.34

The wish to be a member of the other sex.

12.35

The practice of wearing clothes appropriate to the opposite sex; cross-dressing.

12.36

The process through which a task loses some of its intrinsic reinforcing properties because extrinsic reinforcers were delivered after the task was performed.

12.19

A collective term for the events that can affect the nature, strength and persistence of a behavior.

12.20

The need of people to work to overcome obstacles and perform something difficult as well and quickly as possible.

12.21

The need of people to maintain social relationships with others.

12.22

The need to assert authority and control over the behavior of others.

12.23

The need of people to avoid failing; leads people to withdraw from a task or situation.

12.24

The hypothesis that when arousal is too high, less stimulation is reinforcing and when it is low, more stimulation is reinforcing; an attempt to find a common explanation for positive and negative reinforcement.

12.25

An effect of a hormone during development that produces permanent changes that alter subsequent development.

12.26

A sexual disorder in which sexual pleasure is derived from unusual stimuli such as animals, young children, body parts, clothing.

12.27

The tendency to work very hard even though the rewards for work occur infrequently.

Chapter 13
Emotion

Lesson I

Read the interim summary on page 447 of your text to reacquaint yourself with the material in this section.

13-1 *Define emotion, mood, and temperament and describe how people often use emotions to explain behavior.*

Read pages 445-447 and then answer the following questions:

1. Describe some practical and ethical problems encountered in the experimental investigation of human emotions.

2. Define these terms in your own words:

   a. *emotion*

   b. *mood*

   c. *temperament*

3. Indicate which of these statements is an example of emotion, mood of temperament.

   _____ Mike was elected "Friendliest Senior" by his classmates.

   _____ Because Mrs. Robinson was usually unpleasant to work with, few people contributed to her retirement gift.

   _____ Steve detests waiting in line.

   _____ When his mother told him the family dog had died, Juan began to cry.

   _____ Tanya grimaced when she remembered how she had made a fool of herself at the reception.

   _____ Monday sales meetings always make Toby irritable.

4. Briefly explain why we often blame bad behavior on our emotions, but take credit for good deeds. What

189

are some social consequences of this kind of reasoning?

5. Give two reasons why the objective study of emotions is difficult.

Read the interim summary on pages 459-460 of your text to reacquaint yourself with the material in this section.

13-2 *State Darwin's hypothesis of emotional expression and describe cross-cultural studies that support it.*

Read pages 447-450 and then answer the following questions:

1. a. According to Darwin

    1. from what have human emotions evolved?

    2. what is the selective value of emotions?

    b. List two kinds of evidence he used to support his assertion.

    1.

    2.

    c. Briefly explain why he believed facial expressions, especially of people in isolated cultures, supported his assertion.

    d. Later, two investigators suggested that Darwin was wrong. Describe their criticisms.

    e. And much later, Ekman and Friesen (1971) concluded that Darwin had been correct. Define the following types of nonverbal behavior:

    1. *illustrator*

    2. *regulator*

    3. *emblem*

    f. Now, using these three terms, explain their support of Darwin's hypothesis.

2. In Ekman and Friesen's cross-cultural studies of expression:

    a. Why did they choose to study the South Fore tribe of New Guinea?

    b. What did they ask members of the Fore tribe to do?

c. Why did they decide against using single words to describe emotions?

d. What technique did they choose instead? (See Figure 13.1 in your text.)

e. How successful were the Fore people at this task? (See Table 13.1 in your text.)

f. How did the investigators explain the fact that fear and surprise were confused?

3. Describe Ekman and Friesen's second experiment with the Fore people:

a. What did they ask members of the tribe to do? (See Figure 13.2 in your text.)

b. How accurate were the choices of American college students?

4. a. Describe the studies of the facial expressions of the blind children.

b. What conclusions can we make?

c. What happens to the facial expressions of blind children as they grow older? Why?

13-3 *Describe the social nature of emotional expression in humans.*

Read pages 450-454 and then answer the following questions:

1. a. List the three situations in which Kraut and Johnson (1979) observed the emotional expression of subjects.

   1.

   2.

   3.

b. When did the subjects show the greatest reaction?

c. What was the conclusion of the study?

2. a. What did Field and her colleagues (1982) ask adults to do?

b. Why did they videotape the babies' expression?

c. Compare the expressions of the adults and the babies. (See Figure 13.3 in your text and notice your own reactions.)

3. Offer an explanation of why we tend to imitate the emotional expressions of others.

4. Describe two ways we can control our own emotional expressions.

5. State the three *display rules* of Ekman and Friesen. (See Figure 13.4 in your text.)

1.

2.

3.

6. Briefly describe the following studies of social display rules:

a. How did Buck (1975, 1977) elicit emotional expression from nursery school children?

b. What results did he obtain when he showed videotapes of the children to university students?

c. During the showing of a coming-of-age rite how did American and Japanese students react when

1. alone?

2. with others?

d. What does this study suggest about the influence of culture on display of emotions?

e. Explain *leakage* in your own words.

f. Describe how Ekman and Friesen (1974) studied this phenomenon among nursing students

g. What does this study suggest about attempts to mask displays of emotion?

13-4 *Describe research on the recognition of emotion by monkeys.*

Read pages 454-456 and then answer the following questions:

1. Summarize research by Miller and his colleagues using the *cooperative conditioning* procedure:

   a. Describe the first task the monkeys learned and then describe the divided task.

   b. What did the closed-circuit television monitor? (See Figure 13.5 in your text.)

   c. How well did the receiver monkey perform?

   d. What does the success of the monkeys suggest about recognition of emotion?

   e. In later research using the same technique, why did the experimenters use some monkeys who had been reared in isolation?

   f. Describe the performance of the following pairs of monkeys on the cooperative conditioning task: (See Figure 13.6 in your text.)

      1. two isolated monkeys

      2. a normal-isolate pair

      3. an isolate-normal pair

   g. What do the results of this study suggest about the role of socialization in the

      1. organization of facial expression?

      2. recognition of facial expression?

      3. control of facial expression?

2. Describe Sackett's experiment, in which infant monkey's were shown color slides. Compare the results to the cooperative conditioning experiments. (See Figure 13.7 in your text.)

13-5 *Describe the types of stimuli that produce emotional displays by humans and describe research on monkeys' ability to learn to control emotional displays.*

Read pages 456-458 and then answer the following questions:

1. Describe the types of situations that can elicit emotions.

2. Do humans and other animals differ very much in their expressions and feelings of emotion? How, then, do they differ?

3. Describe how judgement affects feelings of emotion.

4. a. Briefly describe how an adult vervet monkey in a group responds when it suddenly sees a

    1. leopard.

    2. martial eagle.

    3. snake.

  b. What is the monkey's response if it sees a predator when it is alone?

  c. What does this behavioral change suggest about emotional displays?

5. a. In general, how do young vervet monkeys react when they see a predator? How do these reactions differ from those of adult monkeys?

  b. How do adult monkeys react when a young monkey gives an alarm?

  c. According to Marler and his colleagues, how do young monkeys eventually learn to discriminate accurately among predators.

13-6 *Describe theories of emotion based on the biological significance of emotional behavior.*

Read pages 458-459 and then answer the following questions:

1. According to Darwin, why have emotional expressions evolved?

2. List Tomkins nine innate emotions which are based on the movements and expressions people make.

Positive Affects	Negative Affects
1.	1.
2.	2.
3.	3.
	4.
	5.
	6.

3. List Plutchik's eight categories of *species-typical behaviors* and the corresponding *emotions* they evoke. (See Table 13.2 in your text.)

1.	3.
2.	4.

5.   7.

6.   8.

Lesson I Self Test

1. Which of the following last the longest?

   a. emotions
   b. moods
   c. temperament
   d. feelings

2. A major difficulty encountered in the objective study of human emotions is

   a. producing intense emotions in the laboratory.
   b. the lack of a generally accepted method of measuring emotional intensity.
   c. rating facial expressions of emotion.
   d. confirming the self-reporting of emotions by subjects.

3. Darwin's assertion that emotional expressions are innate unlearned patterns of movement, especially of facial muscles, is believed to be correct because

   a. all languages have words to express emotion.
   b. expressions of emotion, such as a smile for joy, are consistent across cultures.
   c. facial muscles can be used for tasks other than emotional expression.
   d. blind children must be taught to smile.

4. Ekman and Friesen defined *illustrators* as

   a. bodily movements that are not consistent with facial movements in emotional expression.
   b. facial movements that control the flow of a conversation.
   c. expressions that convey a special meaning.
   d. facial movements that, together with changes in pitch and stress of the voice, emphasize words and phrases.

5. Cross-cultural studies of the Fore tribe

   a. used pantomimed stories to avoid inaccurate translations.
   b. confirmed that emotional expressions are not culturally determined.
   c. could not explain why the tribe often confused fear and surprise.
   d. revealed that the tribe could not successfully identify Western facial expressions.

6. In Western societies, losing athletes do not usually show too much disappointment. Their behavior illustrates

   a. that display rules are culturally determined.
   b. acceptable male emotional expression is innately determined.
   c. defeat is not an innate elicitor of emotion.
   d. Western society discourages public display of emotion.

195

7. Using the cooperative conditioning technique, Miller and his colleagues observed that a normal-isolate pair (with the isolate as receiver)

    a. did about as well as a normal-normal pair.
    b. did as poorly as an isolate-isolate pair.
    c. did as well as an isolate-normal pair.
    d. avoided nearly 90 percent of the shocks.

8. Emotions

    a. do not occur spontaneously.
    b. can be elicited by neutral stimuli.
    c. and their eliciting stimuli cannot be far removed from each other in time.
    d. are independent of cognitive processes.

9. When a young vervet monkey gives an alarm call, adult monkeys

    a. immediately seek cover.
    b. soon take up the alarm..
    c. take up the alarm only if they, too, see a predator.
    d. ignore the alarm of the young.

10. Theories of emotion such as those of Darwin, Tomkins, and Plutchik

    a. question whether emotional expression can be linked to species-typical behavior.
    b. agree there are nine innate emotions.
    c. stress that weaker emotions are more similar to each other than stronger ones.
    d. focus on the functional significance of various classes of behaviors

Lesson II

Read the interim summary on pages 467-468 of your text to reacquaint yourself with the material in this section.

13-7 *Describe and evaluate the James-Lange theory of emotion.*

Read pages 460-463 and then answer the following questions:

1. What important question concerning the relationship between emotions and physiology did the *James-Lange theory* attempt to resolve?

2. State the *James-Lange theory* of emotion in your own words.

3. Why do many people find that this theory contradicts their own personal experiences?

4. Study Figure 13.8 in your text and diagram the relationship between the emotional feelings we all have and the sensory feedback the brain receives from organs in the body hypothesized by the James-Lange theory.

5. Briefly summarize Cannon's (1927) criticisms of the theory.

   a.

   b.

   c.

   d.

   e.

6. What do modern physiologists say about Cannon's criticisms?

7. a. What kind of injury was common to all subjects in Hohman's 1966 study?

   b. What kind of personal reactions did he ask subjects to describe?

   c. How did the responses of subjects with high spinal cord damage differ from those of subjects with low spinal cord damage? (See Figure 13.9 in your text.)

   d. What do these results suggest about the importance of feedback in feelings of emotion?

   e. Explain how these results support the James-Lange theory.

8. a. Subjects in Laird's 1974 study were divided into two groups. What did he ask each group to do?

   b. After watching cartoons, each group was asked to describe the mood that the cartoons produced. What were the results of the study?

   c. What were the results of a later study? (Laird et al., 1982)

9. a. Refer back to Figure 13.1 in your text and describe the particular facial movements Ekman and his colleagues (1983) asked subjects to make.

    b. Explain why the subjects were not given further information or explanations.

    c. What, according to the physiological monitoring, happened to the subjects while they made these expressions?

    d. Suggest two explanations for the results you have just described.

        1.

        2.

13-8 *Discuss Schachter's theory of emotion and research on the role of cognition and physiological responses on emotional states.*

Read pages 463-465 and then answer the following questions:

1. State a current controversy in the field of emotion.

2. According to Schachter (1964), how is emotional state and cognition affected by

    a. a state of physiological arousal for which an individual has no immediate explanation?

    b. a state of physiological arousal for which an individual has an appropriate explanation?

    c. the level of perception of physiological arousal?

3. For Schachter, emotion is _____ plus _____ of _____ _____.

4. Briefly describe how Schachter tested his hypothesis. (Schachter and Singer, 1962)

    a. What were subjects told was the purpose of the study?

    b. Some subjects were given saline injections, but others received "suproxin." What was "suproxin?" Describe the physiological effects of these two substances.

    c. Describe the two testing situations.

    d. What additional information were some subjects given?

e. How did the researchers predict that the subjects would react?

f. Carefully describe the effects of adrenaline and subject expectations on subject emotional states.

   1. adrenaline injections

   2. subject expectations

g. What do these results suggest about the way we respond to our physiological state?

5. a. In a study by Nisbett and Schachter (1966), subjects were given a placebo pill. What were some of the subjects told about the effects of the pill? What were others told?

   b. After taking the pill, what happened to subjects?

   c. Describe the tolerance to pain of subjects who did or did not perceive their reactions as drug-induced.

   d. Explain what these results suggest about the effect of cognition on judgments about emotional states.

6. a. When Nisbett and Wilson (1977) performed a similar experiment and explained the results to their subjects, what did the subjects say?

   b. What do these self-reports suggest about the role of cognition in producing emotional states?

13-9 *Describe differences in emotional behavior that can be attributed to brain damage and hemispheric differences in normal people.*

Read pages 465-467 and then answer the following questions:

1. a. Which hemisphere plays the more important role in emotion?

   b. Within the cerebral hemispheres, what is the particular role of the following lobes in emotion?

   1. temporal and parietal lobes

   2. frontal lobe

2. a. Name and describe the kind of emotional responses to injury that characterizes patients with

   1. left hemisphere damage.

   2. right hemisphere damage.

b. Describe how the patient interviewed in the opening vignette reacted to his impairment.

c. Explain this patient's reaction by carefully describing the general roles of the right and left hemispheres in emotional behavior.

3. a. Within the right hemisphere there appears to be regional _____ for the _____ and _____ of emotional expressions.

b. Study Figure 13.10 in your text and list the kind of damage observed by Ross (1981) in patients with damage to

1. the posterior part of the right frontal cortex.

2. the right parietal and temporal cortex.

3. both regions.

4. a. To study the role of the right hemisphere in normal subjects, what did Ley and Bryden (1979) ask subjects to do?

b. Study Figure 13.11 in your text and describe how subjects performed when information was flashed directly to the

1. right hemisphere.

2. left hemisphere.

5. Briefly state the procedure and results of right hemisphere research by

a. Dimond and his colleagues.

b. Leventhal.

Read the interim summary on pages 470-471 of your text to reacquaint yourself with the material in this section.

13-10 *Describe the stress response, discuss the pervasiveness of stress in modern society, and explain techniques for handling stress.*

Read pages 468-470 and then answer the following questions:

1. a. Cannon has suggested that we have inherited a set of particular physiological responses to physical danger. Name and describe this ancient stress response.

b. Selye also studied physiological responses to physical danger. What name did he give to this reaction and which organ did he particularly study?

    c. Name the hormone produced by the pituitary gland in times of stress.

    d. What effect does this hormone have on the adrenal glands?

    e. What will happen if an animal whose adrenal glands have been removed is subjected to mild stress?

    f. In addition to helping the body ready itself for physical activity, what are some of the other effects of corticosterone?

2. According to Miller (1983), what are some of the direct consequences of long-term stress on health?

3. And what are some of the indirect implications of long-term stress on health?

4. Support your answers to questions 2 and 3 by citing evidence gathered by epidemiologists.

5. List the two major variables that affect the stress response.

    1.

    2.

6. Discuss some of the variables that can mitigate the effect of environmental factors.

7. a. Rats in the experiments by Weiss showed fewer signs of stress under which experimental conditions?

    1.

    2.

    b. Describe the conflict condition to which some rats were exposed.

    c. Compare the responses of the rats in earlier experiments with the responses of the rats in the conflict conditions.

8. Identify another environmental variable that affects the stress reaction.

9. a. What three factors did Cromwell and his colleagues (1977) identify as important for the recovery of

heart attack patients?

1.

2.

3.

b. How did information about their health affect patients who

1. participated actively in recovery?

2. did not participate actively in recovery?

3. initially were anxious?

4. were not anxious?

10. a. Name and describe the two personality types Friedman and Rosenman (1959) identified in a study of susceptibility to cardiovascular disease.

1.

2.

b. Which type may be more susceptible to cardiovascular disease?

c. What must be determined by future research into personality types?

11. According to the Center for Disease Control (1980) three behaviors contribute to 50 percent of the mortality from the 10 leading causes of death. Name them.

1.

2.

3.

Lesson II Self Test

1. The James-Lange theory states that

   a. emotion-producing situations elicit a set of behavioral and physiological responses.
   b. emotions are determined jointly by perception of physiological response and cognitive assessment of a situation.
   c. outward manifestations of emotions are accurate reflections of inner physiological responses.
   d. emotions cause behaviors.

2. Cannon criticized the James-Lange theory on the grounds that

a. the internal organs are relatively insensitive structures.
b. artificially induced physiological changes also cause subjects to experience emotions.
c. the strength of the response of internal organs varies too greatly to account for sustained emotions like rage and fear.
d. James and Lange had discounted the importance of muscular feedback.

3. While subjects made particular facial movements their physiological responses were being recorded. The results revealed that

a. simulated expressions did not alter physiological responses.
b. different facial movements produced somewhat different patterns of response.
c. patterns of response were unique to particular facial movements.
d. the recording procedure influenced the physiological response.

4. The Schachter theory states that

a. emotion-producing situations elicit an appropriate set of physiological responses.
b. emotions are determined jointly by perception of physiological responses and cognitive assessment of a situation.
c. emotions are determined jointly by cognitive assessment of a situation and internal feedback about other people's expressions.
d. emotions are self-reports based on self-analysis of internal physiological responses.

5. In the "suproxin" study

a. none of the subjects were told that the injections they received would produce side effects.
b. the confederate encouraged subjects to reply calmly to insulting questions.
c. adrenaline did not increase the intensity of the subjects' emotional states.
d. uninformed subjects reported feeling especially happy or angry after the testing session.

6. After Nisbett and Schachter (1966) explained the experiment and rationale to the subjects, they

a. recognized that they had gone through the process the researchers had explained.
b. insisted they had not experienced the process the researchers had explained.
c. were skeptical that any subjects would go through the process the researchers had explained.
d. urged the researchers to rethink the study because they had not experienced the process the researchers had explained.

7. Patients with right hemisphere damage

a. often show a catastrophic reaction.
b. do not show any impairment of judgment.
c. realistically accept physical limitations.
d. often show an indifference reaction.

8. Subjects were shown pictures of faces expressing various emotional states in such a way that the information went directly to either the right or left hemisphere.

a. When the right hemisphere was the direct recipient, subjects made more accurate judgments.
b. When the left hemisphere was the direct recipient, subjects made more accurate judgments.
c. The right hemisphere advantage is restricted to visually presented material.
d. The left hemisphere advantage is restricted to visually presented material.

9. Corticosterone

a. is secreted by the pituitary gland.
b. suppresses the body's immune system.
c. stimulates secretion of ACTH.
d. facilitates the body's ability to heal itself.

10. Heart attack patients who participated directly in their recovery and received

a. information about their illness reported feelings of anxiety.
b. no information about their illness reported feelings of helplessness.
c. information about their illness had an increased chance of recovery.
d. no information about their illness had an increased chance of recovery.

Answers for Self Tests

Lesson I		Lesson II	
1. c	Obj. 13-1	1. a	Obj. 13-7
2. a	Obj. 13-1	2. a	Obj. 13-7
3. b	Obj. 13-2	3. c	Obj. 13-7
4. d	Obj. 13-2	4. b	Obj. 13-8
5. b	Obj. 13-2	5. c	Obj. 13-8
6. a	Obj. 13-3	6. b	Obj. 13-8
7. b	Obj. 13-4	7. d	Obj. 13-9
8. a	Obj. 13-5	8. a	Obj. 13-9
9. c	Obj. 13-5	9. b	Obj. 13-10
10. d	Obj. 13-6	10. c	Obj. 13-10

13.1 adrenocorticotropic hormone (ACTH)	13.10 James-Lange theory
13.2 catastrophic reaction	13.11 leakage
13.3 corticosterone	13.12 masking
13.4 display rule	13.13 modulation
13.5 emblem	13.14 mood
13.6 emotion	13.15 regulator
13.7 flight-or-fight reaction	13.16 simulation
13.8 illustrator	13.17 stress response
13.9 indifference reaction	13.18 temperament

13.10 Theory of emotion; feelings of emotions are caused by the awareness of behaviors and physiological reactions caused by important stimuli.	13.1 Hormone secreted by pituitary gland at times of stress; stimulates adrenal glands to produce corticosterone
13.11 Expression of true feeling of emotion despite attempt to hide it.	13.2 severe anxiety and depression following damage to left hemisphere; response to awareness of neurological deficits.
13.12 Attempt to hide an emotion.	13.3 Hormone secreted by adrenal gland; stimulated by ACTH secretion; helps body prepare for intense physical activity; suppresses the immune system and impairs ability of body to heal itself.
13.13 Attempt to exaggerate or minimize the overt expression of emotion.	13.4 Learned patterns that modify facial expression of emotion; usually culturally determined.
13.14 Subjective affective feelings; longer-lived and weaker than emotion	13.5 Facial expressions that convey a specific meaning within a given culture; may be mistaken by members of other cultures as expression of emotion.
13.15 Facial movements used to control give-and-take in conversations.	13.6 Relatively brief subjective feelings elicited by situations that are personally significant.
13.16 Attempt to express an unfelt emotion.	13.7 Response to dangerous circumstances; hormonal secretions and changes in autonomic nervous system that prepare body for vigorous physical activity.
13.17 According to Selye, response pattern of the autonomic nervous system and endocrine system to dangerous or harmful stimuli.	13.8 Facial movements used to emphasize words or phrases.
13.18 A person's general disposition or typical pattern of affective reaction.	13.9 Nonchalance associated with damage to right hemisphere; caused by damage to neural circuits involved in emotion.

13.19

type A pattern

13.20

type B pattern

13.19

Personality pattern characterized by excessive competitive drive, impatience, hostility, fast movements, and rapid speech.

13.20

Personality pattern characterized by less competitive nature, general tolerance, patience, slower movements and speech.

Chapter 14
Social Cognition

Lesson I

Read the interim summary on pages 481-482 of your text to reacquaint yourself with the material in this section.

14-1 *Describe the basic principles of attributional theory.*

Read pages 474-477 and then answer the following questions:

1. a. In what way do we benefit from our ability to learn what to expect from particular people in particular situations?

   b. Define *attribution* and *implicit psychology* in your own words and explain their role in our daily lives.

   c. What is a detrimental consequence of our use of implicit psychology?

2. a. Explain the *covariance method* in your own words.

   b. "Lucia is usually cheerful and relaxed, but when her husband is out of town she tends to worry," one of her friends commented. Use the covariance method to determine the cause of Lucia's behavior.

   c. Define *situational factors* and *dispositional factors* in your own words.

3. a. Under what circumstances do we *discount* someone's behavior?

   b. 1. Suppose that as you are standing in the check-out line of a crowded grocery store you notice that an elderly woman in the next line looks ill. She says to the man in front of her, "I'm not feeling very well, would you mind if I went ahead of you?" "Of course not," the man replies. Would you attribute the man's behavior to dispositional factors? Explain your answer.

2. What if the man had said, "I'm sorry, but I want to get home and watch the football game"?

4. According to Kelley, we decide whether the behavior of other people is due to external, or _____, causes or internal, or _____, causes on the basis of _____, _____, and _____.

5. a. Carefully explain the standards of *consensus*, *consistency* and *distinctiveness* and say how they are used to determine whether behavior is caused by situational or dispositional causes.

   b. Would you attribute the behavior of the people in the following situations to situational or dispositional factors. Explain the basis--consensus, consistency or distinctiveness--of your decision.

      1. William's violin teacher was not surprised that he was unprepared for his weekly lesson, because he is usually ill-prepared.

      2. Nicholas looked nervously at all the cutlery around his plate. When everyone else picked up a small fork to use for the appetizer, he did so, too.

      3. "I don't like the language Peter has picked up from his summer job." Mrs. Lindsey told her husband. "He never spoke like that until he started working."

      4. "Marcy, you have been never been late to school before, but this month you have already been late eight times. Can you tell me what's been going on?" the guidance counselor asked.

14-2 *Describe the common attributional biases and research on their causes.*

Read pages 477-481 and then answer the following questions:

1. a. When the *fundamental attributional error* affects our judgments about the behavior of others, what factors do we tend to overestimate? underestimate?

   b. After playing a contrived "quiz game", subjects rated their own and their opponents level of general knowledge. What factors influenced these judgments when subjects served as questioners? as contestants? (Study Table 14.1 in your text.)

   c. Under what circumstances is a person *least* likely to make the fundamental attributional error?

   d. Study Figure 14.1 in your text, and describe the experimental procedure Storms (1973) used. Be sure to explain why a dummy camera was part of the equipment.

e. When subjects, who had seen videotapes of themselves, were asked to attribute their own behavior to either situational or dispositional factors, which factors had the strongest influence on their judgment? (See Figure 14.2 in your text.)

2. Carefully outline two explanations for the fact that we make the fundamental attributional error when we observe the behavior of others and not when we view our own behavior.

3. a. Explain the *error of false consensus* in your own words.

   b. Explain why students who either agreed or refused to walk around campus wearing sandwich boards gave equally high estimates of the number of their friends who would make the same choice.

4. a. Explain the *credit for success, blame for failure* motivational bias in your own words.

   b. How did "teachers" in an experiment conducted by Johnson et al., (1964) explain student scores on a math tests?

   c. In a similar study by Beckman (1970), how did observers' judgments differ from the "teachers?" What do these results suggest about the way personal involvement affects judgment?

   d. How did more information affect the judgment of subjects in a realistic teacher-student situation? (Ross et al., 1974)

5. a. Explain how attributional judgments are affected by the bias of *motivational relevance*.

   b. According to Harvard undergraduates, why did the person of higher status comply with their requests? the person of lower status? (Thibaut and Riecken, 1955)

6. a. Explain the false belief in *personal causation* in your own words.

   b. Why did people who had selected a lottery ticket place a higher price on it than people who had been given a ticket? (Langer, 1975)

   c. Offer a possible explanation for the basis of this belief.

Read the interim summary on pages 495-496 of your text to reacquaint yourself with the material in this section.

14-3 *Discuss the formation of the affective, cognitive, and behavioral components of attitudes.*

Read pages 482-484 and then answer the following questions:

1. Briefly define these components of attitude.

    a. *affective component*

    b. *cognitive component*

    c. *behavioral component*

2. Explain two means by which affective components of attitude develop and are transmitted.

    1.

    2.

3. Explain how children acquire the cognitive components of attitudes and beliefs through *modeling*.

4. a. How many times were LaPiere and a Chinese couple refused service on a cross-country trip? How did responses to a later letter contradict their experiences?

    b. What did this study seem to indicate about the relation between the cognitive and behavioral components of an attitude?

5. Summarize research on the variables that affect the behavioral components of attitudes:

    a. How does the *degree of specificity* affect predictions about behavior?

    b. Study Table 14.2 in your text and identify the best predictor of membership or volunteer service in the Sierra Club and explain why.

    c. Describe research Sivacek and Crano (1982) that demonstrated the importance of *motivational relevance*.

    d. Most parents agreed it would be thoughtful to do something for the teachers at the end of the school year. However, few volunteered to serve on a committee to sponsor an appreciation luncheon. Offer two explanations, one based on the degree of specificity and the other on the motivational relevance, to explain the behavior of the parents.

    e. An attitude formed through _____ - _____ is an _____ predictor of behavior.

f. How did the opportunity to play with puzzles affect ratings of personal interest in puzzles and "free time" activity? Why?

g. Briefly explain how circumstances may affect the performance of a behavior that someone rates as desirable.

6. Decide whether the following situations illustrate an (A) affective, (B) behavioral, or (C) cognitive component of attitude.

_____ Meg recently told a friend, "When I was little I always thought Mrs. Zinn was abrupt and unfriendly. Later I learned she was in almost constant pain from arthritis, but I still don't like to be the one to answer the phone if she is calling."

_____ "You shouldn't tell ethnic jokes like that," Herb told Mickey firmly. "Why not? Those people are idiots--they deserve all the ridicule they get," Mickey retorted.

_____ "Our teacher has been telling us a lot about what its like to be vegetarian. He thinks its much healthier than eating meat. I've been thinking a lot about becoming a vegetarian, too," thirteen-year-old Ralph told his mother.

_____ "We'll be moving away this summer, so I don't think we'll get involved in building the new playground, even though we certainly think it is a worthwhile project."

14-4 *Describe Festinger's theory of cognitive dissonance and discuss how and why induced compliance affects a person's attitude.*

Read pages 484-486and then answer the following questions:

1. a. Festinger's theory of _____ _____ is an attempt to explain the effect of discrepancies between attitudes, behaviors, and self-images on _____ formation.

    b. Explain the feeling produced by *cognitive dissonance* in your own words. Describe some of the situations that can produce it.

    c. Explain how people can achieve *dissonance reduction*. Be sure to define the term *consonant elements*.

        1.

        2.

        3.

2. Which strategy is the candidate in the following examples using to reduce the dissonance between his self-image and his election loss?

    a. "We just weren't able to raise as much money as my opponent."

b. "It doesn't really matter that much. There are a lot of other ways to be active in county government."

c. "I think if we start earlier and work harder to get out the vote on election day, we can win next time."

3. a. According to dissonance theory, how does induced compliance affect attitudes?

b. In these situations, what causes dissonance?

4. a. Study Figure 14.3 in your text and using dissonance theory, explain why poorly paid subjects rated working with spools on a tray a more interesting task than well paid subjects?

b. Explain why Steele and Liu (1981) asked subjects to write essays against funding for handicapped facilities? What opportunity did they later offer some of the subjects?

c. What effects did this opportunity have on the attitudes of these subjects?

5. a. What is the physiological effect of induced compliance?

b. Why is this finding important to dissonance theory?

c. Describe the task Croyle and Cooper (1983) used to produce various levels cognitive dissonance. Then study Figure 14.4 in your text and describe and explain the results.

d. Cite research that suggests physiological arousal that results from dissonance is necessary for attitude change.

e. What is a possible explanation for alcoholism? (Steele et al., 1981)

14-5 *Describe the role of conflict resolution and expenditures on attitude change and discuss Bem's theory of self-perception.*

Read pages 486-490 and then answer the following questions:

1. According to dissonance theory, how does decision making affect attitudes? Under what conditions is the effect the strongest?

2. a. According to dissonance theory, which items do we tend to value most highly, designer running shoes or

discount running shoes? Why?

b. Study Figure 14.5 in your text. How did the degree of embarrassment that subjects experienced affected their ratings of a very dull conversation? Explain why the results are consistent with dissonance theory.

c. What did later questioning of some subjects appear to indicate about the consciousness of attitude formation?

3. a. Restate the *self-perception theory* in your own words.

b. How do people make judgments about their own or someone else's behavior or attitudes?

c. Under what circumstances is an analysis of the situation insufficient to determine the cause of an event?

4. How does the self-perception theory explain the task ratings of poorly paid subjects?

5. What is an advantage of the self-perception theory?

Lesson I Self Test

1. Implicit psychological theories

   a. are unbiased assessments of the causes of behavior.
   b. are based on group consensus.
   c. tend not to be revised in the light of contradictory evidence.
   d. tend to overestimate dispositional factors.

2. John was a bit drunk and was laughing uproariously at his own jokes--but then, so was everyone else at the party. An attribution about the causes of John's behavior would be based on

   a. consensus.
   b. consistency.
   c. distinctiveness.
   d. heuristics.

3. We make the fundamental attributional error

   a. most often when we explain the causes of our own behavior.
   b. by overestimating the significance of dispositional factors and underestimating situational factors.
   c. by underestimating the importance of distinctive behavior.

d. when we rely more on the observations of others and less on our own.

4. Mrs. Norton liked to buy goods at home demonstration parties, and assumed that everyone did. She was disappointed by the poor sales at a party she hosted. Mrs. Norton made the error of

   a. credit for success.
   b. false consensus.
   c. motivational relevance.
   d. the illusion of personal causation.

5. Like his parents, John never buys anything from door-to-door sales representatives. John has acquired his behavior through

   a. direct classical conditioning.
   b. vicarious classical conditioning.
   c. modeling.
   d. compliance.

6. Attitudes consist of three different components:

   a. dispositional, intuitional, and situational.
   b. covariance method, direct classical conditioning, vicarious classical conditioning.
   c. consensus, consistency, and distinctiveness.
   d. affective, behavioral, and cognitive.

7. Dissonance theory predicts that

   a. dissonance reduction is motivated by an aversive drive.
   b. self-confident people experience the least dissonance.
   c. people habituate to mild physiological arousal.
   d. attitudes, but not behaviors, are resistant to coercion.

8. An experiment in which students wrote essays supporting or opposing alcohol use at Princeton supported Festinger's theory because

   a. subjects showed a preference for talking together to obtain a consensus before writing the essay.
   b. researchers obtained physiological evidence of arousal.
   c. the greater the motivational relevance of the issue the more compelling the essays.
   d. subjects who were paid the least showed the greatest attitude change.

9. Female subjects who were embarrassed the most later

   a. refused to tell prospective subjects the conversation was interesting.
   b. offered the clearest explanation of their ratings.
   c. rated the discussion as the most interesting.
   d. made the fewest comments during the conversation.

10. An advantage of Bem's self-perception theory is that

   a. all attributions about behavior are based on situational rather than dispositional factors.
   b. it is based on principles of classical conditioning.
   c. it does not depend on a motivating aversive drive.
   d. it offers the best explanation of inconsistent behavior.

Lesson II

14-6 *Describe the role played by the characteristics of the communicator and the message in the process of persuasion.*

Read pages 490-493 and then answer the following questions:

1. a. Define *persuasion* in your own words.

    b. List some of the variables that affect this process.

2. What are the three most important factors that affect the communicator's ability to persuade others?

    1.

    2.

    3.

3. a. Briefly describe the experimental procedure that Aronson et al. (1963) used to study the effect of poetry interpretations by "experts" on subjects' interpretation of poetry.

    b. Study Figure 14.7 in your text and identify the group with the largest and smallest opinion shift. Explain the results.

4. a. Under what circumstances do we tend to disregard someone's opinion about a product?

    b. How do advertisers attempt to minimize our suspicions?

    c. Which group of married female college students disregarded the speakers' conclusions that student husbands should spend more time at home? Explain the results.

5. a. Who is likely to be more successful at persuading someone--an attractive or an unattractive person?

    b. Explain why attractiveness is related to persuasiveness.

6. Under what circumstances do people pay more attention to the likability of the persuader? to the arguments that the persuader makes?

7. List the three characteristics of messages that affect their persuasiveness.

   1.   3.

   2.

8. Under what circumstances is it best to attempt to persuade someone with

   a. less emphasis on the arguments?

   b. careful arguments?

   c. one-side arguments?

   d. arguments on both sides on an issue?

9. a. Describe two ways that repetition affects persuasion.

   1.   2.

   b. Use the effects of repetition to explain why subjects preferred

      1. reversed pictures of themselves and unreversed pictures of their friends. (See Figure 14.8 in your text.)

      2. frequently used words and grew to like frequently presented nonwords.

   c. Identify two other factors that affect the effectiveness of repetition.

      1.   2.

10. a. List three factors that influence the effectiveness of fear-producing methods of persuasion. (Rogers, 1975)

      1.

      2.

      3.

    b. Why are specific recommendations especially effective when they are presented in a fear-inducing message?

14-7 *Describe the role played by the characteristics of the recipient in the process of persuasion, describe the effects of supportive and refutational defenses against persuasion, and explain the phenomenon of impression management.*

Read pages 493-495 and then answer the following questions:

1. a. How does the recipient's expertise affect persuasive attempts made by experts and nonexperts?

    b. If the recipient does not have any special knowledge about the topic of a persuasive message, how does the recipient's self-esteem influence its effect?

    c. What is the best way to attempt to persuade an intelligent recipient?

2. a. Explain *supportive defense* and *refutational defense* in your own words.

    b. Under what circumstances is a refutational defense most effective?

3. a. When people change their attitudes in order to make a more favorable impression on others, the phenomenon is called _____ _____.

    b. If you observe someone change their attitudes, under what circumstances are you likely to rate the person positively? negatively?

    c. Under what circumstances is the person who has changed attitudes likely to admit to having done so?

4. a. Briefly describe the four experimental conditions of the experiment by Braver et al., 1977.

    b. Study Figure 14.9 in your text and identify the situation in which subjects made the greatest shift in opinion. What is the most likely explanation?

Read the interim summary on page 500 of your text to reacquaint yourself with the material in this section.

14-8 *Describe research on the origins of prejudice and some of its damaging consequences, and reasons for hope for change.*

Read pages 496-500 and then answer the following questions:

1. a. Define and carefully distinguish between a *prejudice* and a *stereotype*.

    b. Define *discrimination* in your own words.

2. a. Briefly recount the experiences of the "Rattlers" and the "Eagles." What do the findings of this experiment suggest is an important factor in the development of prejudice?

Chapter 14

b. What are some of the desires that motivate competition? In general, what is the social status of people who are motivated by a need to increase their self-esteem?

c. Describe how Meindl and Lerner (1985) manipulated the self-esteem of subjects. How did English-speaking Canadians whose self-esteem had been threatened then rate French-speaking Canadians?

3. a. Explain how the use of the representativeness heuristic contributes to prejudice.

b. What kind of adjectives did subjects associate with the words "black" and "white?" What do these associations suggest about the kinds of characteristics associated with racial groups?

c. Explain how the use of the availability heuristic contributes to the *illusory correlation*.

d. Mrs. Devlin, who lived near the college, was frequently disturbed by loud music coming from the dormitories. She was often heard to comment, "College students are so thoughtless." Explain Mrs. Devlin's attitude as an example of the *illusion of out-group homogeneity*.

4. a. List three serious consequences of prejudice.

1.

2.

3.

b. Explain a *self-fulfilling prophecy* in your own words.

5. Snyder et al., 1977 asked male subjects to have a phone conversation with females. The men were shown a photograph of either attractive or unattractive woman who was identified as their partner.

a. How did men talk to women they thought were unattractive? attractive? How did women respond to men who thought they were attractive? How were the women's reactions verified?

b. Explain the results as an example of the self-fulfilling prophecy.

6. Summarize research on how prejudices are perpetuated:

a. What are some of the excuses used to explain behavior contradictory to a stereotype? (Miller and Turnbull, 1986)

b. How did subjects react to friendly partners who subjects had expected to be unfriendly? (Ickes et al., 1982)

7. a. Explain how prejudices perpetuate exploitation of one group by another. Why is this kind of prejudice especially resistant to change?

b. What is the best way to minimize prejudice that results from inadvertent stereotypes and preconceptions?

c. In what specific ways did school children, who had received training about some of the difficulties of the handicapped, show changes in their attitudes? (Langer et al., 1985)

Lesson II Self Test

1. Advertisers often quote from unsolicited letters praising their product because potential customers tend to believe the writer is

   a. an expert.
   b. not motivated by greed.
   c. attractive.
   d. persuasive.

2. A one-sided presentation is most effective when the audience

   a. favors the communicator's viewpoint to some degree.
   b. disagrees with the communicator viewpoint.
   c. is already familiar with the issues.
   d. has a limited time to make a decision.

3. A fear-inducing message is persuasive if it

   a. does not dwell on the most noxious aspects of the situation.
   b. suggests recipients develop their own solutions.
   c. makes specific recommendations to prevent aversive results.
   d. minimizes the likelihood the feared event will actually occur.

4. Repetition of a message is most effective if the message is

   a. brief.
   b. long.
   c. simple.
   d. complex.

5. A refutational defense is more effective than a supportive defense when the

   a. topic is complex.
   b. topic is simple.

   c. listener is well-informed.

   d. topic is a cultural truism.

6. Recipients with high self-esteem

   a. resent complex arguments because they prefer to develop arguments for themselves.

   b. are less resistant to persuasion.

   c. find complex arguments more persuasive.

   d. find simple arguments more persuasive.

7. Subjects seem more favorable to shortening the medical training of doctors when they were

   a. alone with the persuader.

   b. alone with the observer.

   c. all alone.

   d. with the persuader and the observer.

8. A prejudice is

   a. the treatment of people based on their membership in a particular group.

   b. a negative belief about the characteristics of members of particular groups.

   c. a positive or negative belief about the characteristics of members of particular groups.

   d. an attitude toward a group of people defined by the racial, religious, ethnic or occupational background.

9. Which is the most accurate statement about prejudice?

   a. The tendency to affiliate with a group is accompanied by the tendency to be suspicious of others.

   b. Competition is the cause of all prejudice.

   c. The increased use of heuristics would decrease errors in judgment about people.

   d. We are more likely to form prejudices about people who are similar to ourselves.

10. What is an effective way to change prejudicial attitudes?

   a. Point out that prejudices are harmful to other members of society.

   b. Explain that prejudices are based on misinterpretations and misperceptions.

   c. Teach people to think of members of other groups as individuals.

   d. Present statistics that refute unfair charges against minority groups.

Answers for Self Tests

Lesson I			Lesson II		
1.	d	Obj. 14-1	1.	b	Obj. 14-6
2.	a	Obj. 14-1	2.	a	Obj. 14-6
3.	b	Obj. 14-2	3.	c	Obj. 14-6
4.	b	Obj. 14-2	4.	d	Obj. 14-7
5.	c	Obj. 14-3	5.	d	Obj. 14-7
6.	d	Obj. 14-3	6.	c	Obj. 14-7
7.	a	Obj. 14-4	7.	a	Obj. 14-7
8.	b	Obj. 14-4	8.	d	Obj. 14-8
9.	c	Obj. 14-5	9.	a	Obj. 14-8
10.	c	Obj. 14-5	10.	c	Obj. 14-8

14.1 attribution	14.10 distinctiveness
14.2 cognitive dissonance	14.11 false consensus
14.3 consensual behavior	14.12 fundamental attributional error
14.4 consistency	14.13 illusion of out-group homogeneity
14.5 covariance method	14.14 illusory correlation
14.6 discounting	14.15 implicit psychology
14.7 discrimination	14.16 impression management
14.8 dispositional factor	14.17 modeling
14.9 dissonance reduction	14.18 personal causation

14.10 The occurrence of a behavior by a person only in a particular situation; leads to attribution of external causes.	14.1 The process by which people infer the causes of other people's behavior.
14.11 An attributional error; the tendency to believe that one's own behavior represents the general consensus and that different behaviors are deviant.	14.2 An unpleasant state of tension resulting from a discrepancy between a person's behavior and self-image or one attitude and another.
14.12 The tendency to overestimate the significance of dispositional factors and underestimate the significance of situation factors in controlling the behavior of other people; the source of many other attributional errors.	14.3 Behavior shared by a large number of people; usually attributed to external causes.
14.13 The false belief that other groups are much more homogeneous than one's own; contributes to prejudice.	14.4 The regular occurrence of a behavior by a person; leads to attribution of internal causes.
14.14 The tendency to see a relationship between two distinctive elements that does not actually exist; e.g., to conclude that minority groups commit a greater number of violent crimes because they are more distinctive.	14.5 A method of determining the cause of behavior or natural phenomena by observing which events occur together or vary together.
14.15 A set of inferences (attributions) that people make in everyday life about the causes of other people's behavior, including predictions of what they are likely to do.	14.6 The tendency, when making attributions about the cause of behavior, to give little significance to behavior that would be expected of most people in a particular situation.
14.16 Altering one's behavior in an attempt to make oneself appear in a more favorable light.	14.7 Treating people differently because of their membership in a particular group.
14.17 A way of forming attitudes by observing and imitating the attitudes of people who play an important roles in one's life.	14.8 Individual personality characteristics that affect a person's behavior.
14.18 The false belief that one's actions will have an affect on later events even when these events cannot possibly be related to one's own behavior.	14.9 Motivation to perform behaviors that reduce aversive states of dissonance; accomplished through reducing the importance or changing one of the dissonant elements or adding consonant elements.

14.19

prejudice

14.20

refutational defense

14.21

self-attribution

14.22

self-fulfilling prophecy

14.23

self-perception theory

14.24

situational factor

14.25

social cognition

14.26

stereotype

14.27

supportive defense

14.19

A negative attitude toward a group of people defined by distinctive features such as race, religion, sexual orientation, or occupation.

14.20

A form of argumentation used to persuade people to change their opinions; the communicator first presents arguments opposing an issue and then offers counterarguments to refute them.

14.21

Determining one's own attitudes by observing one's own behavior.

14.22

The tendency for the members of a particular group who are subjected to prejudice to adopt the characteristics that are attributed to them.

14.23

According to Bem, many attitudes are based on self-observation and examination of the situation for clues to the causes of behavior, such as probable reinforcers and punishers.

14.24

Stimuli in the environment that affect a person's behavior.

14.25

The study of the ways people interpret and use information about the attitudes and behavior of others.

14.26

A positive or negative belief about the characteristics of a particular group that are generally accepted in a particular culture.

14.27

A form of argumentation used in an attempt to persuade people to change their opinions; the communicator only presents arguments in favor of an issue.

Chapter 15
Social Interaction

Lesson I

Read the interim summary on pages 517-518 of your text to reacquaint yourself with the material in this section.

15-1 *Describe research on the nature and effects of conformity and the conditions that facilitate or inhibit bystander intervention.*

Read pages 504-508 and then answer the following questions:

1. Give several examples of beneficial social conventions.

2. Outline research by Asch (1951) on group conformity:

   a. Briefly describe the

      1. task. (See Figure 15.1 in your text.)

      2. group composition.

      3. seating arrangement and its significance.

      4. results.

      5. subjects' reasons for their responses.

   b. What do the results suggest about the strength of the tendency to conform (the Asch effect)?

3. Briefly describe research that used the tendency to conform to encourage subjects

   a. to review pamphlets. (Schofield, 1975)

   b. to laugh more during television shows despite the content or the subjects' personal opinion. (Fuller et al., 1974)

4. According to Baron and Byrne (1987), what are the two primary reasons for conformity?

5. a. Following the death of Kitty Genovese, what explanation was given for the indifference of the bystanders?

   b. Define *bystander intervention* in your own words.

   c. Briefly describe how Darley and Latané (1968) used a staged seizure to study bystander intervention.

   d. Study Figure 15.2 in your text and identify the circumstances in which subjects responded and failed to respond to the "seizure?"

   e. From talking with subjects who did not respond, what did the researchers conclude were some of the reasons for the subjects' behavior?

6. Describe and explain some of the conditions that

   a. deter people from intervening. (Cialdini, 1984)

   b. encourage people to intervene. (Clark and Word, 1972, 1974; Shotland and Heinold, 1985)

15-2 *Describe research on situations that require reciprocity: returning favors, atoning for causing harm, and making reciprocal concessions.*

Read pages 508-510 and then answer the following questions:

1. a. Define *reciprocity* in your own words.

   b. Give several examples of social situations in which one party will feel the need to make a reciprocal gesture.

   c. Under what circumstances will a person avoid a social situation that will require a reciprocal gesture later?

   d. Explain the relation between reciprocity and trade.

2. Summarize research on the strength of reciprocity in social interactions:

   a. In an experiment by Regan (1971) some subjects were given a soft drink by the confederate or experimenter and others were not. Study Figure 15.3 in your text and describe the conditions that led subjects to purchase raffle tickets.

   b. What do the results suggest about the phenomenon of reciprocity?

3. Explain why companies frequently offer free samples.

4. Use the concept of reciprocity to explain why more teachers who had "shocked" learners complied with a request from the learner after the experiment. (Carlsmith and Gross, 1969)

5. a. Explain the concept of reciprocal concessions in your own words.

   b. Explain why demands at the start of contract negotiations are usually excessive.

   c. Use the concept of reciprocal concessions to explain why more subject in the high-low group agree to donate blood than students in the low-only group. (Cialdini and Ascani, 1976)

6. What concepts are illustrated by the following situations?

   _____ "Would you like a taste of our new frozen yogurt?"

   _____ Everyone thought he was drunk, and he died on the sidewalk.

   _____ "Mom, please don't put tofu in my lunch anymore. No one brings that kind of food to school."

   _____ The citation read in part, "For your prompt action that saved the life of . . . ."

   _____ "I'd like to have a dinner party for everyone who helped my family while I was in the hospital."

   _____ "Christopher's mother said he was hurt that you did not invite him to your birthday party. I think you should ask him if he would like to go to the movies with you on Saturday."

   Choices:
   a. conformity
   b. failure to intervene
   c. reciprocity
   d. bystander intervention
   e. atoning for causing harm

15-3 *Describe research on the effects of making a commitment.*

Read pages 510-512 and then answer the following questions:

1. How did making a bet on a horse affect a person's confidence in his or her choice? (Knox and Inkster, 1968)

2. Over 55 percent of homeowners, who had previously accepted a small sign, later agreed to display a huge sign in front of their homes. However, less than 20 percent of homeowners who had not been previously contacted agreed to display the huge sign. Refer to the *foot-in-the-door technique* to explain the response of each group.

3. Describe legislation that allows people to break a commitment made under pressure as well as a sales technique designed to combat the legislation.

4. How do salespeople using the *low-balling technique* get people to make a commitment?

5. Summarize some of the reasons why making a commitment strengthens compliance:

   a. How may commitment affect self-image?

   b. Study Figure 15.4 in your text and identify the subjects who volunteered the highest number of hours and rated volunteering least unpleasant. What caused this effect?

15-4   *Explain research on the compliance with the requests of attractive people and authority figures.*

Read pages 512-513 and then answer the following questions:

1. a. What was the response of Canadians voters who were asked whether the attractiveness of a candidate influenced their decision to vote for that candidate?

   b. What are two possible reasons for their denial?

2. How did mock jury awards to attractive plaintiffs compare with awards to unattractive plaintiffs?

3. a. Describe research that confirms that attractive models can affect people's judgments about products and then explain why this effect occurs. (Smith and Engel, 1968)

   b. Explain why is it easier for attractive people to get others to comply with a request.

   c. How do sports fans demonstrate the need to belong to a select group?

4. a. In general, how do we respond to the request of authority figures? Cite research to support your answer. (Cohen and Davis, 1981)

   b. Study Figure 15.5 in your text and state the relationship between estimated height and status. Explain what these estimates suggest about people's perception of authority figures.

5. a. Study Figures 15.6 and 15.7 in your text and describe the experimental procedure Milgram (1963) used to study obedience to authority.

   b. Study Figure 15.8 in your text and state the percentage of subjects who delivered what they believed to be a 450 volt shock to the "learner."

   c. How was the experimental procedure changed in later research? Under these conditions, what percentage of subjects shocked the learner?

   d. What do these results suggest about the tendency to obey authority figures?

   e. Explain why people found these results surprising. (Ross, 1977)

15-5 *Describe research on reactance and on the situations in which people act automatically or carefully consider relevant evidence.*

Read pages 515-517 and then answer the following questions:

1. a. Define the phenomenon of *psychological reactance* in your own words.

   b. Use this phenomenon to explain the reaction of Miami women to a ban on phosphate detergents.

2. a. Describe the experimental procedure Brehm and Weintraub (1977) used to study reactance in two-year-olds.

   b. Study Figure 15.9 in your text and describe how the barrier height affected boys' behavior.

   c. How did barrier height affect girls' behavior?

   d. How do some researchers explain the different reactions of boys and girls?

3. a. What may be the role of self-esteem in psychological reactance?

b. What evidence suggests that self-esteem is not the only cause of psychological reactance?

4. a. In what ways is the tendency to conform to social influences beneficial to our species? (Cialdini, 1984)

b. What is the best defense against harmful social influence?

5. a. Under what circumstances do people react rationally in response to social influences? (Petty and Cacioppo, 1981)

b. Describe the experimental procedure used by Petty et al. (1981) to study variables that affect a subject's response.

c. What were the results and conclusions of their study?

Lesson I Self Test

1. Subjects who were asked to estimate the length of lines went along with the group decision in spite of some doubts showed that

a. they misunderstood the instructions.
b. they found the other members of the group to be very attractive.
c. group pressure is a powerful force.
d. they did not want to disrupt the experiment.

2. A common reason that people fail to intervene in an emergency is that they

a. are indifferent.
b. fear ridicule.
c. prefer anonymity.
d. cannot atone for causing harm.

3. Companies that offer free samples are trying to

a. overcome bystander indifference.
b. encourage bystander intervention.
c. take advantage of the reciprocity rule.
d. atone for causing harm.

4. One of the best ways to get someone to do something is to

a. present a well-reasoned request.

b. threaten self-esteem by suggesting that someone else could do the task better.
c. take advantage of the desire to belong to a select group by suggesting only a few people have been asked.
d. make a large request and, when that is rejected, make a smaller request.

5. The *foot-in-the-door technique* is based on the knowledge that once people

a. make a commitment they are more likely to comply with other requests.
b. try a product they are reluctant to criticize it even if it is poor.
c. think a sales representative has sold a product to someone they know, they will find it difficult to refuse to make a purchase.
d. allow a sales representative into their home, they will find it difficult to refuse to make a purchase.

6. Commitment may increases compliance because

a. of changes to a person's self-image.
b. habits are difficult to break.
c. of the tendency to avoid the obligations of reciprocity.
d. of the tendency to avoid confrontation.

7. The majority of subjects in a series of experiments on obedience by Milgram (1963)

a. urged other subjects to shock the learner too.
b. repeatedly shocked the learner in spite of obvious signs of his distress.
c. asked the experimenter to confirm that the learner would not suffer permanent harm.
d. stopped shocking the learner at the first signs of his distress.

8. The reason most people find the results of Milgram's studies surprising is because of the tendency to

a. believe that most people do not wish to harm others.
b. overestimate empathy for others.
c. underestimate bystander indifference.
d. make the fundamental attributional error.

9. Psychological reactance

a. is a calculated, not automatic, response.
b. is unrelated to self-esteem.
c. occurs at a very early age.
d. is more common among females.

10. Responses that have become automatic through the influence of social variables are

a. almost always bad.
b. often the best and most efficient responses for most situations.
c. increase the likelihood of being manipulated.
d. learned through operant conditioning.

Lesson II

Read the interim summary on page 524 of your text to reacquaint yourself with the material in this section.

15-6   *Describe research on the effects of positive evaluation, similarity, physical appearance, and familiarity on interpersonal attraction.*

Read pages 518-522 and then answer the following questions:

1. a. The _____ of other people is the our most important source of _____ and
    _____ stimuli.

    b. Define interpersonal attraction in your own words.

2. Summarize research on the relationship between interpersonal attraction and the need to be evaluated positively:

    a. Study Figure 15.10 in your text. When subjects were asked to evaluate their feelings of attraction for a stranger, what factor affected their decisions the most? (Byrne and Rhamey, 1965)

    b. How did subjects who were ignored during a conversation evaluate the experience and themselves? (Geller et al., 1974)

    c. Briefly describe the experimental procedure used by Major et al., (1984).

    d. Study Figure 15.11 in your text and identify the group of students in this experiment who discounted their positive evaluation. Why did they do so?

3. a. We tend to choose mates and friends who have looks, attitudes and opinions that are _____ _____ our own.

    b. Explain why we make this choice and cite research to support your answer.

    c. Study the scatter plot in Figure 15.12 in your text and state the relationship between similarity in attitudes and ratings of attraction.

4. a. Explain why both men and women prefer physically attractive people.

    b. Briefly describe the experimental procedure and results of research by Walster et al. (1966) on the effects of physical appearance.

    c. Review how physical appearance affects our choice of a partner.

    d. In general, how do we rate the attitudes, personalities, marriages, and occupations of unfamiliar, but physically attractive, people? Explain why our evaluations based on a single factor tend to be accurate.

5. a. What is the most important variable that influences people's attraction to others who are not especially attractive?

b. How has the effect of exposure been documented by research on friendship patterns in apartments, suburban neighborhoods, and classrooms?

c. Study Figure 15.13 in your text and summarize the results of research by Saegert et al. (1973) on how the number of interactions among subjects during an experiment affected their attraction for each other.

15-7 *Describe research on the role of negative reinforcement on feelings of romantic love.*

Read pages 522-524 and then answer the following questions:

1. Why do some researchers believe love is qualitatively different from liking?

2. a. Describe the two conditions in which male college students were interviewed by an attractive female interviewer. (Dutton and Aron, 1974)

b. Describe how the responses of men interviewed on the wobbly suspension bridge differed from those made by men interviewed on the sturdy bridge.

c. Dutton and Aron explained the results by referring to attribution theory. Summarize their explanation.

d. Summarize a different explanation suggested by Kendrick and Cialdini (1977).

e. Describe other research by Dutton and Aron (1974) that supported Kendrick and Cialdini's assertion that the presence of another person does reduce aversive arousal.

f. How can the negative reinforcement hypothesis explain the stronger attachment of couples of different backgrounds?

Read the interim summary on page 529 of your text to reacquaint yourself with the material in this section.

15-8 *Define research on social facilitation and social loafing and the conditions under which each occurs.*

Read pages 524-526 and then answer the following questions:

1. Define *social facilitation* in your own words.

2. Compare the results of research by Triplett (1897) with that of other early investigators.

3. Summarize Zajonc's (1965) explanation of social facilitation. Be sure to refer to *arousal* and *dominant response* in your answer.

4. Describe the task and the results of research by Martens (1969), which tested Zajonc's explanation.

5. Subjects who had spent different amounts of time pronouncing some fictitious Turkish words were asked to guess which word was flashed on a screen. Study Figure 15.14 in your text and describe how the presence of an audience affected the kind of words subjects recalled. (Zajonc and Sales, 1966)

6. a. What factor influences how people respond in the presence of an audience?

   b. What modification did Cottrell et al. (1968) make to the procedure used by Zajonc and Sales? Describe and explain the results.

7. Define *social loafing* in your own words.

8. Now use this concept to explain why a tug-of-war team (Ringelmann) and a group of shouting subjects (Latané et al., 1979) made a smaller combined effort than the simple combination of individual efforts.

9. Summarize research on the factors that determine whether the presence of other people causes group facilitation or social loafing:

   a. What information did some subjects in a study using the shouting format (Williams et al. 1981) receive? Describe the results.

   b. Explain why identifiability deters social loafing.

   c. Which testing conditioning encouraged subjects to take the most responsibility for identifying a moving dot? (Harkins and Petty, 1982)

   d. Explain why *responsibility* deters social loafing.

10. Summarize research on the relevance of social loafing to situations outside the laboratory:

    a. Study Figure 15.15 in your text and identify the situation in which weak arguments will be the most effective.

b. Why is it difficult to maintain high quality control on assembly lines such as those at pickle factories? (Turner, 1978)

15-9 *Discuss some of the variables that affect decision making by groups.*

Read pages 526-529 and then answer the following questions:

1. a. What common belief about group decisions was challenged by research by Stoner?

   b. Briefly describe the experimental task, the surprising results, and Stoner's conclusions.

   c. Study Figure 15.16 in your text and determine the circumstances in which group opinion favors more or less risk taking.

   d. Describe how polarization affects decisions made by subjects pretending to be jurors and by people involved in collective bargaining.

2. List the two principal causes of group polarization.

   1.   2.

3. Cite research to support the notion that the social desirability of being better than average is well-established.

4. Outline Brown's hypothesis (1974) of how social comparison leads to group polarization.

5. a. Define the *autokinetic phenomenon* in your own words.

   b. What incorrect information about this phenomenon did Baron and Roper (1976) give some subjects but not others?

   c. Which group of subjects stated more extreme positions? What do the results suggest about the causes of group polarization?

6. a. How does the exchange of persuasive arguments contribute to group polarization?

b. Study Figure 15.17 in your test and identify the conditions in which subjects showed the greatest shift in attitude. (Ebbesen and Bowers, 1974)

c. What kind of arguments do people avoid presenting? How does this reluctance influence group polarization? (Vinokur and Burnstein, 1974)

Lesson II Self Test

1. We tend to disregard the positive evaluation of others if we

   a. are accustomed to being positively evaluated.
   b. find the other person physically unattractive.
   c. perceive the other person wants something from us.
   d. wish to avoid reciprocity.

2. People tend to choose

   a. partners who are about as physically attractive as they are.
   b. the most attractive partner they can.
   c. a less attractive partner to reduce the likelihood of rejection.
   d. a less attractive partner because they tend to have more interesting personalities.

3. For people who are not especially attractive or unattractive the most important variable that effects other people's attitudes toward them is

   a. intelligence.
   b. personality.
   c. exposure.
   d. occupation.

4. Men interviewed on a wobbly suspension bridge

   a. could not accurately identify the source of their arousal.
   b. found the female interviewer more attractive than men interviewed on sturdy bridge, and contacted her later.
   c. experienced embarrassing anxiety and avoided later contact with the woman.
   d. thought the purpose of the experiment was to measure response to stress.

5. A good explanation for the men's reaction is that the woman

   a. became a conditioned reinforcer because the presence of another person can reduce aversive arousal.
   b. was the source of heightened arousal.
   c. modeled acceptable behavior in times of stress.
   d. became an aversive stimulus that threatened their self-esteem.

6. The presence of others

   a. increases arousal.

b. inhibits the dominant response.
c. makes a simple task more difficult.
d. heightens fear of failure.

7. Although the fans urged their friends in the tug-of-war contest to do their best, research suggests that _____ will occur.

a. social facilitation.
b. social loafing.
c. induced compliance.
d. polarization.

8. Social loafing occurs

a. only when the task requires physical effort.
b. when people must work alone.
c. when the contingencies of reinforcement are present.
d. when individual contributions to the group effort are anonymous.

9. If the average opinion of the members of a group is moderately conservative, the final group opinion will be

a. less conservative.
b. moderately conservative.
c. more conservative.
d. the mean of the individual opinions.

10. The two principal causes of group polarization may be

a. identifiability and responsibility.
b. social comparison and exchange of persuasive arguments.
c. similarity and familiarity.
d. physical appearance and authority.

Answers for Self Tests

Lesson I

1. c Obj. 15-1
2. b Obj. 15-1
3. c Obj. 15-2
4. d Obj. 15-2
5. a Obj. 15-3
6. a Obj. 15-3
7. b Obj. 15-4
8. d Obj. 15-4
9. c Obj. 15-5
10. b Obj. 15-5

Lesson II

1. c Obj. 15-6
2. a Obj. 15-6
3. c Obj. 15-6
4. b Obj. 15-7
5. a Obj. 15-7
6. a Obj. 15-8
7. b Obj. 15-8
8. d Obj. 15-8
9. c Obj. 15-9
10. b Obj. 15-9

15.1

autokinetic phenomenon

15.2

bystander intervention

15.3

psychological reactance

15.4

reciprocity

15.5

social facilitation

15.6

social loafing

15.1

The tendency for people to perceive that a fixed point of light in a dark room moves slightly.

15.2

The helpful actions of people who witness a situation in which someone appears to need aid.

15.3

The tendency for people who perceive that their freedom of choice is being constrained to react in a way that affirms their ability to choose.

15.4

The tendency for people to pay back favors others have done for them.

15.5

The positive effect of the presence of other people on a person's performance.

15.6

The tendency for people working in groups in which they are not identifiable to make a smaller effort than they would make if they were working alone.

Chapter 16
Personality

Lesson I

Read the interim summary on pages 540-541 of your text to reacquaint yourself with the material in this section.

16-1 *Distinguish between personality types and traits and summarize the personality traits identified by Cattell, Eysenck, and the five-factor model.*

Read pages 532-538 and then answer the following questions:

1. What two kinds of efforts are required to study human personality?

2. a. The _____ _____ was the earliest explanation for personality _____.

   b. Study Figure 16.1 in your text and complete this table summarizing the humoral theory.

Personality Type	Predominant Humor	Characteristics
1.		
2.		
3.		
4.		

3. a. Define and distinguish between *personality types* and *personality traits*. (See Figure 16.2 in your text.)

   b. Why do most researchers prefer a classification system based on personality traits rather than personality types?

4. Allport suggested that personality traits were organized in a hierarchy. Name and give some examples of the most powerful and less powerful traits.

5. a. Describe Cattell's use of the method of factor analysis to identify personality factors or traits.

b. Study Figure 16.3 in your text and list some of the factors he identified.

6. a. Name and define the three factors that Eysenck identified through factor analysis. Make sure you identify both ends of each dimension.

b. See Table 16.1 and Figure 16.4 in your text and give some examples of questions that a neurotic individual would answer yes. What are some other likely characteristics of this individual?

c. Which two factors are considered the most important?

d. According to Eysenck and Eysenck (1985), what is the biological basis of extraversion-introversion?

e. See Figure 16.5 in your text and briefly explain an alternate set of pairings of Eysenck's three factors proposed by Gray (1970, 1987).

7. a. Name the five personality factors identified through a factor analysis of words related to personality. Define the unfamiliar factors, including both ends of each dimension.

b. What were the results of a factor analysis of adjectives from the California Q-Set? (See Table 16.2 in your text.)

16-2 *Describe the effects of heredity on personality characteristics and discuss the biological influences on personality.*

Read pages 538-540 and then answer the following questions:

1. a. Summarize the results of studies that compared the extraversion and neuroticism of fraternal and identical twins and twins reared apart and together.

b. What do these results suggest about the heritability of personality traits?

2. a. Summarize the results of studies that compared a large number of personality characteristics of fraternal and identical twins.

   b. What do most experts believe may account for the heritability of some personality characteristics?

   c. What kind of personality characteristics are influenced by environment rather than heredity?

3. a. What is known about neural circuits controlling approach and avoidance behaviors and changes in the autonomic nervous system? What causes these circuits to become active?

   b. In novel situations, what factor appears to influence an animal's tendency to approach a stimulus? Cite research with kittens to support your answer.

4. a. What question did Kagan et al. (1988) investigate? Describe the experimental groups especially the basis used to place subjects in a particular group. How long did testing continue?

   b. Describe the social and physiological responses of both groups in test situations.

   c. What do the results suggest about the biological basis of shyness?

Read the interim summary on page 546 of your text to reacquaint yourself with the material in this section.

16-3 *Describe the behaviorist and social learning approaches to personality and compare them with trait theories.*

Read pages 541-546 and then answer the following questions:

1. Skinner believes that if we wish to understand human behavior we must study a person's _____ to the environment rather than his or her _____ or _____ _____. This approach to the study of human behavior, which uses the principles of _____ _____ conditioning, is called _____ _____.

2. How would Skinner respond to the following questions?

   a. Does behaviorism ignore the person or self?

   b. Why do we make the responses that we do?

   c. What accounts for personality traits such as laziness?

d. What is the role of heredity?

3. Social learning theorists believe that _____ is the most important factor in personality development and that the most important experiences are _____ with other people. It makes use of _____ _____, which are not directly _____ and thus differs from Skinner's radical behaviorism.

4. a. Define *process rewards* and *content rewards* in your own words.

   b. Study Table 16.3 in your text and give several examples of both kinds of rewards, their opposite dimensions, and resulting personality traits. At what level are process rewards reinforcing? content rewards?

   c. What are the most important personality characteristics? (Mischel, 1973) What is the relation between these characteristics and perceptions, goals, and behaviors?

   d. Define *self concept* and *self-control* and these responses: *self-praise*, *self-criticism*, and *delay of gratification*.

   e. Explain Bandura's concept of self-efficacy.

5. Behaviorists believe that learning does not take place without _____ and social learning theorists believe that learning can take place through _____ or _____.

6. a. After watching an adult either in person or on television beat a Bobo doll, how did children later treat the Bobo? (See Figure 16.6 in your text.) By what means did they learn their responses?

   b. When the adult who beat the Bobo doll was rewarded or punished in the presence of the children, how did they then treat the Bobo?

   c. When this same group of children was offered a reward for imitating the adult's behavior, how did their behavior change? Now explain why their behavior changed.

7. a. What was Mischel's (1968, 1976) early view of the predictive value of stable personality traits?

   b. Define *cross-situational consistency* in your own words and explain how this concept tended to support Mischel's views.

c. Outline Epstein's (1977) two arguments that personality traits are actually more stable than previously believed.

d. Explain how Mischel (1977, 1979) has modified his views on the predictive value of personality traits and situations.

8. a. Describe evidence that personality traits and situations are not independent. (Bem and Allen, 1974)

b. How has this evidence changed the way psychologists now study the reasons for people's behavior?

Lesson I Self Test

1. Assertiveness is an example of

   a. a personality type.
   b. a personality trait.
   c. temperament.
   d. a cardinal trait..

2. Eysenck's personality theory is based on these three factors:

   a. self-praise, self-criticism, and self-control.
   b. stimuli, responses, and reinforcement.
   c. extraversion, neuroticism, and psychoticism.
   d. heredity, environment, and experience.

3. Eysenck and Gray

   a. agree that extraversion and introversion are bipolar opposites.
   b. agree that biological differences are important.
   c. disagree on the importance of each of the three factors.
   d. disagree on the value of factor analysis.

4. The five-factor model is based on

   a. the theoretical framework of Galen's four original temperaments.
   b. the cross-situational consistency of word use.
   c. a factor analysis of adjectives appearing in the California Q-Set.
   d. a factor analysis of the words used to describe differences in temperament.

5. Studies of the personality traits of identical twins found

   a. a correlation of more than .50 for the traits of neuroticism and extraversion.
   b. a high correlation only if the twins had been reared together.
   c. that all personality characteristics are influenced to a high degree by heredity.

    d. that personality traits could not be accurately assessed until adolescence.

6. Whether or not an animal approaches a novel stimulus may be influenced by

    a. past experiences with the stimulus.
    b. differences in temperament.
    c. species-typical responses.
    d. its innate ability to learn.

7. The results of a study that attempted to assess the biological basis of shyness found that

    a. children outgrow their shyness around 7.5 years of age.
    b. no correlation exists between physiological responses and behavioral responses
    c. shyness is an enduring personality trait.
    d. there are structural differences in the brains of the shy and nonshy children.

8. Skinner believes that

    a. we must study a person's responses to the environment in order to understand human behavior.
    b. heredity does not influence enduring personality traits.
    c. superstitious behavior is culturally determined.
    d. conditioned reinforcers must be closely linked to primary reinforcers.

9. Social learning theorists believe that

    a. learning takes place through reinforcement and observation.
    b. enduring personality traits have a stronger influence on behavior than environment.
    c. social rewards are reinforcing at high levels.
    d. self-discovery is the most important learning experience.

10. Children who beat the Bobo doll

    a. had a high need to demonstrate authority.
    b. might be termed "bold" children with highly excitable neural circuits.
    c. had seen a film of other children beating the Bobo.
    d. learned their aggressive behavior through observation.

Lesson II

Read the interim summary on page 555 of your text to reacquaint yourself with the material in this section.

16-4 *Describe how Freud's training influenced his psychodynamic theory of personality development and explain the structures of the mind and defense mechanisms that he hypothesized.*

Read pages 546-550 and then answer the following questions:

1. Explain how Freud's early training with

    a. von Brücke influenced his approach to research.

    b. Charcot influenced his thinking about the sources of problems of the mind.

2. Briefly summarize the case of Anna O. as it was originally presented by Freud and Breuer and the new evidence that challenges their description. Does this information invalidate psychoanalysis?

3. Outline the structures and functions of the mind as conceived by Freud. Be sure to pay careful attention to the terms he introduced to the language:

    a. What are the names and functions of the major structures of the mind?

        1.

        2.

        3.

    b. What is the function of the *reality principle*?

    c. What are the names and functions of the divisions of the *superego*?

    d. What are the two primary drives? What holds them in check?

    e. What conflict is resolved through *compromise formation*? Be sure to mention Freudian slips in your answer.

    f. Compare the manifest content of a dream with its latent content. What purpose do these separate forms serve?

4. Summarize the Freudian defense mechanisms:

    a. Which structure of the mind contains the *defense mechanisms*? When are they needed?

    b. Briefly explain each of these defense mechanisms.

        1. *repression*

        2. *reaction formation*

        3. *projection*

        4. *sublimation*

        5. *rationalization*

        6. *conversion*

16-5 *Explain Freud's psychodynamic theory of personality, how it influenced the theories of Jung, Adler, and Erikson, and discuss modern research on the Freudian concepts of repression and self-deception.*

Read pages 550-555 and then answer the following questions:

1. Outline the stages hypothesized by Freud in his psychosexual theory of personality development.

    a. *Oral stage*   age:

        1. source of gratification:

    b. *Anal stage*   age:

        1. source of gratification:

        2. Distinguish between the expressive and retentive period.

    c. *Phallic stage*   age:

        1. source of gratification

        2. Describe the *Oedipus* and *Electra complexes*. Be sure to explain the source of the conflict and how it is resolved.

    d. *Latency period*   age:

    e. *Genital stage*   age:

        1. source of gratification:

2. a. Explain a development *fixation* in your own words.

    b. What kinds of disorder may result from a fixation at the oral, anal, and phallic stages?

3. In general, which of Freud's ideas did neo-Freudians accept? reject?

4. a. In what ways did Jung disagree with Freud's view of the unconscious?

    b. What important distinction did Jung suggest?

5. According to Adler, how do feelings of inferiority influence children?

6. a. In what ways did Erikson disagree with Freud's views on the motivation and timing of personality development?

    b. According to Erikson, what are life crises and how do they influence psychosocial development? (See Table 16.4 in your text.)

7. Describe the negative effects that Freud's teachings about causes of mental disorders have had on the families of people with these disorders.

8. a. Briefly describe the general design of repression experiments? How must the design be changed to better study repression and why is it unethical to do so?

   b. How well did subjects recall words they believed were associated with latent homosexuality? (D'Zurilla, 1965)

   c. How well did the same subjects recall the words after they learned the words were not linked to latent homosexuality?

   d. How would Freudian theory explain the results?

   e. Provide a simpler explanation.

9. a. Explain the process of *self-deception* in your own words.

   b. What three conditions must be met for self-deception to occur? (Gur and Sackheim, 1979)

   c. Describe how the experimental design of Quattrone and Tversky (1974) met the three conditions for self-deception.

   d. Describe how information about heart types affect tolerance to pain and explain why the results support the concept of self-deception.

Read the interim summary on page 562 of your text to reacquaint yourself with the material in this section.

16-6 *Describe the humanistic approach to personality and outline and evaluate Maslow's theory of self-actualization.*

Read pages 556-557 and then answer the following questions:

1. a. What is the emphasis of the holistic view of behavior?

   b. What aspects would behaviorists such as Skinner accept? reject?

c. Why do humanistic psychologists resist the use of the scientific method? What method and which subjects do they prefer?

2. a. What is the basis of Maslow's theory of self-actualization?

   b. What is the source of needs? What is the result of the failure to satisfy needs? the consistent satisfying of needs?

3. a. Study Figure 16.7 in your text and draw Maslow's hierarchy of needs.

   b. Briefly define each need in your own words.

4. List some of the objections to Maslow's theory and evaluate their importance.

16-7 *Explain how personality test are constructed using the rational and empirical strategies and describe these personality tests: the MMPI, the Rorschach Inkblot Test and the Thematic Apperception Test.*

Read pages 557-562 and then answer the following questions:

1. a. Describe the *rational strategy* of test construction.

   b. What two conditions must be met if the test is to be successful?

2. a. Describe how test questions are selected following the *empirical strategy*. Be sure to use the term *criterion group* in your answer.

   b. When is the empirical strategy used most often?

3. What are some of the characteristics of an *objective test*?

4. Describe the *Minnesota Multiphasic Personality Inventory (MMPI)*:

   a. What was the purpose of the first MMPI?

   b. Describe how test questions were originally selected following the empirical strategy. Be sure to describe both the criterion and the control group.

   c. What is the general purpose of the MMPI validity scales? Study Table 16.5 in your text and explain what each of the validity scales indicates about people whose responses to a particular category of questions exceeds the criterion.

      1. *? scale*

      2. *L scale*

      3. *F scale*

      4. *K scale*

   d. In what ways is the MMPI used?

   e. Why do advocates of the five-factor model object to the MMPI?

5. Why are *projective tests* designed to be ambiguous?

6. a. See Figure 16.8 in your text and describe the Rorschach inkblots and their use.

   b. Describe two methods of interpreting a person's descriptions of the inkblots and their features.

7. a. See Figure 16.9 in your text and describe one of the card from the *Thematic Apperception Test (TAT)*. How are the cards used during testing?

   b. Why are the results often difficult to interpret?

Lesson II Self Test

1. Freud divided the mind into three structures:

a. the ego, the superego, and the ego-ideal.
b. the ego, the ego-ideal, and the conscience.
c. the id, the ego, and the superego.
d. the id, the ego, and the libido.

2. What are internalized prohibitions?

a. guilt feelings
b. forbidden sexual fantasies
c. rules of behavior learned in childhood
d. Freudian slips

3. The physician found no physical cause for the patient's amnesia for the event and suggested it might be caused by a defense mechanism called

a. repression.
b. reaction formation.
c. sublimation.
d. conversion.

4. During the latency period the sexual instinctual drive

a. is almost completely submerged.
b. finds an outlet in heterosexual activity.
c. is directed toward the parent of the other sex.
d. emerges.

5. Erikson believed that personality development

a. is a struggle between the personal and collective unconscious.
b. continues throughout life.
c. is motivated not only by sexual desires but also by religious and spiritual concerns.
d. is a striving for perfection.

6. D'Zurilla suggested that subjects had difficulty remembering words that they believed were associated with latent homosexuality because

a. the words were repressed.
b. they worried about their responses, and their preoccupation interfered with recall.
c. they engaged in self-deception.
d. of internalized prohibitions.

7. Humanistic psychologists stress the importance of studying the

a. person through scientific experimentation.
b. abnormal person.
c. average person.
d. entire person.

8. According to Maslow, the highest need is the need for

a. safety.
b. belongingness or love.
c. self-actualization.

d. esteem.

9. A high score on the K scale of the MMPI indicates the person may be

a. lying.
b. careless.
c. defensive.
d. evasive.

10. Projective personality tests

a. measure the degree to which a subject agrees or disagrees with the examiner's interpretation of an ambiguous situation.
b. are based on the assumption that an ambiguous situation will elicit the subject's true feelings.
c. are not as difficult to score as empirical tests.
d. require that subject responses be realistic.

Answers for Self Tests

Lesson I

1. b Obj. 16-1
2. c Obj. 16-1
3. b Obj. 16-1
4. d Obj. 16-1
5. a Obj. 16-2
6. b Obj. 16-2
7. c Obj. 16-2
8. a Obj. 16-3
9. a Obj. 16-3
10. d Obj. 16-3

Lesson II

1. c Obj. 16-4
2. c Obj. 16-4
3. a Obj. 16-4
4. a Obj. 16-5
5. b Obj. 16-5
6. b Obj. 16-5
7. d Obj. 16-6
8. c Obj. 16-6
9. c Obj. 16-7
10. b. Obj. 16-7

16.1 anal stage	16.10 cross-situational consistency
16.2 anxiety	16.11 defense mechanism
16.3 cardinal trait	16.12 delay of gratification
16.4 central trait	16.13 ego
16.5 compromise formation	16.14 ego-ideal
16.6 conscience	16.15 Electra complex
16.7 content reward	16.16 empirical strategy
16.8 conversion	16.17 extraversion
16.9 criterion group	16.18 five-factor model

16.10

The likelihood that a person will act in similar ways in different situations.

16.11

According to Freud, patterns of behavior controlled by the ego; used to reduce the anxiety produced by intrapsychic conflict.

16.12

According to social learning theory, a form of self-control; the ability to forego a reinforcer in order to receive an even more desirable one later.

16.13

One of Freud's three structures of the mind; the self, motivated by the reality principle; mediates between the id, superego and reality; uses defense mechanisms when demands of the id cannot be fulfilled.

16.14

According to Freud, one of the two divisions of the superego; represents the internalization of what a person would like to be.

16.15

Freud's belief that girls form an attachment to their fathers during the phallic stage; he later rejected this concept.

16.16

A method of developing psychological tests; a variety of items are presented to a criterion group; those that are regularly answered in one way by members of the criterion group are retained; the others are discarded.

16.17

A personality trait; the tendency to seek the company of other people, to be lively, and to engage in conversation and other social behaviors with them.

16.18

A personality theory derived from factor analyses of the words we use to describe temperament: neuroticism, extraversion, openness, agreeableness, and conscientiousness.

16.1

According to Freud, the second stage of psychosexual development during which the infant obtains gratification by passing or retaining feces.

16.2

An unpleasant condition which Freud believed resulted from intrapsychic conflict; the ego uses defense mechanisms to reduce the anxiety level.

16.3

According to Allport, powerful, all-encompassing personality characteristics that can be used to predict the behavior of some people in almost all situations.

16.4

According to Allport, personality traits that determine what kind of behaviors a person will engage in during a particular situation.

16.5

According to Freud, the result of the struggle between the demands of the instinctual drive and the suppressive effects of internalized prohibitions; examples include dreams and slips of the tongue.

16.6

According to Freud, one of the two divisions of the superego; internalized rules and restrictions of society; determines which behaviors are acceptable; punishes mistakes with guilt feelings.

16.7

According to social learning theory, a bipolar social reward; one end is reinforcing, the other is aversive (e.g.: praise/criticism).

16.8

A Freudian defense mechanism; intrapsychic conflict is relieved through the formation of a physical symptom such as blindness or paralysis.

16.9

A group of subjects whose behavior is used to validate a psychological test.

16.19	16.28
fixation	L scale
16.20	16.29
F scale	Minnesota Multiphasic Personality Inventory (MMPI)
16.21	16.30
genital stage	neuroticism
16.22	16.31
id	objective test
16.23	16.32
internalized prohibition	Oedipus complex
16.24	16.33
introversion	oral stage
16.25	16.34
K scale	personality trait
16.26	16.35
latency period	personality type
16.27	16.36
libido	phallic stage

16.28	16.19
Validity scale on the MMPI; lie scale; helps identify people who are not answering questions truthfully; a high score indicates results must be interpreted with caution.	According to Freud, an arrest in development during one of the stages of psychosexual development, which results in neurotic behaviors.
16.29	16.20
An objective test of personality traits; various patterns of response on more than one scale correlate with some distinct personality problems; 566 items grouped into 10 clinical scales and 4 validity scales.	Validity scale of the MMPI; frequency scale; 90 percent of normal people answer particular items in one way; a high score on this scale indicates carelessness, poor reading ability or very unusual personality traits.
16.30	16.21
According to Eysenck, a personality factor; filled with anxiety and guilt; bipolar opposite is emotional stability.	According to Freud, the final stage of psychosexual development in which a person receives gratification through heterosexual genital contact.
16.31	16.22
A test that can be scored objectively, such as a multiple-choice or true/false test.	One of Freud's three structures of the mind; provides energy for all psychic process and is completely unconscious.
16.32	16.23
Freud's belief that boys form an attachment to their mothers during the phallic stage.	According to Freud, behaviors learned in childhood that become a part of the superego; protect a person against guilt feelings that would result from allowing the instinctual drives to express themselves.
16.33	16.24
According to Freud, the first stage of psychosexual development, during which the infant obtains gratification first through sucking, and then biting and chewing.	A personality trait; the tendency to avoid the company of other people, especially large groups of people; shyness.
16.34	16.25
An enduring characteristic of a person that helps to explain consistent and recurring patterns of behavior.	Validity scale of the MMPI; defensiveness scale; identifies people who are attempting to hide their feelings to avoid emotional distress.
16.35	16.26
A pattern of traits or characteristic behaviors that can be used to assign people to one of several distinct categories.	According to Freud, an interval after the phallic stage and before the genital stage in which the child's sexual instinctual drive is inactive.
16.36	16.27
According to Freud, the third stage of psychosexual development; children begin playing with their genitals and discover the sex roles of their parents and form attachments to the parent of the opposite sex.	According to Freud, the psychic energy or motivation associated with instinctual drives; a part of the id.

16.37 process reward	16.46 repression
16.38 projection	16.47 Rorschach Inkblot Test
16.39 ? scale	16.48 self-concept
16.40 psychoticism	16.49 self-control
16.41 radical behaviorism	16.50 self-criticism/self-praise
16.42 rationalization	16.51 self-deception
16.43 rational strategy	16.52 sublimation
16.44 reaction formation	16.53 superego
16.45 reality principle	

16.46

A Freudian defense mechanism; intrapsychic conflict causes amnesia for events that cause guilt.

16.47

A projective test; people describe what they see in a set of ambiguous ink blots.

16.48

A person's perception of his or her own personality and ability.

16.49

The ability to withhold a response normally elicited by a particular situation.

16.50

Positive or negative responses people make to themselves after perceiving their own behavior and its consequences.

16.51

Simultaneously holding contradictory beliefs, at least one of which is not recognized for reasons related to motivation.

16.52

A Freudian defense mechanism; diversion of psychic energy from an unacceptable drive to an acceptable one.

16.53

One of Freud's three structures of the mind; subdivided into the conscience and the ego-ideal.

16.37

According to social learning theory, a social reward that is pleasant at moderate levels but aversive at very high or very low levels.

16.38

Freudian defense mechanism; intrapsychic conflict is relieved when a person denies his or her own unacceptable desires and discovers these desires in the behavior of others.

16.39

Validity scale of the MMPI; cannot say scale; number of questions not answered; a high score indicates the person finds some questions irrelevant or is evading issues.

16.40

According to Eysenck, a personality factor; aggressive, egocentric, and antisocial; bipolar opposite is self-control.

16.41

Skinner's approach to the study of behavior; a form of behaviorism that denies the importance of mental structures, which cannot be observed.

16.42

A Freudian defense mechanism; intrapsychic conflict is relieved by finding acceptable (but fictitious) reasons for a behavior.

16.43

A method of developing psychological tests; items are selected because of their theoretical relevance to the characteristic in question.

16.44

A Freudian defense mechanism; intrapsychic conflict is relieved by experiencing feelings opposite to a prohibited drive.

16.45

According to Freud, the tendency for the ego to be able to delay gratification of the desires of the id.

Chapter 17
The Nature and Causes of Mental Disorders

Lesson I

Read the interim summary on page 568 of your text to reacquaint yourself with the material in this section.

17-1 *Explain the value of a classification system for mental disorders and describe the most commonly used system*

Read pages 566-568 and then answer the following questions:

1. Explain how classifying a person's mental disorder may have serious consequences for the patient.

2. a. Briefly describe how Rosenhan (1973) demonstrated the tendency to regard all patient behavior as symptomatic of the diagnosis.

   b. What did some people conclude about the value of any attempt to classify mental disorders after learning of the results of this study? How did Spitzer (1975) refute their assertion?

3. a. Explain an advantage of classification by summarizing how an accurate description of *Graves' disease* eventually benefited its victims.

   b. State two other advantages of the accurate classification of mental disorders.

4. a. What is the name of the classification system most commonly used in North America?

   b. Study Table 17.1 in your text and describe its organization.

Read the interim summary on page 579 of your text to reacquaint yourself with the material in this section.

17-2 *Describe the symptoms and possible causes of the major anxiety disorders: panic disorder, phobic disorders, and obsessive compulsive disorder.*

Read pages 570-575 and then answer the following questions:

1. a. Define *neuroses* in your own words.

    b. Complete these sentences.

        1. Neurotics never

        2. Neurotics almost always

    c. Describe how neuroses can disrupt a normal daily life.

2. a. Briefly describe a panic attack.

    b. People with panic disorder often suffer from _____ _____ between panic attacks. Explain why they do.

    c. Explain how panic attacks may cause phobias. Be sure to refer to classical conditioning in your answer.

3. Discuss evidence that panic disorder may be a medical problem rather than a "mental" one:

    a. evidence for heritable trait (Slater and Shields, 1969; Crowe et al., 1983, 1987)

    b. artificially induced attacks (Gaffney et al., 1988; Woods et al., 1988)

    c. possible link with heart disease (Gorman et al., 1981)

    d. sensitivity to bodily sensations

4. Define and distinguish between a fear of an object or situation and a *phobic disorder*.

5. Describe the following forms of phobic disorders recognized by the DSM-III-R. Be sure to mention the incidence in the general population and between the sexes, heritability, age of onset of symptoms, chance of recovery, and explain how severely they disrupt daily life.

    a. *agoraphobia*

b. *social phobia*

c. *simple phobia*

6. a. Explain how Miss E.M., the young secretary, developed a phobic disorder through classical conditioning.

   b. Now explain why most people do not develop phobias even though they may experience a traumatic event. (Lacey and Lacey, 1962; Goodwin, 1983; Goodwin and Guze, 1984)

7. Define the two components of *obsessive compulsive disorder* in your own words.

8. State the incidence of obsessive compulsive disorder in the general population and between the sexes, age of onset of symptoms, and how it disrupts daily life.

9. List the two principal kinds of obsessions and give an example of each.

10. List the four categories of compulsions and give an example of each.

11. a. Explain how a normal behavior such as thinking about other things can develop into an obsession. Be sure to mention role of reinforcement in your answer.

    b. Describe *Tourette's syndrome* and explain how it may be associated with obsessive compulsive disorder. (Pauls and Leckman, 1986; Pauls et al., 1986)

17-3 *Describe the symptoms and possible causes of somatization disorder and conversion disorder.*

Read pages 575-578 and then answer the following questions:

1. a. Describe *somatization disorder* and the criteria set by the DSM-III-R for this diagnosis.

   b. Describe *hypochondriasis* and explain how it differs from somatization disorder.

   c. Define the terms *symptom* and *sign* in your own words and explain why people with somatization disorder complain of symptoms rather than signs.

2. Study Figure 17.1 in your text and explain how somatization disorder affects daily life.

3. Describe the following evidence that suggests that somatization disorder may be hereditary:

    a. incidence among first degree female relatives of people with the disorder (Coryell, 1980)

    b. evidence of association with other mental disturbances (Guze et al, 1967; Woerner and Guze, 1968)

    c. incidence of mental disturbances in first-degree relatives reared apart (Cadoret, 1978)

4. Describe the case of the new father, Mr. L. in order to explain the origins and symptoms of *conversion disorder*.

5. Define *malingering* in your own words.

6. Briefly explain how to distinguish between conversion disorder and

    a. malingering

    b. somatization disorder

    c. psychosomatic disorder (See Figure 17.2 in your text.)

    d. organic disorders (Whitlock, 1967)

7. a. Describe the two conditions that suggest that conversion disorders may be learned. (Ullman and Krasner, 1969)

   b. Now describe the case of the soldier with an eye injury that illustrates how both of these conditions contribute to the problem.

17-4 *Describe the symptoms and possible causes of the major dissociative disorders: psychogenic amnesia, psychogenic fugue, and multiple personality disorder.*

Read pages 578-579 and then answer the following questions:

1. Define *dissociative disorder* in your own words.

2. According to psychoanalytic theory, what are the origins of dissociative disorders?

3. Define and distinguish between *psychogenic* and *organic* amnesia.

4. Summarize the case of Miss K.B. to illustrate both the symptoms and apparent origin of her psychogenic amnesia.

5. What is the distinguishing characteristic of

   a. *psychogenic fugue*?

   b. *multiple personality disorder*?

6. a. In general, what kind of conflicts may cause a person to develop a dissociative disorder?

   b. What advantage does each of the three principal forms of dissociative disorder offer a person?

Read the interim summary on page 583 of your text to reacquaint yourself with the material in this section.

17-5 *Describe the symptoms and possible causes of antisocial personality disorder.*

Read pages 580-583 and then answer the following questions:

1. Define personality disorder in your own words.

2. a. Outline some of the diagnostic criteria set by the DSM-III-R for *antisocial personality disorder*.

   b. What are some of prominent personality characteristics of psychopaths, as identified by Cleckley (1976)?

3. Refer to both the diagnostic criteria and Cleckley's list and describe the life style of a psychopath.

4. a. What are the three primary defects that most investigators believe are characteristic of antisocial personality disorder?

   b. What do some investigators believe to be the cause of their inability to experience normal emotions?

   c. Describe how investigators believe these defects contribute to a propensity for criminal behavior (Quay, 1965).

5. Summarize research on the emotional responses of psychopaths:

   a. Describe the procedure and results of research by Hare (1965a) on how sociopaths react to painful stimuli. (Study Figure 17.3 in your text.)

   b. Now describe the procedure and results of research again by Hare (1965b) on anticipatory fear responses of sociopaths. (Study Figure 17.4 in your text.)

   c. Finally describe the procedure and results of research by Schmauk (1970) on the degree to which sociopaths respond to various forms of punishment. (Study Figure 17.5 in your text.)

6. Summarize research on a heritable factor in antisocial personality disorder:

   a. What is the incidence of antisocial personality disorder or other disorders among

      1. females in families with psychopathic males?

      2. relatives of both men and women convicted of felonies? (Guze et al., 1967; Cloninger and Guze, 1973)

      3. identical and fraternal twins? (Christiansen, 1970)

   b. What were the conclusions of research by Mednick et al., 1983 on the affect of being the biological son of a convicted criminal being raised by a criminal and noncriminal father? (See Table 17.4.)

   c. What do these studies suggest about a biological cause of antisocial personality disorder?

Lesson I Self Test

1. Rosenhan (1973) asked normal volunteers to commit themselves to mental institutions in order to expose the

   a. dangers of the tendency to view all patient behavior in terms of the original diagnosis.
   b. substandard conditions in mental institutions.
   c. uselessness of DSM-III-R diagnostic criteria.
   d. lack of standards for voluntary admissions.

2. The Diagnostic and Statistical Manual III-R diagnostic criteria

   a. discourage treatment of hopeless cases.
   b. facilitate research on the causes and treatments of mental disorders.
   c. are cross-indexed to accepted treatments.
   d. are not used as frequently as originally anticipated because of distrust of any classification system.

3. Panic attacks can

   a. be controlled through injections of lactic acid.
   b. last for several days.
   c. occur for no apparent reason.
   d. are a result of inconsistent treatment by the parents during childhood.

4. People with obsessive-compulsive disorder

   a. fail to recognize how their compulsive behavior controls their lives.
   b. use compulsive behaviors as a defense against anxiety.
   c. may also suffer from Tourette's syndrome.
   d. sometimes develop phobias through classical conditioning.

5. People with somatization disorder

   a. have an excessive fear of becoming ill.
   b. complain of symptoms that have no physiological cause.
   c. have a real illness that is made worse by physiological problems.
   d. have a neurological problem with a psychological rather than a physical cause.

6. People with conversion disorders

   a. are almost always women.
   b. do not appear to be upset by their symptoms.
   c. are reluctant to talk about their symptoms.
   d. rarely suffer from organic diseases as well.

7. Behaviorists believe that conversion disorders

   a. are hereditary.
   b. can be learned.
   c. are primarily sexual in origin.
   d. result from hormone imbalances.

8. The most common form of dissociative disorder is

   a. psychogenic amnesia.
   b. psychogenic fugue.
   c. multiple personality disorder.
   d. malingering.

9. A common trait of a psychopath is

   a. truthfulness.
   b. lack of interest in sex.
   c. feelings of guilt and remorse.
   d. superficial charm.

10. Psychopathic subjects who were taught an avoidance task learned best when the aversive stimulus was

   a. an electric shock.
   b. the experimenter saying "wrong."
   c. loss of a quarter.

d. disapproval from confederate subjects.

Lesson II

Read the interim summary on pages 591-592 of your text to reacquaint yourself with the material in this section.

17-6 *Describe the characteristic symptoms of schizophrenia.*

Read pages 584-585 and then answer the following questions:

1. Explain the two traditional positions regarding the forms of schizophrenia. What has modern research contributed to the search for an answer?

2. How is the term *schizophrenia* often misused?

3. What is the most important symptom of schizophrenia and how did a schizophrenic, during a lucid period, describe the feeling?

4. Define *neologism* in your own words.

5. Define *hallucination* in your own words and describe some of the different kinds of hallucinations that schizophrenics experience.

6. What appears to be an important cause of the anxiety schizophrenics experience?

7. What may be the reason schizophrenics exhibit emotional withdrawal?

8. Define *delusion* in your own words and explain the following types of delusion:

   a. *delusions of persecution*

   b. *delusions of grandeur*

   c. *delusions of control*

17-7 *Describe catatonic schizophrenia, paranoid schizophrenia, and disorganized schizophrenia.*

Read pages 586-588 and then answer the following questions:

1. Define *undifferentiated schizophrenia* in your own words. When is it an appropriate diagnosis?

2. Describe the characteristics of *catatonic schizophrenia*.

3. Why were catatonic schizophrenics sometimes put in straitjackets?

4. a. What are the most important symptoms of *paranoid schizophrenia?*

   b. Why are the delusions of paranoid schizophrenics often rich in detail?

5. a. Describe the prominent symptoms of *disorganized schizophrenia*. Be sure to use the term word salad in your answer.

   b. What is the prognosis for this form of schizophrenia?

17-8 *Discuss and evaluate research on the early predictors of schizophrenia, the role of heredity, and the dopamine hypothesis.*

Read pages 588-591 and then answer the following questions:

1. Define and distinguish between *reactive and process schizophrenia* first suggested by Bleuler.

2. Why is it important to identify the early signs of schizophrenia?

3. a. Briefly describe the subjects and the control group that Watt and Lubansky (1976) studied in an attempt to identify the early signs of schizophrenia.

   b. In what ways did children who later became schizophrenic differ from normal control subjects? What do these results suggest about the early signs of this disorder? What questions remain unanswered?

4. a. Briefly describe how Kety et al., 1968 studied the heritability of schizophrenia. Be sure to refer to the Danish *folkeregister* in your answer.

   b. What was the most important difference between adoptive children who later developed schizophrenia and those who did not?

c. In addition, which form of the disease appears to be hereditary?

5. Carefully explain how most investigators believe heredity and environment interact to cause schizophrenia.

6. a. What is the general effect of cocaine and amphetamine and the antipsychotic drugs on the symptoms of schizophrenia?

b. Describe the progression of symptoms that subjects displayed when they received high doses of dextroamphetamine during an experiment. (Griffith et al., 1972)

c. Describe the effect of amphetamines on patients with naturally occurring schizophrenia. (Davis, 1974)

d. Study Figure 17.7 in your text and describe the effect that *chlorpromazine* has on the treatment of schizophrenics. How does the effect of chlorpromazine differ from that of tranquilizers?

e. Outline the dopamine hypothesis of schizophrenia that was suggested by the differing effects of drugs that you have just described.

7. Summarize the evidence that the dopamine hypothesis is not a complete explanation of the cause of schizophrenia:

a. When antipsychotic drugs were first used to treat schizophrenia, what inconsistency did clinicians observe?

b. How did Crow and his colleagues (1980, 1982) attempt to explain the lack of effect on some patients?

c. List the positive and negative symptoms of schizophrenia they proposed.

8. Describe the kinds of brain damage discovered in the brains of schizophrenics that may account for the negative symptoms of this disease.

9. How does evidence of brain damage

a. confirm the existence of two different kinds of symptoms?

b. explain the failure of antipsychotic drugs to relieve symptoms in all schizophrenics.

10. Summarize evidence that the observed brain damage in schizophrenics may be caused by a virus:

   a. seasonal variation (Torrey et al., 1977)

   b. analysis of cerebrospinal fluid (Torrey et al., 1982)

   c. infection during pregnancy (Mednick et al., 1988)

11. According to Stevens (1982a), what may be the interaction between heredity and environmental factors in the development of schizophrenia?

12. To summarize: According to recent research, what may be the best way to classify the various forms of schizophrenia?

Read the interim summary on page 596 of your text to reacquaint yourself with the material in this section.

17-9 *Describe the symptoms of bipolar disorder and major depression.*

Read pages 592-593 and then answer the following questions:

1. Briefly describe the most severe *mood disorders*: *bipolar disorder* and *major depression*. Be sure to mention the incidence in the general population and between the sexes, age of onset of symptoms, and most characteristic symptom.

2. Distinguish between major depression and two other forms of depression: *dysthymic disorder* and *cyclothymic disorder*.

3. Discuss the emotional episodes of mania and depression:

   a. Describe the thoughts and behavior that people often experience during an episode of *mania*.

   b. According to many therapists, how does mania appear to differ from happiness?

   c. _____ _____ is an effective treatment for bipolar disorder.

   d. List the five cardinal symptoms of depression identified by Beck (1967).

   e. Find examples of some of these symptoms in the conversation between Mr. H. and his therapist reported in your text.

f. In general, how do patients suffering from major depression judge themselves and their behavior?

17-10 *Discuss psychoanalytic and cognitive theories of the causes of mood disorders, the role of heredity, research on biochemical factors, and the relation to biological rhythms.*

Read pages 594-596 and then answer the following questions:

1. a. Briefly summarize how psychoanalytic theory accounts for depression.

   b. Discuss three objections raised against this explanation.

2. a. According to Beck (1967), what is the principal cause of depression?

   b. What is the utility of this approach?

3. a. Cite evidence that suggests mood disorders are heritable. (Rosenthal, 1970; Allen, 1976)

   b. Which two chromosomes may be involved?

4. _____ _____ and _____ _____ are both effective treatments for severe depression.

5. What are the biochemical effects of the antidepressant drugs?

6. How does the blood pressure drug *reserpine* affect the brain? What side effect results and what does it suggest about the cause of major depression?

7. a. How does the brain biochemistry of depressed people differ from that of nondepressed people?

   b. Describe research that suggests a biochemical imbalance may not be the first stage of depression. (Miller et al., 1977)

8. a. Compare the sleep patterns of people suffering from a severe mood disorder and people suffering from

the less severe dysthymic disorder.

b. How does the REM sleep cycle of depressed people differ from normal?

c. If depressed people are deprived of REM sleep in the laboratory, how is depression affected?

d. Review how ECT and antidepressant drugs act to support the role of REM sleep in depression.

9. a. Define *zeitgeber* in your own words and give an example of a physical and a social zeitgeber.

b. Explain the cause and describe the treatment for *seasonal depression*.

10. a. Summarize the hypothesis suggested by Ehlers, Frank, and Kupfer (1988) that accounts for both biological and environmental events that seem to trigger depression.

b. What changes were observed in the biological or behavioral rhythms of depressed people who were

1. recently widowed? (Flaherty et al., 1987)

2. going through a divorce? (Cartwright, 1983)

Lesson II Self Test

1. Hallucinations are

   a. feelings of persecution.
   b. beliefs contrary to fact.
   c. perceptions of stimuli that are not present.
   d. periods of emotional withdrawal.

2. The schizophrenic who believed he had discovered "the secrets of the universe" suffered from a delusion of

   a. persecution.
   b. grandeur.
   c. control.
   d. innocence.

3. Catatonic schizophrenics

   a. often make inappropriate emotional response especially silly laughter.
   b. are among the most intelligent of psychotic patients.

c. sometimes believe they are being persecuted, sometimes believe they possess special powers.

d. were often restrained with straitjackets before effective medications were developed.

4. A survey of all patients in Massachusetts mental institutions (Watt and Lubansky, 1976) revealed

a. people who develop schizophrenia were different from others even in early childhood.

b. early childhood differences were caused by physiological disorders.

c. early childhood differences were defense mechanisms against the unpredictable behavior of their families.

d. few sex differences between boys and girls who later developed schizophrenia.

5. Amphetamine and cocaine _____ symptoms of schizophrenia presumably because they _____ dopamine receptors.

a. reduce; stimulate

b. reduce; block

c. cause; stimulate

d. cause; block

6. The negative symptoms of schizophrenia

a. improve if the patient is given antipsychotic drugs.

b. result from the loss of brain tissue.

c. are the classic symptoms: delusions, hallucinations, and thought disorders.

d. do not have their origin in early childhood.

7. Mania is

a. characterized by wild, excited behavior.

b. indistinguishable from true happiness.

c. seldom seen in women.

d. often triggered by an environmental event.

8. One of the difficulties with the psychoanalytic explanation of depression is that

a. the death of a loved one is often viewed as a release from pain and suffering.

b. the hypothesized stages of psychosexual development are still disputed.

c. it cannot account for depression that does not result from environmental stress.

d. almost everyone whose development is fixated at the oral stage becomes depressed.

9. The cerebrospinal fluid of depressed people contains significantly lower than normal levels of

a. lithium carbonate.

b. dopamine.

c. a compound produced by the breakdown of serotonin.

d. chlorpromazine.

10. Treatments that reduce or alleviate the symptoms of depression

a. reduce the amount of REM sleep.

b. increase the amount of REM sleep.

c. desynchronize daily biological rhythms.

d. synchronize daily social rhythms.

Answers for Self Tests

Lesson I		**Lesson II**	
1. a Obj. 17-1		1. a Obj. 17-6	
2. b Obj. 17-1		2. b Obj. 17-6	
3. c Obj. 17-2		3. d Obj. 17-7	
4. c Obj. 17-2		4. a Obj. 17-8	
5. b Obj. 17-3		5. c Obj. 17-8	
6. b Obj. 17-3		6. b Obj. 17-8	
7. b Obj. 17-3		7. a Obj. 17-9	
8. a Obj. 17-4		8. b Obj. 17-10	
9. d Obj. 17-5		9. c Obj. 17-10	
10. c Obj. 17-5		10. a Obj. 17-10	

17.1 agoraphobia	17.10 cyclothymic disorder
17.2 anticipatory anxiety	17.11 cytomegalovirus (CMV)
17.3 antidepressant drug	17.12 delusions of control
17.4 antisocial personality disorder	17.13 delusions of grandeur
17.5 bipolar disorder	17.14 delusions of persecution
17.6 catatonic schizophrenia	17.15 Diagnostic and Statistical Manual III-R (DSM-III-R)
17.7 chlorpromazine	17.16 disorganized schizophrenia
17.8 compulsion	17.17 dissociative disorder
17.9 conversion disorder	17.18 dysthymic disorder

17.10

A mood disorder that resembles bipolar disorder but is less severe; the person does not experience delusions or hallucinations.

17.1

The fear of finding oneself in "places or situations . . . in which help might not be available in the event of a panic attack . . . ." (DSM-III-R); may be so disabling that individuals hide in their own homes for years.

17.11

A herpeslike virus that may cause brain damage; antibodies for CMV have been found in the cerebrospinal fluid of some schizophrenics.

17.2

The fear of having a panic attack suffered by people with panic disorders; can lead to agoraphobia.

17.12

The false belief that one is being controlled by other people or forces; symptom of schizophrenia.

17.3

Drugs such as lithium carbonate and imipramine, used to alleviate the symptoms of severe depression.

17.13

The false belief that one is powerful, famous, or even divine; symptom of schizophrenia.

17.4

People who consistently exhibit traits such as superficial charm, habitual lying, lack of remorse, failure to learn from experience, inability to form lasting relationships and repeated criminal activity.

17.14

The false belief that other people are plotting against one; symptom of schizophrenia.

17.5

A mood disorder characterized by alternating periods of mania and depression.

17.15

The system and manual developed by the American Psychiatric Association that provide specific criteria for the diagnosis of mental disorders.

17.6

A form of schizophrenia; motor disturbances in which the person shows wild movements or maintains bizarre, stationary poses for many hours.

17.16

A progressive and irreversible form of schizophrenia; people often make inappropriate emotional responses such as silly laughter and, when seriously deteriorated, their speech is called a "word salad."

17.7

One of the first antipsychotic drugs; reduces symptoms of schizophrenia by blocking dopamine receptors.

17.17

A category of mental disturbance that includes such disturbances as amnesia, fugue, and multiple personality

17.8

The performance of a behavior with the feeling that it cannot be resisted.

17.18

A mood disorder that is less serious than major depression, the person does not experience delusions or hallucinations.

17.9

A somatization disorder in which a person experiences symptoms similar to neurological disorders such as blindness, but which have no organic cause.

17.19	17.28
Graves' disease	obsession
17.20	17.29
hypochondriasis	obsessive compulsive disorder
17.21	17.30
lithium carbonate	panic disorder
17.22	17.31
major depression	paranoid schizophrenia
17.23	17.32
malingering	phobic disorder
17.24	17.33
mania	process schizophrenia/reactive schizophrenia
17.25	17.34
mood disorder	psychogenic amnesia
17.26	17.35
multiple personality disorder	psychogenic fugue
17.27	17.36
neurosis	psychosomatic disorder

17.28

Recurrent, persistent, and inescapable thoughts and ideas.

17.29

A mental disorder in which people suffer from obsessions and compulsions; may severely interfere with daily living.

17.30

An anxiety disorder in which people suffer from intermittent attacks of terror that occur for no apparent reason and may last from a few seconds to a few hours.

17.31

A form of schizophrenia in which the person suffers from delusions of persecution, grandeur, or control.

17.32

A mental disturbance in which an excessive fear of a particular object or situation makes daily living difficult.

17.33

According to Bleuler, the process form apparently begins in early childhood and is chronic, the reactive form is apparently a reaction to stressful circumstances and is usually limited to one episode.

17.34

The most common dissociative disorder, amnesia with no apparent organic cause.

17.35

Amnesia with no apparent organic cause accompanied by a flight away from home.

17.36

A real illness caused by psychological stress.

17.19

A syndrome caused by oversecretion of thyroxine by the thyroid glands; originally thought to be a mental disorder; identified first by Robert Graves.

17.20

A somatoform disorder in which one is excessively fearful of illness and misinterprets minor physical sensations as symptoms of a serious disease.

17.21

An antidepressant drug that is effective in treating bipolar disorder.

17.22

A feeling of profound sadness and hopelessness; does not alternate with bouts of mania.

17.23

The deliberate pretense that one in sick in order to gain some advantage; two criteria, a reluctance to describe symptoms and the lack of indifference, aid in distinguishing it from a conversion disorder.

17.24

Extreme exuberance characterized by restlessness and hyperactivity, rapid speech, and grandiose plans; alternates with depression in bipolar disorder.

17.25

A disturbance of normal emotional response; the most severe forms are bipolar disorder and major depression.

17.26

A rarely seen dissociative disorder in which two or more distinct personalities exist within the same person; each personality dominates in turn.

17.27

A nonpsychotic mental disorder in which perceptions of the world and strategies for living become maladaptive; people do not suffer from delusions or hallucinations and recognize that they have a problem.

17.37

reserpine

17.38

schizophrenia

17.39

seasonal depression

17.40

sign

17.41

simple phobia

17.42

social phobia

17.43

somatization disorder

17.44

somatoform disorder

17.45

symptom

17.46

Tourette's syndrome

17.47

tricyclic antidepressant drug

17.48

undifferentiated schizophrenia

17.49

zeitgeber

17.46

Disorder characterized by muscular and vocal tics, facial grimacing, uncontrollable sounds, and repetition of words; appears in childhood and may be genetically related to obsessive compulsive disorder.

17.37

Drug that lowers blood pressure and can cause depression; blocks release of norepinephrine and serotonin in the brain.

17.47

One of two types of antidepressant drugs used to alleviate the symptoms of psychotic depression; stimulating effects on synapses that use serotonin and norepinephrine.

17.38

A serious mental disorder characterized by thought disturbances, hallucinations, anxiety, emotional withdrawal, and delusions.

17.48

Category of schizophrenia characterized by delusions, hallucinations, and disorganized behavior but not the symptoms of catatonic, paranoid, or disorganized schizophrenia.

17.39

A mood disorder that may be caused by changes in a susceptible individual's biological clock by decreasing amount of sunlight in winter; treatment consists of exposure to bright light several hours each day.

17.49

Stimulus that synchronizes daily biological rhythms, which are controlled by an internal biological clock located in the hypothalamus; the most important is light.

17.40

Tangible evidence of a physical malfunction such as a rash.

17.41

Phobias other than agoraphobia and social phobia; fear of specific objects or situations often caused by a traumatic event; easily treated.

17.42

A phobic disorder; excessive and irrational fear of situations in which the person is observed by others.

17.43

A type of somatoform disorder characterized by complaints of symptoms that do not have a physiological basis; almost exclusively seen in females.

17.44

A category of mental disorders characterized by symptoms of physical disorders including conversion disorder, somatization disorder and hypochondriasis.

17.45

Patient reports of feelings of illness such as perceptions of pain.

Chapter 18
The Treatment of Mental Disorders

Lesson I

Read the interim summary on page 609 of your text to reacquaint yourself with the material in this section.

18-1 *Describe the early treatment of the mentally ill and the historical development of psychotherapy.*

Read pages 600-605 and then answer the following questions:

1. a. Summarize some of the earliest beliefs about the causes of mental illness and the first attempts at "treatment" beginning with *trephining*. (See Figures 18.1 in your text.)

    b. How did Johann Wier in the 16th century and Saint Vincent de Paul in the 17th century attempt to change prevailing attitudes toward the mentally ill?

    c. Describe how, despite changing attitudes, the mentally ill continued to be mistreated (See Figures 18.2-18.4 in your text.)

    d. Briefly describe Philippe Pinel's reforms and their effect, especially on reform in the United States led by Dorothea Dix. (See Figure 18.5 in your text.)

2. What treatment did Mesmer develop? (Be sure to use the word *mesmerism* in your answer.)

3. How did the apparently successful treatment of hysteria through hypnosis change the direction of Charcot's research?

4. How did Charcot influence Freud?

18-2 *Describe and evaluate the treatment of mental disorders by means of psychoanalysis and client-centered therapy.*

Read pages 605-609 and then answer the following questions:

1. a. Define *insight psychotherapy* in your own words, paying special attention to the presumed cause and cure of mental conflicts.

    b. Give two examples of therapies based on insight psychotherapy.

2. Define *psychoanalysis* in your own words.

3. a. Why are patients undergoing psychoanalysis encouraged to engage in *free association?*

    b. When patients show *resistance,* how do they behave? What do therapists believe resistance indicates?

    c. What is a another source of insight into the unconsciousness?

4. Summarize the role of the therapist in psychoanalysis:

    a. How does the therapist use information revealed during free association? When are these interpretations most helpful? least helpful?

    b. Describe the *transference neurosis* that develops between therapist and patient.

    c. How does the therapist encourage transference neurosis to develop and attempt to guard against *countertransference?* Be sure to use the term *training analysis* in your answer.

    d. Why do therapists decline to help patients with everyday problems? How do they justify their position?

5. Evaluate the effectiveness of psychoanalysis:

    a. Outline the reasons why it is impossible to obtain a random sample of patients for evaluation.

    b. Explain the difficulty of assessing changes in patient behavior, especially why a patient's increased insight is not a sufficient basis for evaluation.

    c. How do therapists explain away their failures and thus contribute to the difficulty of evaluation?

    d. What emotional problem and what kind of patient respond best to psychoanalysis?

e. Why do some critics object to techniques that encourage a transference neurosis?

6. a. According to Carl Rogers, who developed _____-_____ therapy, people are basically _____ and possess a drive toward _____-_____.

    b. What then causes emotional problems to occur?

    c. And how can emotional problems be overcome?

7. Summarize the role of therapists in client-centered therapy:

    a. Describe an atmosphere of *unconditional positive regard* and its importance in treatment.

    b. Why must client-centered therapists be empathetic individuals in order to be effective?

    c. What are some of the other characteristics of effective therapists?

8. Evaluate the effectiveness of client-centered therapy:

    a. In what way did Rogers encourage evaluation of his own technique?

    b. How did Truax analyze Rogers's interactions with his clients and what did the analysis reveal about Rogers's responses?

    c. What change did Rogers make as a result of Truax's findings?

    d. Outline Davison and Neale's (1982) objection to Rogers's assumption that maladaptive behaviors will disappear when a person heeds his or her own feelings.

    e. What conditions and what kind of patients respond best to this therapy?

    f. Describe an objection to Rogers's basic assumption about human worth.

9. What is Rogers's chief contribution to psychotherapy?

Read the interim summary on page 616 of your text to reacquaint yourself with the material in this section.

18-3 *Describe the treatment of mental disorders by means of systematic desensitization and aversive classical conditioning.*

Read pages 609-611 and then answer the following questions:

1. a. Behavior therapy focuses on changing maladaptive _____ rather than understanding its _____ and its techniques are based on the principles of _____ and _____ conditioning.

   b. State once again the differences between classical conditioning and instrumental conditioning.

2. a. Define the goal of *systematic desensitization* in your own words.

   b. Carefully describe the steps that are followed during the desensitization procedure. (See Table 18.1 in your text.)

   c. Refer to the principles of classical conditioning to explain why each step in the procedure is essential. Cite research to support your answer. (Johnson and Sechrest, 1968)

   d. Describe two ways that therapists present clients with the objects or situations they find frightening. Compare the effectiveness of each.

   e. How do these encounters differ for clients undergoing *implosion therapy?*

   f. What is the presumed reason why anxiety-reducing drugs taken by clients before implosion therapy sessions interfere with treatment?

3. a. Define *aversive classical conditioning* in your own words.

   b. Describe how inappropriate behaviors can be treated using aversive classical conditioning, explain why such therapy must be voluntary, and evaluate its effectiveness.

18-4 *Describe the treatment of mental disorders by means of techniques based on instrumental conditioning.*

Read pages 611-614 and then answer the following questions:

1. a. In general, what kind of behaviors should be reinforced? punished?

b. Which is the more effective method?

c. Describe two situations that often undermine the effectiveness of punishment.

2. a. Define *covert* reinforcement and punishment in your own words.

   b. Summarize the case of the housewife with a clothes-folding compulsion to illustrate the use and effectiveness of covert reinforcement and punishment. Be sure to note what kind of behaviors Wisocki (1970) vicariously punished or reinforced.

3. a. Summarize Bandura's (1971) description of a modeling session to help people overcome a severe fear of snakes.

   b. Explain why modeling is effective.

   c. Describe *behavior rehearsal*. Be sure to note the circumstances in which it is an appropriate therapy.

4. a. Explain why a system of *token economies* was developed and how it operates in large institutions for the mentally ill.

   b. Summarize long-term research by Paul and Lentz (1977) on the effectiveness of token economies.

   c. Give two reasons for the fact that token economies are difficult to implement.

18-5 *Evaluate behavior therapy and describe the types of situations in which its use is inappropriate.*

Read pages 614-616 and then answer the following questions:

1. a. Some traditionally oriented psychotherapists object to behavior therapy because they believe that if only the _____ and not the _____ of a psychological problem are treated, new symptoms may develop through a process called _____ _____.

   b. Describe how bed-wetting was successfully treated without the occurrence of symptom substitution. (Baker, 1969)

2. a. What difficulty with behavior therapy was revealed by work with chronic alcoholics?

b. List three techniques behavior therapists use to facilitate generalization of new behaviors to daily life.

1.

2.

3.

c. Why do behavior therapists refrain from reinforcing every positive behavioral response?

d. Describe the goal of self-observation in your own words.

e. Describe how Drabman et al., 1973 taught a group of disruptive boys to evaluate their own behavior. Explain why self-observation remained effective after the training sessions.

f. Why are family members often asked to participate in behavior therapy?

3. Explain how methods of *self-control* can maintain desirable behavior learned during therapy or establish new behaviors.

4. Explain some of the ethical problems raised by some forms of behavior therapy.

Lesson I Self Test

1. The idea that mental illness was no different from other physical diseases

    a. was one of the few advances during the Middle Ages.
    b. gained widespread acceptance through the efforts of the Church.
    c. gradually brought an end to inhumane "treatments."
    d. was renounced by Saint Vincent de Paul.

2. The early use of hypnosis to treat hysteria is attributed to

    a. Johann Wier
    b. Anton Mesmer
    c. Jean Charcot.
    d. Sigmund Freud.

3. Insight therapies are based on the assumption that insight

    a. leads to behavioral change.
    b. is less important than behavioral change.
    c. is a frightening realization that should only be attempted with an empathetic therapist.
    d. results from transferring emotional problems to the therapist.

4. It is difficult to evaluate psychoanalysis because

    a. most informants were dissatisfied with treatment and do not constitute a random sample.
    b. goals are constantly changing as treatment progresses.
    c. failure is often attributed to the client and not to the treatment.
    d. few clients complete treatment.

5. Behavior therapies are based on the assumption that

    a. symptom substitution is an important problem with insight therapy.
    b. people are basically good and problems are the result of faulty learning.
    c. a sound scientific basis reduces the importance of the therapist.
    d. behavioral change is more important than understanding the cause of the behavior.

6. Systematic desensitization is an effective therapy for

    a. the mentally ill who do not readily communicate with others.
    b. specific phobias.
    c. generalized fears or anxieties.
    d. maladaptive behaviors that are harmful to the individual.

7. Wisocki asked a woman with a clothes-folding compulsion to imagine herself vomiting each time she tried to refold clothes. This technique is an example of vicarious

    a. reinforcement.
    b. punishment.
    c. modeling.
    d. symptom substitution.

8. In a token economy, tokens

    a. are conditioned reinforcers for appropriate behaviors.
    b. can be exchanged for money depending on the pay scale.
    c. are conditioned punishers for inappropriate behavior.
    d. can be exchanged to reduce a patient's workload.

9. Self-observation is a technique to

    a. encourage unconditional positive regard.
    b. help patients recognize the first signs of symptom substitution.
    c. identify the sources of anxiety in daily life.
    d. insure that positive behavioral changes generalize to real life situations.

10. Behavior therapy is inappropriate if

    a. the patient has been confined in a mental institution for a long period of time.
    b. ethical issues cannot be resolved.
    c. the patient's family does not agree to take part in treatment.
    d. the patient does not understand the causes of the maladaptive behavior.

Lesson II

Read the interim summary on page 619 of your text to reacquaint yourself with the material in this section.

18-6 *Describe and evaluate the treatment of mental disorders by means of rational-emotive therapy and methods using a combined behavioral-cognitive approach.*

Read pages 616-619 and then answer the following questions:

1. Briefly compare these aspects of *cognitive behavior therapy* and behavior therapy:

   a. focus

   b. methods

   c. interest in origins of mental disorder

   d. presumed causes of behavioral changes

2. _____-_____ therapy, which was developed by Albert Ellis, asserts that psychological problems are the result of irrational _____ which must be exposed and challenged by the therapist.

3. State the formula that Ellis devised to express the relationship between emotions and cognition and state what each symbol represents. Go on to explain how inappropriate emotions such as guilt or depression develop.

4. Describe the value of *cognitive restructuring* in rational-emotive therapy.

5. Compare and contrast rational-emotive therapy and client-centered therapy, especially with respect to the role of the therapist.

6. a. What are some of the characteristics of people who are most likely to benefit from this kind of therapy?

   b. What kind of emotional problems have been treated successfully and unsuccessfully using this approach? Cite research to support your answer.

7. Therapists who use a combined approach attempt to change both their clients _____ and _____ behavior.

8. a. Define *self-efficacy* in your own words.

   b. According to Bandura (1977a), how does self-efficacy--a private behavior--develop and how does it affect public behavior.

9. a. Define *self-talk* in your own words.

   b. Indicate which of the following examples of self-talk are likely to have a positive or negative influence on behavior.

   _____ "Left over right and then right over left."

   _____ "I didn't understand this the first time and I won't understand it next time either."

   _____ "It will be easier the next time."

   _____ "I'm just naturally pessimistic."

   c. Describe the technique Meichenbaum (1977) developed to change self-defeating self-talk.

10. a. Explain why cognitive behavior therapists concentrate on both cognitive and behavioral changes in their clients.

    b. Summarize the evaluation of Emmelkamp et al. (1978) of the role of cognitive restructuring in cognitive behavior therapy.

11. Although cognitive behavior therapists and insight therapists stress the importance of unobservable thought processes, they differ in several important ways. State three of them.

    1.

    2.

    3.

Read the interim summary on page 622 of your text to reacquaint yourself with the material in this section.

18-7   *Describe some of the benefits of group psychotherapy and describe and evaluate psychodrama, family therapy, and group behavior therapy.*

Read pages 619-622 and then answer the following questions:

1. a. Briefly describe the origins and structure of group psychotherapy.

   b. List four advantages of group sessions.

2. a. Describe how therapist and clients act out problems through *psychodrama*. Be sure to state who plays the role of actor, audience and director.

   b. Why are clients asked to *mirror* each other?

   c. How effective is psychodrama?

3. a. Explain why *family therapy* is often a good way to help solve the problems of an individual.

   b. What are some of the interactions a family therapist is careful to observe during a session?

   c. Describe how Minuchin (1974) organizes observed family relationships using the *structural family therapy* approach.

   d. List two kinds of alliances that are always regarded as unhealthy.

   1.   2.

   e. What are some of the ways a therapist attempts to restructure unhealthy relationships?

   f. List two changes that must take place before family therapy can be evaluated.

   1.   2.

4. a. Describe two advantages of *group behavior therapy*. Provide an example by citing research by Lewinsohn et al., 1970.

   b. What is the likely future of group behavior therapy? Refer to the advantages that you have just described.

Read the interim summary on page 628 of your text to reacquaint yourself with the material in this section.

18-8 *Describe and evaluate the treatment of mental disorders with antipsychotic, antidepressant, and antianxiety drugs.*

Read pages 622-624 and then answer the following questions:

1. List three forms of biological treatment of mental illness.

   1.

   2.

   3.

2. Explain the use and some of the advantages and disadvantages of antipsychotic drugs.

   a. Name the two prominent positive symptoms of schizophrenia that antipsychotic drugs alleviate and explain how these drugs are presumed to work.

   b. What is the location of the dopamine-secreting neurons thought to be involved in schizophrenia?

   c. What kind of activity does a different system of these neurons control?

   d. Explain how a dual system of dopamine-secreting neurons complicates the use of antipsychotic drugs.

   e. Describe an early motor impairment caused by anti-psychotic drugs and explain why it is sometimes made worse.

   f. Now describe the symptoms and treatment of a motor impairment that can develop later, *tardive dyskinesia*.

   g. Why is there reason to hope that the side-effects of antipsychotic drugs may someday be eliminated?

3. Explain the use and some of the advantages and disadvantages of antidepressant drugs.

   a. _____ _____ drugs are most effective for treating major depression and _____ _____ is most effective for treating bipolar disorders or simple mania.

   b. Briefly summarize some of the side effects and difficulties resulting from the use of lithium carbonate.

   c. Under what circumstances should tricyclic antidepressant drugs be used? (Reda, 1984) When should they be discontinued? What other treatment should be started?

   d. What are the therapeutic effects of tricyclic antidepressant drugs? psychotherapy?

   e. Describe an important side effect of these drugs and the dilemma it creates in prescribing them.

   f. Identify some of the other anxiety disorders that respond to antidepressant drugs.

   g. Explain the importance of the drug clomipramine. (Zahn et al., 1984)

   h. Carefully explain why antidepressant drugs are neither a "cure" nor a long-term solution to the treatment of antianxiety disorders.

4. Explain the use and some of the advantages and disadvantages of antianxiety drugs:

   a. Antianxiety drugs are more commonly called _____.

   b. Describe the conditions for which antianxiety drugs are most appropriate.

   c. Explain why chronic use of these drugs can occur and why it is not beneficial.

18-9 *Describe and evaluate the treatment of mental disorders with electroconvulsive therapy and psychosurgery.*

Read pages 624-628 and then answer the following questions:

1. Describe the preparation for and administration of an electroconvulsive therapy (ECT) session. (See Figure 18.10 in your text.)

2. The _____, not the _____, produced by the brief surge of electricity, produces the therapeutic effect of ECT.

3. What change resulting from the seizure may account for the lifting of depression?

4. Describe the case of a middle-age widow hospitalized for severe depression to illustrate the effects of ECT: (Fink, 1976)

   a. Why did the woman fail to show improvement during early treatment?

   b. When did she and her therapist notice a change in her mood?

   c. What does this case demonstrate about the effectiveness of ECT?

   d. List three situations in which ECT is the preferred treatment for severe depression.

      1.

      2.

      3.

   e. Describe a serious side effect of the excessive use of ECT reported by Squire, et al. (1981) and the dilemma that it creates for patients and therapists.

   f. What precaution is now taken to reduce the occurrence of adverse side-effects?

5. Define *psychosurgery* in your own words. Be sure to point out how it differs from other forms of brain

surgery.

6. a. Retell the experiences of Jacobsen and his colleagues (1935) with Becky, the chimpanzee, that led to the first *prefrontal lobotomy*.

b. Study Figure 18.11 in your text and describe the procedure.

c. How did Becky's behavior change following surgery?

d. What observation led Moniz to perform the first prefrontal lobotomy on a human patient?

e. Study Figure 18.12 in your text and describe how this procedure was simplified, thus increasing the extent of its use.

f. List some of the serious side effects of these early operations.

g. How has the procedure been refined? What kind of effects does the more restricted technique produce?

h. Briefly summarize the case study of Ms. A. reported by Tippin and Henn (1982), which illustrates the condition for which psychosurgery is most valuable.

i. If psychosurgery is performed, it should only be as a _____ _____.

Read the interim summary on pages 631-632 of your text to reacquaint yourself with the material in this section.

18-10 *Describe the eclectic approach to psychotherapy and discuss research on the effectiveness of therapies and therapists.*

Read pages 628-631 and then answer the following questions:

1. Describe the *eclectic treatment* of mental disorders in your own words.

2. Carefully explain these problems of evaluating the effectiveness of particular therapies and therapists.

a. measurement

b. ethics

c. self-selection

d. control group

3. Summarize Eysenck's (1952) conclusions concerning the effectiveness of psychotherapy and its implications for the field.

4. a. Define *meta-analysis* in your own words.

   b. Outline the findings of Smith et al. (1980) who used this technique to compare the effectiveness of several forms of treatment.

5. a. List the three kinds of variables that Luborsky et al. (1971) investigated in their evaluation of psychotherapy.

   1.

   2.

   3.

   b. Next to each variable summarize the significant findings.

   c. Explain why it is inaccurate to conclude that more treatment sessions are more effective than fewer treatments.

6. a. Explain why it is encouraging to learn that experienced therapists are more effective.

   b. What do some researchers believe is the most important function of the therapist? (Fix and Haffke, 1976; Truax and Carkhuff, 1964)

   c. What are some of the characteristics of effective therapists?

   d. Describe how Strupp and Hadley (1979) tested this assertion with the aid of some college professors.

   e. State the results and explain what they suggest about most important factors in psychotherapeutic treatment.

Lesson II Self Test

1. Rational-emotive therapy asserts that

   a. psychological problems are the result of unhappy childhoods.
   b. a directive, argumentative approach is counterproductive.
   c. a feeling of full self-acceptance is essential.
   d. the therapist must be empathetic in order to be effective.

2. Self-efficacy is

   a. a generalized reduction in fear.
   b. the degree to which a person feels able to cope with difficult situations.
   c. the ability to recognize the source of one's psychological problems.
   d. a technique to reduce maladaptive self-statements.

3. The role of the therapist in psychodrama is to

   a. mirror unhealthy behavior exhibited by group members.
   b. serve as a director and focus the "action" in a useful direction.
   c. explain the events to family members who serve as the audience.
   d. prevent unhealthy alliances between group members.

4. Family therapists believe that the healthiest family structure contains

   a. a child-oriented marriage.
   b. an alliance between one parent and one or more children.
   c. a three-generation household.
   d. a healthy relationship between husband and wife.

5. Tardive dyskinesia results because antipsychotic drugs

   a. cannot discriminate between dual systems of dopamine-secreting neurons in the brain.
   b. sometimes cause degeneration of dopamine-secreting neurons in the hypothalamus.
   c. are often discontinued by patients as soon as their symptoms decrease.
   d. interfere with REM sleep cycles.

6. Lithium carbonate is most effective in the treatment of

   a. bipolar disorder.
   b. obsessive compulsive disorder.
   c. schizophrenia.
   d. high blood pressure.

7. The most important objection to the use of electroconvulsive therapy is that

   a. even a few treatments produce brain damage and excessive use results in permanent memory loss.
   b. it is generally too slow-acting to be an effective treatment for depression.
   c. it is very difficult to evaluate the therapeutic effects of a treatment that produces permanent brain damage.
   d. even a few treatments blunt the effect of antidepressant drugs.

8. Cingulectomies

a. are no longer performed because more refined techniques have been developed.
b. are performed to remove diseased or damaged brain tissue.
c. appear to be of most value in the treatment of affective disorders and severe compulsions.
d. disconnect the two hemispheres of the brain.

9. A comprehensive study using meta-analysis to compare the effectiveness of several kinds of treatment concluded that

a. institutionalized patients who received no therapy showed almost as much improvement as patients who received treatment.
b. psychotherapy is effective if patients remain in treatment as long as their therapists advise.
c. psychotherapy combined with drug therapy was more effective than either approach by itself in treating neuroses.
d. the benefits of psychotherapy are permanent.

10. Several studies suggest that an important characteristic of a successful therapist is the ability to

a. create patient anxiety which motivates desire to improve.
b. form a warm relationship with client.
c. remain dispassionate and objective.
d. conclude treatment before patients form harmful dependent relationships with the therapist.

Answers for Self Tests

Lesson I			**Lesson II**		
1.	c	Obj. 18-1	1.	c	Obj. 18-6
2.	c	Obj. 18-1	2.	b	Obj. 18-6
3.	a	Obj. 18-2	3.	b	Obj. 18-7
4.	c	Obj. 18-2	4.	d	Obj. 18-7
5.	d	Obj. 18-3	5.	a	Obj. 18-8
6.	b	Obj. 18-3	6.	a	Obj. 18-8
7.	b	Obj. 18-4	7.	a	Obj. 18-9
8.	a	Obj. 18-4	8.	c	Obj. 18-9
9.	d	Obj. 18-5	9.	c	Obj. 18-10
10.	b	Obj. 18-5	10.	b	Obj. 18-10

18.1 antianxiety drug	18.10 countertransference
18.2 antidepressant drug	18.11 eclectic approach
18.3 antipsychotic drug	18.12 free association
18.4 aversive classical conditioning	18.13 implosion therapy
18.5 behavior rehearsal	18.14 in vivo
18.6 cingulectomy	18.15 insight psychotherapy
18.7 client-centered therapy	18.16 meta-analysis
18.8 cognitive behavior therapy	18.17 mirroring
18.9 cognitive restructuring	18.18 prefrontal lobotomy

18.10 During psychoanalysis, the inadvertent and inappropriate communication of the therapist's own feelings and opinions about the client to the client.	**18.1** "Tranquilizers," frequently used to reduce anxiety; also useful in reducing symptoms of alcohol or drug withdrawal or to reduce anxiety of panic disorders or panic attacks.
18.11 Approach to therapy that incorporates elements of many different specific types of therapy.	**18.2** Drugs used to treat major depression (tricyclic antidepressant drugs) or bipolar disorder and simple manias (lithium carbonate).
18.12 Psychoanalytic technique; patients are encouraged to relax and discuss everything that comes to mind.	**18.3** Drug used to treat the positive symptoms of schizophrenia; therapeutic effect presumed to result from blocking dopamine receptors in the brain.
18.13 A form of therapy that attempts to help patients get rid of their fears by confronting them as vividly as possible either through imagination or in vivo.	**18.4** Technique employed by behavior therapists that attempts to link an unpleasant response such as fear or disgust to the object or action that produces the undesired behavior.
18.14 A real life encounter with the object or situation that a person fears the most; used in both systematic desensitization and implosion therapy.	**18.5** A technique of behavior therapy in which the therapist shows the client how to behave in particular situations with other people and then gives the client an opportunity to practice the skill.
18.15 A general approach to psychotherapy; people's problems will be solved once they understand their nature and causes.	**18.6** A psychosurgical procedure; the cingulum bundle, which connects the prefrontal cortex with parts of the limbic system, is cut; therapeutic effects without profound side effects caused by prefrontal lobotomies.
18.16 A statistical method for estimating the strength of an experimental effect by examining the literature describing experiments that others have performed.	**18.7** Developed by Carl Rogers; people are basically good and can overcome mental disturbances caused by disparity between the concepts of the ideal self and the real self; atmosphere of unconditional positive regard.
18.17 A technique developed as a part of psychodrama in which one of the members of the group is asked to act out the maladaptive behavior of another member.	**18.8** Therapy combining cognitive approach with behavior therapy; less interested in the possible childhood causes of mental disturbances than in altering a client's behavior.
18.18 The first psychosurgical treatment in which parts of the frontal lobe are disconnected from the rest of the brain in order to reduce severe anxiety; no longer performed because of serious behavioral effects.	**18.9** Therapeutic process used by rational-emotive therapists to help clients overcome counterproductive thoughts and behaviors.

18.19 psychoanalysis	18.28 symptom substitution
18.20 psychodrama	18.29 systematic desensitization
18.21 psychosurgery	18.30 tardive dyskinesia
18.22 rational-emotive therapy	18.31 token economy
18.23 resistance	18.32 training analysis
18.24 self-control	18.33 transference neurosis
18.25 self-efficacy	18.34 trephining
18.26 self-talk	18.35 unconditional positive regard
18.27 structural family therapy	

18.28 During behavior therapy, the hypothetical replacement of one symptom of a psychological problem that has been eliminated with another, possibly more serious, one; no good evidence for its occurrence.	18.19 Form of psychotherapy developed by Freud; during therapy the client gradually learns the unconscious sources of mental disturbances and once these are understood they will be resolved.
18.29 Technique of behavior therapy developed by Joseph Wolpe, used to treat specific phobias; hierarchy of feared situations (CS) are paired with learned relaxation responses (US).	18.20 A form of group therapy developed by Jacob Moreno; members of the group act out their problems with some members serving as actors and others as the audience; the therapist is the "director."
18.30 A serious side effect of the long-term use antipsychotic drugs to treat schizophrenia; involuntary motor disturbances.	18.21 The destruction of brain tissue in the absence of any evidence of disease or damage in an attempt to treat mental disturbances.
18.31 A technique based on instrumental conditioning used in institutions; patients' performance of useful or socially desirable tasks is rewarded with tokens that can be exchanged for privileges.	18.22 A form of cognitive behavior therapy developed by Albert Ellis; asserts that people often develop irrational behaviors which the therapist must replace through argumentation and explicit directions.
18.32 Part of the education of psychoanalysts during which they learn to recognize and understand their own problems in order to avoid reacting inappropriately toward clients.	18.23 During psychoanalysis, a strong reluctance by the client to confront painful topics by avoiding some subjects, changing the subject, or "forgetting," sessions.
18.33 During psychoanalysis a client may pass his or her feelings about an important childhood figure to the psychoanalyst; considered essential, therapist remains vague to facilitate its development.	18.24 Methods used by behavior therapists to teach clients to reward and punish their own behavior.
18.34 The earliest known attempt to treat mental disturbances by drilling holes in the skull of the disturbed person.	18.25 The degree to which a person is able to cope with a difficult situation; strengthening this characteristic is an important goal of Bandura's method of cognitive behavior therapy.
18.35 An integral part of client-centered therapy; the total acceptance and approval of the client as a person by the therapist.	18.26 Private "conversations" we have with ourselves; in cognitive behavior therapy clients are taught to alter their behavior by learning appropriate verbalizations that guide behavioral changes.
	18.27 An approach to family therapy developed by Salvador Minuchin; unhealthy family alliances are observed, diagramed, and restructured.